S0-AYI-553

The Changing Nature of Man

J. H. Van den Berg, M.D.

The Changing
Nature of Man

Introduction to a Historical Psychology

W · W · NORTON & COMPANY · New York · London

First published as a Norton paperback 1983

COPYRIGHT © 1961 BY W. W. NORTON & COMPANY, INC.

Originally published in the Netherlands under the title
of *Metabletica, of Leer der Veranderingen*. Translated
from the Dutch by H. F. Croes, M.D.

Library of Congress Cataloging in Publication Data

Berg, J. H. (Jan Hendrik van den), 1914–
The changing nature of man.

Translation of: Metabletica.
Bibliography: p.
Includes index.
1. Genetic psychology.   2. Change (Psychology)
I. Title.
BF702.B4713   1983   150′.1   83–4199

ISBN 0-393-30115-X

PRINTED IN THE UNITED STATES OF AMERICA

W. W. Norton & Company, Inc., 500 Fifth Avenue,
New York, N.Y. 10110
W. W. Norton & Company Ltd., 37 Great Russell Street
London WC1B 3NU

1 2 3 4 5 6 7 8 9 0

Contents

Preface

The whole science of psychology is based on the assumption that
man does not change. Even the theory of the neurosis and its
therapy leans on this supposition: a neurotic is a person whose
faculties are obstructed; the therapy consists of the removal of
the obstruction. Nothing is added to the person himself and
nothing is taken away from him. How much more should this be
true for the normal person; certainly he will not change at all.
If he should go and live in another country, or under different
circumstances, he would take his whole personality with him,
and if one day he should return to his old environment, he would
return just as he had been before, exactly the same person, entirely unchanged. There is nothing basically new in human
existence—that is what psychology has always assumed, except, perhaps, for a very few exceptions.

This book stems from the idea that man *does* change. And so,
consequently, it deals with the history of man. Whereas, in traditional psychology, the life of a previous generation is seen as a
variation on a known theme, the supposition that man does
change leads to the thought that earlier generations lived a differ-

ent sort of life, and that they were *essentially* different. It is this thought which, in principle, defines historical psychology.

Historical psychology compares the past and the present with the object of finding in what ways modern man differs from man in previous generations. It also seeks the reasons and the causes of the changes. And, inevitably, it must consider why and how psychology itself has changed in the course of the years. Ultimately, therefore, historical psychology has to concern itself with its own principles. It has to analyze every change in the psychology of the past and explain why a change occurred and what kind of living and thinking necessitated the change. It has to find the causes of every new principle.

Historical psychology is not the history of psychology. The history of psychology is the history of a science, exactly like the history of any other science, or like history in general. The historian of psychology tries to distinguish eras, to trace fundamental thoughts, and to define the significance of the most prominent psychologists and schools of thought. He is not primarily concerned with the causes of the changes in fundamental principles, and certainly not with the changes in man himself of which they were a reflection—although no good historian can altogether ignore these. But there is a similarity: historical psychology, as a science of changes, is also concerned with the past eras of psychology.

To avoid misunderstanding, and to make it clear from the start that this book is not a book on history, the term *historical psychology* is omitted from the title. This book will try to explain psychology on the basis of the assumption that man changes. This means that it is based on an understanding of human existence which differs from the conventional one; it is based on the belief, ignored by science but so common in every day life, that nothing is more liable to change than man.

The Changing Nature of Man

Up till now we have had no historical psychology.
. . . Why did the Middle Ages and the Renaissance produce entirely different types of men?

Karl Mannheim, Man and Society

CHAPTER 1

The need for a theory of changes

The idea of eternity in the psychology of the nineteenth century

Psychologists of the previous century would be astonished if they could see what work their modern colleagues do. In their day, psychology was a science of distinction, related by old ties to timeless philosophy. The psychologists bore the marks of this distinction. Like philosophers they sat behind desks laden with books and counters, writing theoretical treatises. They contemplated the differences between observation and fantasy, they classified emotions, and they compiled codes of associations. And when, in 1878,[1] it became fashionable for them to leave their desks now and then, it was only to repair to laboratories where experiments were conducted which remained true to the serenity of their contemplations; and true, mainly, to the timeless character of those contemplations. The psychologist worked for eternal science. He remained remote from daily life. He considered the walls of his study and of his laboratory the limits of his science. He was able to do so because nobody ever asked him anything.

A *lost tranquillity*

In the twentieth century his idyll was disturbed, and his tranquillity vanished. People began to ask questions, a few at first, but more and more as time went on; at last they asked so many questions that the psychologist could hardly find time to answer them all. And yet he had to answer them, for the questions concerned important matters. For instance: "What is the best way to educate my child?" Could the psychologist disappoint the father who asked this question? "How should I treat my wife?" "How should I, as an employer, deal with my employees?" "How can I know if there is a suitable person among the twenty who applied for my position?" "How do I find what occupation suits me best?" "How can I grow old blamelessly?" It is undeniable that these are important questions, all of them; and it is apparent that the psychologist had to answer them.

The *psychologist learns to answer questions*

And so he did answer them. Hurriedly he invented a respectable system of examination, checked and applied it, and discovered the words to express his conclusions and advice. Faith in psychology grew; people did not ask questions in vain. And the psychologist, in his turn, grew in the faith that people appeared to have in him. He put down his thoughts in businesslike articles, books, and practical guides. The difference between twentieth-century publications and those of the nineteenth century is striking: the contemplative character has almost entirely disappeared. The twentieth-century psychologist speaks of extremely practical subjects. He knows about ordinary daily life. He comes to factories and homes, business firms and schools; he is to be found in recreation areas and instruction centers. He is busy and he knows what to do. He speaks, examines, tests, discusses, and—answers questions.

Is *the psychologist capable of answering the questions?*

A few psychologists, however, view all this practical activity with critical eyes. It is their opinion that the psychologist, in spite of his equipment and his choice of words, is not really justified in answering most of these questions, for the simple reason that his answers and his recommendations are based on a foundation which does not exist.

Let us presume that these few psychologists are right. What, then, is the psychologist to do with the questions? He has just learned how to answer them; should he now send them back to those who asked? Should he block his letterbox, close his doors and windows, and return to the old subjects? He would not succeed: the questioners would know how to find him, and so much need, so much faith, would appear in their interruptions that he would have to get his tests and his tape-recorder out of the cupboard and start to work again.

It has to be admitted that in any case it was the questions which had made him give the advice in the first place. It would never have occurred to the psychologist to write reports and to give advice if people had not urgently requested him to do so. The nineteenth-century psychologist could permit himself the luxury of unconcern because nobody ever felt the need to ask him even a single question.

Nobody asked questions

Did people in the nineteenth century know the answers, then? Did they know how to educate their children, how to treat their wives? Did employers know how to handle employees? Did people know the tricks of the different phases of life and could they recognize the dangers where the one phase changes into the next? Did they know which occupation suited them best? Did no one ever have doubts about being the right man in the right place?

Apparently they did know the answers: for no one asked. At one point people must have begun to ask. It is not clear why or from whom. Certainly they did not learn to ask from the psychologist: the questions were there before he even thought of answering them. What then had happened? What knowledge had been lost? and how?

Martin Buber and a modern inability

Once Martin Buber lectured in Czernowitz; afterward, as he was sitting in a restaurant continuing the discussion with a few of his audience, a middle-aged Jew came in. He introduced himself, and then sat down and followed the abstract discussion, which must have been unusual to his ears, with great interest.[2] He declined every invitation to advance a comment, but at the close of the discussion he came to Buber and said, "I want to ask you something. I have a daughter and she knows a young man who has been studying law. He passed all his examinations with honors. What I would like to know is: would he be a reliable man?" Buber was taken by surprise by this question, and answered, "I assume from your words that he is industrious and able." But apparently this was not what the other man really meant to ask, for he proceeded, "But could you tell me—I would like to know this particularly—would he be clever?" "That is rather more difficult to answer," Buber said, "but I presume that merely with diligence he could not have achieved what he did." The other man was still not satisfied, and finally the question he really meant to ask came out. "Herr Doctor, should he become a solicitor or a barrister?" "That I cannot tell you," answered Buber, "for I do not know your future son-in-law, and even if I did know him, I would not be able to give you advice in this matter." The other man thanked him and left, obviously disappointed.

In this conversation an ancient certainty—the certainty that wise men are men who know—was shattered by a modern inability. Buber ought to have said, "He should become a solicitor," or, "He should become a barrister."

"How could he know?" cries out Buber's modern contemporary, as if action were founded on knowledge. Of course Buber could not know. But nobody asked him to know. What he had been asked for was advice—judgment, not knowledge. Advice and judgment, of course, fitting the occasion, and applicable to this man: someone who entered in this particular way, who asked his question in this particular manner, and who looked like him; a man who presumably had such-and-such kind of a daughter; advice which fit this vague, very vague, totality, but primarily advice, a certainty, a wise word, a word that would have brought structure to this vague totality; an answer which would have erected a beacon, so that the sailing would no longer be dangerous. "He should become a barrister." These words, if spoken by Buber, by a sage, by a man who looked and spoke like one, a man who apparently *knew*,—these words would have been the strongest foundation for the future son-in-law's choice of profession. How could he have gone wrong if his career had been initiated by such advice? The answer would have created its own rightness; it would have created truth. Is not truth, truth in the relation between man and man, basically the effect of a fearlessness toward the other person? Is not truth, above all, a result, a made up thing, a creation of the sage? The person who knows creates the future by speaking.

But Buber is a modern man. To the sudden question—a question which, as he himself confessed later on, could have opened his eyes because of its suddenness—to the sudden question, "Is my daughter's fiancé a reliable man?" he replies (as if he had studied psychology), "According to your own words he must be industrious and able." He could have added, "Don't you think so yourself?" Imagine, however, the consternation that would have been caused by this answer. It would have seemed inconceivable that Buber would throw back the question—the sage must be joking. Another attempt is made: "Is he clever?" which is met by the inevitable, though not less shocking, answer: "Merely with diligence—the diligence, dear questioner, which you yourself mentioned in your description of your future son-in-law and to which I can refer—merely with diligence he could not have achieved what you, yourself, dear questioner, indicated when you said that he had passed all his examinations with honors—merely with diligence he could not have achieved all that, don't you think so yourself?"

"Leave me alone," says Buber, "don't tempt me. For—being a modern man—I don't know; or rather I firmly believe that all inter-human actions should be based on knowledge, and as I don't possess this particular knowledge, I am not permitted to make a guess." And so his final answer is quite understandable: "I don't know," he says, "I don't know him. But even if I knew him, I still would not know."

The psychologist and the modern inability

The modern psychologist undoubtedly would agree with Buber. He would have given the same answers. But he would not have left it at that. He would have said, "I don't know, nobody knows; you should not formulate your questions like that, for you will only get the wrong answers. If you want your questions answered, let your future son-in-law come to my office."

And when the son-in-law came, the psychologist would have held a long and cunning conversation with him; he would have taken from his cupboard a few very apparently innocent but even more cunning papers, and he would have invited the future son-in-law to interpret ten or so inkspots, to complete a series of uncompleted sentences, and to describe a few disquieting pictures. Then he would have correlated these acquired data and summed up the effects of his labour in straightforward advice.

That is what the psychologist would have done, with faith and conviction. But is his faith as sure as it once was? His belief in the correctness of his advice has been taken away from him a little. It has become clear "that from a test or a psychological examination *nothing* can be concluded about what should be done, about what is right, about what is justified or what is suitable." [3] The test says *nothing*. It was not by accident that the author of this quotation put *nothing* in italics.

In the same speech, given by B. J. Kouwer in 1955, he stated what the psychologist can do. He can "put his knowledge and experience at the client's disposal, but his assistance can only be effective to the extent that the client is able to learn the possibilities and to start to find for himself the solution of his problems or his conflicts. The insight in his problems which the psychologist is able to give a person *may* help him to solve his problems. But the solution should rest with the client himself; for to point out the future way, in whatever manner, is beyond science."

The psychologist thus says in effect: "You do not know what occupation would suit you best? Please, realize that I do not know either. But we can talk it over and there is a fair chance that together we might be able to find the right solution."

It seems to me that these words open a wide and honest field of activity for the psychologist. Yet Professor Kouwer's speech created anxiety among quite a few of them. Actually, his words should have created anxiety in all of us. For they disclose a secret, which has, not by chance, been carefully kept.

We do not know

This secret is: we do not know. At first it seemed as if psychology would be able to abolish our ignorance, and so it created a feeling of relief for many people. The psychologist knows all the answers! If my son does not know what he is going to be and I do not know either—my opinion does not count, anyway—then there is always the psychologist who can find out; he will tell us what to do and we shall act accordingly. If my daughter does not know whether she should marry the boy with whom she has been going for six years, and neither do I—which is of no consequence—there is the psychologist, who will unravel the secret of her affections and disclose a few oedipal inconveniences; then he will tell her what to do. Or he will refer her to the psychiatrist, which, of course, would be a disappointment, but which will still be a beacon.

Only now it is the psychologist himself who does not believe this anymore. Soon his disbelief will spread to his questioners, and there will be great consternation. For it should be realized that the questioner does not share the conscience problems of the psychologist; to him it is the certainty that matters, it is the fact that *there is an answer* to his problem that matters; what the answer is, is secondary. He wants to be able to say, "Here it is, written in black and white; he is to be a solicitor. So stop quibbling, for Pete's sake—or rather, for the psychologist's sake—go, and be a solicitor. That's all there is to it." It is this relief that the questioner wants. And why doesn't the psychologist co-operate? Why doesn't he comply with the desire for certainty, that certainty which is built on the words of the sage—actually, the only possible certainty? Why is he haunted by a scientific conscience, while the questioners awake in him with their frightened questions another and more real conscience. Does he have a right not to comply, not to answer?

Advising psychology, a dubious emergency bridge

Whether he has a right to withhold what is obviously expected from him or not, he cannot very well avoid losing faith in what he is doing. After all, his scepticism is not based on a conclusion reached in a scientific manner, the conclusion that no psychology can support advice which includes the future; ultimately his scepticism is caused by an inability from which everybody is suffering, the inability to build on the certainties of old. His science is refinding Buber's scepticism. His science is leading him to the acknowledgment of the fact (which has always been known, but which has been kept a secret) that the gap of not-knowing which divides one person from the other, and which divides anybody from his future, cannot be bridged by psychology. He is discovering the *raison d'être* of his science, he is discovering that psychology is an emergency bridge between two banks which had never been separated before; banks which became banks because the earth we live on has split apart. The connection between them has disappeared to such an extent, that no sage, not even a modern hesitating sage like the psychologist, can repair it with his words— or even bridge the gap. This is what the modern psychologist is discovering. The realization of this fact leads to the idea that the emergency bridge called psychology fails because nobody knows how to identify the bridgeheads.

What are the bridgeheads?

What is the nature of the modern inability to mold the future? As long as this question is not answered, every psychological aid concerned with the connection between now and the future will be blind. And other questions, too: What is the nature of the relationship between young and old? Why does nobody know any more how to act in this relationship? What has happened to us elders, that our grip on the child is hesitating, unsure, timorous? What has happened to the child, that it does not let itself be caught, that it escapes, that it seeks its own way, often losing it, often wandering, but finally, as if by a miracle, maturing after all? As long as these questions are not answered, every pedagogic advice will remain floating in the air. And finally: What has happened to the relationship between husband and wife? What has made them need the almost unbelievable spate of books on sexology? As long as this question is not answered, every attempt to help solve marital problems will be founded on quicksand.

What has happened to us? This is the question to which this book intends to make a first and therefore undoubtedly preliminary answer. It will describe how we change; and since the theme of change will occupy the center of our attention, this book is about *metabletics*, a word derived from the Greek μεταβάλλειν, to change.

CHAPTER 2

Adults and children

Pedagogic manuscripts of the past do not contain anything on the nature of the relationship between old and young. Even the greatest authors do not mention the subject. Apparently they were not interested at all in what appears to us the first and most important subject of pedagogy. If the student wants information on the nature of the relationship between old and young in earlier times, he has to be satisfied with hints, allusions, and side remarks, which suddenly, almost by accident, allow us to catch a glimpse of how elders treated the young in those days. These incidental observations are actually present in the works of every pedagogical author, but the student has to discover them. The search is worth the trouble; let us open the first book of Montaigne's *Essays* to the first chapter, devoted to the education of children: "De l'institution des enfans."

Montaigne's advice

This part of Montaigne's work is dedicated to the Countess of Curson, Diane de Foix, who, expecting her first child, asked Montaigne for enlightenment about the pedagogic task which lay before her. When it was written, Europe, in many ways, had detached itself from the middle ages, but was still related to it to a certain extent. A few years after Montaigne died, Descartes was born; and Descartes, supported by the experience of his century, went on to outline a pedagogical program with a few fundamental treatises. Montaigne stands on the threshold of this new era; what he thought about the way adults should treat the young is therefore significant.

Montaigne's composition on education is not very entertaining. It seems unlikely that the countess was thrilled when she read it; anyway it is improbable that she learned much from it. To our eyes, it is pompous, scholarly, and too unreal to be of much practical value; it bristles with classical quotations. Until, suddenly, this sentence attracts our attention: "A few years of life," says the author, "are reserved for education, not more than the first fifteen or sixteen; make good use of these years, adult, if you wish to educate the child to the right maturity. Leave out superfluous matters. If you want to do something constructive, confront the child with philosophical discourses, those that are not too complicated, of course, yet those that are worth explaining. Treat these discourses in detail; the child is capable of digesting this matter from the moment that it can more or less manage for itself [Montaigne actually wrote: "from the moment it is weaned," but probably he did not mean this too literally]; "the child will, in any case, be able to stand philosophical discourses much better than an attempt to teach it to write and to read; this had better wait a little."

The Decameron *is not children's reading matter*

Philosophical discourses! and Montaigne then adds, in all seriousness, that these are to be preferred to Boccaccio's *Decameron*. Really, he says, philosophical explanations are much more comprehensible to the child.[1]

This remark indicates that Montaigne, who has such sound and wise judgment on so many matters, seems to be off the mark when it comes to advising expectant mothers. And he is not the only one. Every writing on pedagogy of those days breathes the same unreality. Every one of them evidences an unchildlike interpretation of the child; not one of them gives us the impression that the child had really been observed and understood. The child is absent in this pompous, solemn writing.

John Locke's advice

A hundred years later, the literature on the relationship between old and young still seems very unreal to us. When John Locke wants to convey the spirit in which adults should treat children, he emphasizes that children should be treated as creatures who are willing and eager to understand *reason*. Children desire "a gentle Persuasion in Reasoning," writes Locke. "They understand it as early as they do Language; and, if I misobserve not, they like to be treated as rational Creatures." [2] Let us illustrate this with an example.

One day your five-year-old daughter wants only peanut butter for her breakfast; but not only for her breakfast, she wants it for her lunch as well; and even for her dinner she does not want anything but bread and this desirable food. Anxious to avoid the ill effects of a one-sided nutrition, you want to help her to get rid of this new habit. According to Locke, the thing to do would be to tell her quietly and completely why it is not right to eat nothing but peanut butter. You make her realize that her diet would become too one-sided and that the result of her preference could well be an undermining of her health.

But perhaps this example is not well-chosen. For today there is always the chance that you might not want to deprive your daughter, anxious as you are not to cause some harm to the child's soul which might well burden your conscience with guilt-feelings for years. So you just let her eat peanut butter until she asks for something else herself. Let us imagine, however, that there is a bottle of medicine on the table. It is yours; and the child implores you with tears in her eyes to let her consume the contents. You know it would kill her, so you do not let her have it. Would you talk with her in the way John Locke recommends—that is, convince her rationally that she is wrong? You would not. You would be ridiculous if you did, and as far as the child is concerned, you would be leading her into a mock maturity.

Rousseau's comment

This was Rousseau's opinion, anyway. Another century later, he exclaims, with the vehemence so characteristic of him, that he knows of nothing so ridiculous as this kind of persuasive treatment of a child. Reasonableness, he argues, commenting on Locke's views, is not the first but the last effect of education; to begin with reason is to begin at the end. If it were possible to argue reasonably with children there would be no need to educate them; they would be mature.[3] Rousseau then gives an example of a persuasive conversation between an adult and a child which inevitably arrives at silly reasoning in circles. Please realize, says Rousseau, that the child is a child, that it is not an adult; your pedagogic actions cannot be right if they do not originate from this very difference.[4]

Rousseau understood. He was the first to view the child as a child, and to stop treating the child as an adult.

We might finish our historical excursion here. At the end of the sixteenth century Montaigne showed an almost unbelievable misunderstanding; a century later Locke still shows the same misunderstanding, although to a lesser degree; a hundred years later again, we come to the first understanding of the childlike in the child. All the manifestations of the correct treatment of the child —the publishing of children's books, the manufacturing of children's clothes, the construction of playgrounds, and the furnishing of correct pedagogic advice—all these modern proofs of understanding of the child are implicit in Rousseau's work. After many years of misunderstanding, the first tendency toward a better understanding appeared in the second half of the eighteenth century. This understanding, in the twentieth century, has led to great, not to say impressive, results.

What stirred Rousseau?

That is how it seems. In Rousseau's *Émile*, however, there are passages which give rise to another interpretation. "Do not talk with the child," says the author. In a way we are inclined to agree with him. "The child is a child, not an adult; you are the adult."

We agree again. "There should be reasonableness between adults; use [moral] force when dealing with the child." [5]

This turn is not what we expected. Does it fit in with the acknowledgment of the childlike in the child? Hardly, it seems to us. Was Rousseau perhaps paying his respects to a past from which he could not free himself? But if so, then it is not clear why he advocates the supremacy of the adult just as emphatically as the childishness of the child. He may have been trying to convey to his contemporaries an idea then just as novel as the idea that the child is a child and should be treated as one. This is what he says:

"What the child should know is that it is weak and that you, adult, are strong; and from this difference it follows that it is under your authority. That is what the child should know, that is what it ought to learn, that is what it must feel." [6]

This plea for parental authority [7] may look like a toll paid to the past, but actually we have to admit that it is in agreement with his rejection of Locke's ideas. Talking with the child admits accepting him as an equal; and then it is hard to justify the parents' authority and their right to intimidate the child. Thus the acknowledgment of the inequality of child and adult leads to using compulsion and intimidation as means of education. This is the more remarkable because, at present, we do accept the first part of this logic even eagerly, while we emphatically reject the second, which we consider inhuman and not pedagogic. To intimidate a child? No! Our authority? How dangerous to refer to it. And besides, what distance would there be between child and adult if compulsion should take the place of reason?

It seems as if Rousseau is pushing the child away. Stay there, he says, you cannot come to where I am, for I am an adult and you are a child. Why? Can it be that Rousseau made a mistake? He must have. Of course the child is a child and we are not; to that extent there is a distance, but this distance should be absent as much as possible in our attitude toward it. And yet, is this really possible? Is not this a contradiction? I would prefer to let this important problem rest a while and first point out another peculiarity of Rousseau's *Emile*.

Émile's second birth

In the fourth chapter, Rousseau states that man is not born once, but twice. At his first birth he comes into existence; at his second he comes into life. It is quite apparent what Rousseau meant by this: the first birth is the physical one, out of the mother; the second birth involves puberty, the psychic maturation which is inseparable from physical maturation, although the latter usually takes place a little earlier. Psychic maturation (which from now on I shall denote by the term *maturation*) is what Rousseau calls a state of crisis—and we agree immediately. The child who is maturing is moody and erratic, and has a more or less strong aversion toward parental authority; it does not want to be led anymore. In this period (I am still quoting Rousseau) it does not want to have anything to do with the adult, it is unreasonable and mutinous; in short, it is unmanageable. It should be kept in mind, however, says Rousseau, that all this is of the greatest significance. The child is maturing; after this crisis nothing human will be foreign to it.

This description of maturation agrees with our experience. The only thing which surprises us is that Rousseau speaks of "a *moment* of crisis," of a "rather short" period.[8] We think that maturation takes a rather long time—even an unbelievably long time. According to some textbooks, it takes about five years. Some authors feel that even this estimate is far too short, and speak of seven, nine, ten years. Rousseau must have underestimated the time it takes the child to mature; for that maturation should show such variation in the time it takes does not tally with our idea that it is related to biological change. Or is it not so related?

Maturation: an absent subject

Before Rousseau, nobody ever mentioned maturation. Locke does not and neither does Montaigne; and this, particularly, is surprising. For Montaigne writes about literally everything in his *Essays*: about vanity, sadness, lies and truth, friendship and loneliness, the right way to die, praying, being drunk, cruelty, stagecoaches, fleas—and this is just a small list. He even wrote a chapter on life's duration, with valuable comments on the different phases. And yet this man, who observed everything and who described accurately what he saw, does not even mention maturation, the most noticeable phase of life to us, which is apparent to us both in terms of our own lives and of our experiences with our children. Had his observation failed in this one respect? Odd. Did all authors before Rousseau have a blind spot as far as maturation was concerned? For, except for a few lines of Aristotle's and a few sparing, and, for that matter, doubtful, autobiographical notes from writers in the Renaissance, there is nothing on maturation in all European literature.[9] Were all our ancestors' eyes closed to this matter, which to us has such prominence? Can we really believe this? Or is it more probable that all authors before Rousseau did not notice anything because there was nothing to see?

Maturation: an absent phase of life

But this would imply that the child before Rousseau's time was a child in a different way from the children during and after his time, so different a way that a period of maturation—by which is meant *a period of inwardly and outwardly difficult and rebellious life*—failed to appear. Could this be possible? But what was a child like in Montaigne's time, for instance? Could he have been so close to adulthood that he need not muddle through a turbulent period to reach it?

These questions are difficult to answer, for data on the nature of the child's life are extremely scarce. Later on I shall invite the reader to consider why these data are so scarce. But first, I shall discuss a few short communications on the child which have reached us: isolated data from complete, but almost entirely unknown, lives; data which quite unexpectedly throw light on the child of earlier times.

Théodore Agrippa d'Aubigné

We do have some data on the child's nature in Montaigne's time—the life of Théodore Agrippa d'Aubigné, Huguenot, friend of Henri IV, born in 1550. Montaigne was born in 1533, so he had reached the age of discretion when d'Aubigné was still a child.

Observing young contemporaries of this d'Aubigné, Montaigne did not notice anything about maturation. Of d'Aubigné it is told that he read Greek, Latin, and Hebrew when he was six years old, and that he translated Plato into French when he was not yet eight.[10]

Plato. Montaigne recommended the reading and explaining of philosophical discourses to children—well, if an eight-year-old child can translate Plato, what objections can there be to reading a translated version to him when he is four?

When d'Aubigné was still eight years old, he went through the town of Amboise, accompanied by his father, just after a group of Huguenots had been executed. He saw the decapitated bodies; and at the request of his father he swore an oath to avenge them. Two years later he was captured by *Inquisiteurs*; the ten-year-old boy's reaction to the threat of death at the stake was a dance of joy before the fire. The horror of the Mass took away his fear of the fire,[11] was his own later comment—as if a ten-year-old child could know what he meant by that. And yet a child who has translated Plato and who has been used to reading the classics for four years, could not such a child know what he wants, and know what he is doing? But he can hardly be called a child. A person who observes the effects of an execution intelligently, who swears an oath to which he remains true through life, who realizes for himself the interpretation of the Holy Communion, and who fathoms the horror of death at the stake—he is not a child, he is a man.

Blaise Pascal

At the time Montaigne died another child was standing on the threshold of great discoveries: Blaise Pascal, born in 1623, wrote, when he was twelve years old, without assistance, a treatise on sound which was taken seriously by expert contemporaries. At about the same time he happened to hear the word *mathematics*; he asked his father what it meant, and he was given the following incomplete answer (incomplete, because his father was afraid that an interest in the mathematics might diminish his interest in other sciences): "Mathematics, about which I shall tell you more later on, is the science which occupies itself with the construction of perfect figures and with the discovery of the properties they contain." Young Pascal brooded over this answer during his hours of leisure,[12] and unassisted, he constructed circles and triangles which led him to the discovery of the sort of properties his father must have meant—for instance, that the sum of the angles of a triangle equals two right angles. Certainly, his father was impressed, from which it appears that these mature achievements were not usual in those days, either—but to us they seem absolutely incredible. There were tears of joy in Pascal's eyes when he looked at his son's constructions. Would we not be frightened and think: Where will this end? What is it that this child is lacking?

Pascal's father was won over, and presented Blaise with Euclid's *Elements,* which he devoured as if it were a children's book. The boy was then twelve years old; four years later he wrote a treatise on conic sections, which, according to his learned contemporaries, was superior to anything written on the subject since Archimedes.

Small adults

The precociousness of talented children in earlier days is astonishing to us. Even after Rousseau there are examples of this precociousness which, although not as striking as Pascal's extravagances, are amazing. Goethe, for instance, was able to write German, French, Greek, and Latin before he was eight. He picked up Italian while his father was teaching this language to his little seven-year-old sister. Turnvater Jahn could read and write when he was four. The Jesuit monk, Père Joseph (1597), recited the drama of Golgotha, standing on his own little table at a dinner party given by his father, when he was four years old. A Dutch commander of a company of infantry, Menno van Coehoom, was sixteen years old when he was transferred from Friesland to a garrison in Maastricht. And so on—an almost endless series of precocious children, children who evidently at a very young age were considered able enough to go to a university and who appeared capable of digesting the very mature matters offered to them. If a girl were educated at all, she too started when she was two or three years old. There were girls who had read the Bible before they were five; well, if they had read the Bible before they were five, there could hardly be any objection to reading a story from the *Decameron* to them once in a while at this charming age, even though Montaigne was against it. For one cannot get away from it by saying that the child did not understand what it had been reading. Pascal apparently did understand quite a few mature matters. When it is recorded of Heinrich Jung-Stilling, a youthful friend of Goethe's, that he read Luther and Calvin when he was eleven,[13] can it really be assumed that the young man merely pronounced words, or rather, stumbled over words, and remained ignorant of their meaning? Can one really believe that our ancestors were all stupid? stupid, naive, blind, or whatever they may be called to express the idea that they did not understand a thing, nothing at all, of the child?

Campe's complaint

From the time of Goethe and Jung-Stilling, the complaint arises that youth is being maltreated, that it is not delightful at all to see an eight- or ten-year-old boy "who has read a whole library of books, who can converse about the plants and animals of India, who speaks many languages, who knows all the paradigmata of Latin Grammar by heart, who calculates like a merchant and who explains the classical authors with an ability which brings tears of joy to every true schoolmaster's eyes." [14] This cry of distress was uttered at the time of Rousseau, the author who was the first to describe maturation—not because he observed more intelligently than his predecessors, but because for the first time there was something to see at the border between youth and adulthood— the author who was the first to be confronted with the distance between old and young, and who therefore did not grudge the child his childlike qualities (which had just come into existence) and who, for the same reason—like his follower, Campe—advocated different methods of teaching.

Although it appears irrefutably from Campe's book that the child had come into serious difficulties even in the eyes of its own contemporaries, it is just as apparent from his book that these contemporaries did not consider the didactic methods to which the child had to conform as impossible. That is how we should have considered them. Would it not seem impossible (apart from being undesirable) for a ten- or twelve-year-old to have read a whole library of books (do you remember how much trouble you had getting through your own modest list?), to speak many languages (do you remember how laboriously the few you learned were spoken by your eighteen-year-old lips?), to know all paradigmata of Latin grammar by heart (it took you many years, and that was after your twelfth birthday), and to explain the classics in a way that moves one to tears (and you?)?

A matter of talent

Usually, although not always, this evidence of change in the child is rejected with the observation that the examples used are children who even in their own time were considered infant prodigies. And this is partly true. But that the precociousness only concerned the very talented children becomes doubtful when it is realized that Rousseau and Campe described the—to them, untenable—situation as generally existing. Rousseau does not speak of a few children, and neither does Campe; [15] both of them criticize a method of education that was common.

Besides, what about the great men of our day? If they are like the talented of the past, they too should have been precocious. There is no evidence of this. The youth of those who in our century have been scientific pioneers cannot stand comparison with d'Aubigné, Pascal, Grotius, or Goethe.[16] Instead, instances of a late maturation are easier to find among the great of the present. Are not we, ourselves, as parents, considerably less disturbed when we are told that our child is a bit young for his age and that it might be better not to let him pass to the next grade, than we are when we notice that our child is far ahead of the other children, and that he sits with a book on his lap when his classmates are swimming, romping, or contradicting their elders? We would not feel happy about this, and it would not be hard to convince us that we should consult the child psychiatrist.

The child has become a child

The child has become a child. If we do not accept this, we will not understand how for centuries the child could have been confronted with reading matter which, in our opinion, it could not digest at all. And it will remain equally incomprehensible why the child was treated in such an ostentatiously unpedagogic way. The *Colloquia* of 1522, edited by Erasmus himself, and dedicated by him to the six-year-old son of his friend and publisher, Froben, begins with a dialogue between a young man and his girl friend on the value a woman should attach to her virginity, on the right she does or does not have to refuse sexual intercourse in marriage, and on the question of whether sexual enjoyment in itself can be considered sinful. In the second chapter the reader encounters a discussion between a young man and a prostitute. The man, returning from the errors of his way, means to read her a moral lecture in private; she, of course, misunderstands his reason for wanting privacy, and says, when they are alone, "Here we are, as safe as you wish, my darling; we can do and say anything we want, my dear little sensualist, nobody can see what we are doing," words which give him his opportunity. For he answers, "No, I do not think so; for could we prevent God from seeing us?"

It may be assumed that this book, although dedicated to a six-year-old, would never be put in his hands; but this assumption is doubtful. The old literature bristles with remarks which, because of their incidental nature, make it obvious that children were indeed confronted with extremely mature matters. Here is another example.

In Elias' *Process of Civilization* [17] it is recorded that in the seventeenth century a six-year-old princess of Bouillon was told, as a joke, that she was pregnant. The little one denied it, but the joke was carried further. When she woke up one day, she found a newborn baby in her bed, put there by the ladies-in-waiting when she had been asleep. She was surprised, and said that it was apparently not only the Holy Virgin to whom a thing like that could happen. Everybody was delighted at this remark, and she got lying-in visits, and the queen herself offered to be the child's godmother. Eventually she was asked who might be the father. The little one thought deeply for a moment, and then replied that only the King and the Count of Guiche could be considered, for, said she, "Only those two had kissed me." Nobody considered this joke the least improper; in all probability because in those days there was nothing improper about it. But imagine such a joke being played on a six-year-old child today! Bad effects would be unavoidable.

The child has today become separated from everything belonging to the adult's life. Yet this can only mean that nowadays two separate states of human life can be distinguished: the state of maturity, with all the very mature attributes belonging to it, like birth, death, faith, and sexuality; and the state of immaturity, which lacks these attributes.

The child has become a child.

But this unusual conclusion has barely been reached when we are confronted with the question as to what causes were responsible for making the child a child. What caused the child, formerly hardly distinguishable from the adult, to be so different, so radically different from the adult? What caused the gap which today exists between young and old, a gap, so wide and deep, that it is impossible to carry the things of maturity to the other side?

In this general form, this question is easy to answer. The child is only childlike in comparison to what is not childlike, the adult. The causes of the change in the child's nature must lie in the changes in the nature of maturity. Is the adult mature in a way different from the way he was in the past? Is our maturity characterized by qualities which were less prominent or even entirely lacking in the past? Or did maturity in the past have qualities which have been lost in the course of time?

THE ADULTS

Je respire l'odeur d'une rose, et aussitot des souvenirs d'enfance me reviennent à la memoire.[18]

Turning over the leaves of Erasmus' *Colloquia* to verify a quotation, I became aware of the smell so peculiar to old books; and suddenly the memory of my own youth came back to me, still vague and not exactly determined in time, but alive, real, and pregnant, more real than it would have been if I had tried to recall it without opening the book. But it was more fleeting, more transient as well; only a minute later the impression had gone again, the past was submerged, from then on to emit unconnected facts until once more a smell, a sound, a word, an incident, or an object recalls the past as it was; as it can speak to me as "my past."

There is nothing that evokes a memory more faithfully than a smell. Occasionally we are reminded, with this fierce, almost overpowering clarity, by a melody of long ago that we happen to hear again; the song mother used to sing, the tune the boy next door endlessly practised on his flute. It is odd to realize that if we had not heard the melody again this memory, which we perhaps find to our surprise is the most precious memory we have, would never have entered our thoughts. Of course we would have been able to say: This is where I lived, my mother used to sing when she was in the kitchen, or, there was a boy next door who endlessly played on his flute—we would have been able to remember these facts, but the memory, the memory itself, would have stayed away forever. It is the facts that stay, being the skeleton of the past; but the essence of the facts, the thing that causes the facts to be "past," to be the past which, when it announces itself, makes us catch our breath, is as fleeting as nothing else. Even yesterday is foreign to us.

We do not notice it though, for yesterday's facts suggest a memory—which actually is not there at all. All the time the facts are suggesting that time is faithful to us; while actually time is more unfaithful than any lover could ever be.

The facts: skeleton of the past

We know that the war began on the 10th of May, 1940. But this knowing is still not a memory; we are only remembering a fact, nothing else. The actual memory of the day of May 10th, 1940, is another matter altogether. We could not do without the day itself: the day as it began, the warm day in spring with a clear blue sky and whirring metal airplanes in it; the early hour and all the pyjama-clad people looking at the sky. We need all the attributes of the event, we can hardly omit even one of them if we are to tempt the day to show itself. And then, suddenly, there it is, the day, just as it all happened; thousands of impressions are there at the same time, unabridged and full of meaning, still nameless. And before they get a name, they have sunk back in that immense grave called the past.

It is even more difficult to recall a past when we have not been there ourselves. It is not impossible, though. It is still "our" past; wherever we look into the past, it is always a past of human beings; because historical events are human events, they cannot be entirely foreign to us, and therefore they cannot be inaccessible. Just as a good storyteller takes us with him in reality (although not physically) to countries where we have never been, and to incidents we have never witnessed ourselves, so does the historian recall a past simply by narrating this past of which he knows the facts. To narrate means to convey the audience to the place and the time of the incident. In this authentic sense, history is still a "narrative science." But to tell a story is an art. World War I does not become real to us if we are told only about the initial murder, the Battle of the Marne, and the lagging end. This World War only begins to be real when we are told how columns of immature soldiers were mowed down, some of whom remained alive for days, moaning, beyond the reach of their desperate fellow soldiers; or how the horses died that became entangled in barbed wire; or how the rain beat down on the mud of the shot-up ground; or how wounds, covered with paper when there were no more bandages, began to rot.

The past is accessible, but only at the price of much effort and talent. The accessibility is achieved with cunning and with exertion. But I am putting this the wrong way: for it is not so much a matter of the past being or not being available to us; the past wants nothing else but to penetrate to us. That is what we notice in those moments when it jumps or flies at us in a smell or a sound. It is more a matter of liberating the past, of removing an obstruction, of removing a covering layer. The past is always ready for us, pure and complete; only a word is needed, a chord, a small constellation of things, something incidental, whatever it is. It seems as though the past can only come to us through a back entrance; the front door is closed.

Unknown past

Or is the front door closed? The complaint that it is so difficult to let the past come to us—our personal past as well as our mutual past—was uttered seldom in earlier days. And this is all the more striking when we consider how frequently we hear the complaint today. François Villon's sighs about the disappeared *"neiges d'antan"* [19] expresses a sorrow different from the complaint of the Goncourt brothers, that all memories can be stored in an extremely small corner: *"dans une toute petite bière, dans un bien petit coin de mémoire."* [20] Equally striking is the fact that at the beginning of this century two scientific attempts, independent and different in nature, were made to explain why youthful memories are lost during the course of human life.[21] Had this phenomenon become so prevalent that for the first time in history it induced a closer examination? In the same years Proust wrote his lifework, a long almost desperate struggle against the amnestic character of his life.[22] Never before had such a book been written. The popularity of this, in a way monotonous, story proves that Proust had touched on a problem that was felt by many. Has our past become less accessible, less visible?

Another fact leads to this question. When, at the beginning of this century, a first attempt was made to cure neurotics, nothing appeared so efficacious as a complete exploration, a bringing to light as completely as possible, of the hidden, disguised, and inaccessible memories of youth. It remains a mystery why hardly anybody had thought of this technique before. Is it too far fetched to assume that neurotics were the first to show that the entrance to the past had been barricaded, not only for them but for everybody? Were they not suffering from a disturbance affecting everybody, but which made only them manifestly ill? When, based on these therapeutical experiences, a new general conception of the human mind emerged which stressed the significance of the psychotraumatic character of forgotten youth-memories, many were ready to accept this conception. Would this have occurred if there had not been a change in the way man saw himself in relation to his own past? It seems hard to accept the idea that the wisdom of ages missed noticing something that we feel is a most natural state of affairs.

Has our mutual past also become unknown?

Perhaps it is not only our personal past that has become less accessible; perhaps it is the past of all mankind. Why is it that the science of history recently became extraordinarily obsessed by recalling the past as it had been *in daily life* for everybody—which means, in the most real, the most alive, form, in the form that speaks most to us? Why is it that at present a series on "Daily Life in Earlier Times" is appearing in France? [23] Why has the book, *Medieval People,* by Eileen Power, sold by the thousands? The subtitle says that the author wishes to recall past ages by describing the daily lives of ordinary people; [24] but what could there be of interest in the daily lives of ordinary people if things had not been different, if they were not unknown?

Did no one in the old days—that is, in the days before Carlyle, for according to Eileen Power he was the first to call for this "new history" [25]—did no one in the old days feel a need for such books? Did the past penetrate into the present freely, unimpeded, and undiminished? This is one of those questions which is difficult to answer for the reason that satisfied needs are not expressed. The very silence of the authors of the past leads us to believe that in the old days the past penetrated into the present much more easily than it does now. This does not mean that it passed into the present faultlessly. Mistakes have always been made; but these mistakes were aberrations within matter which was accessible as a whole. It certainly is the intention of the authors of the new history to prevent error, but it is not their first intention. Their first aim is to make the past live again, to reincarnate the past in the way that the smell of old books brought back my memory, so that the past in its purest form appeared before me, and I really did not consider it very important whether all the facts, without exception, were in their right place. This does interest me, but not in the first place, and I can even imagine that a correction in the arrangement of the facts might disturb my memory.

In that case, I would gladly sacrifice the facts to the memory. And the historian, when he wants the past to live again, when he wants to reincarnate the people of the past to make them speak to us, to our times, will also sacrifice the facts—if he has to—to this incarnation. For it should be realized that the past, in its real, alive form, is not the same past which was the present when the incidents occurred. The past, as past, is the past as it appears to us *now*: what happened then as it speaks to us now.

The past is the past observed from the present

The youth which emanates from the smell of old books is my youth in relation to my whole life, and not the youth of the years in which that youth had been the present. The memory of my youth is real, even if it is not identical with what happened in those days. That is what I notice when I am aware of the smell; the youth is there, just as it had been, then; but it also has the aspect of the far past, an aspect it did not have when it was the present. That is why eye witness accounts often lack exactness. Worded paradoxically: the memory is only real when it is not real. An autobiography is necessarily a work of art, which violates the facts—but violates them as little as possible. In my opinion the same is true for history. Great historians are great stylists. History is not just what has happened; what has happened is, at the most, a recording of the facts. History is what has happened in relation to the times. And this relation may disagree with the relation between the facts.

The facts are admitted, not the past

Facts can still penetrate to us unhampered. Open an account or a recording of a lawsuit and the facts march up. But the other component of memory, the factor which is the bearer of the facts, is elusive.

It has become elusive in the course of history. The reason is quite obvious. Whereas, in the old days, a conformity of life guaranteed a continuity from generation to generation which in turn made an unhampered transition from the past to the present possible, nowadays this continuity has been lost and we look back with wonder upon a time which does not speak to us any more. In those days "how it was" and "how it speaks to us" were the same thing, for the language spoken by the past was the same language the present spoke, the more so when the past had not been divided from the present by too long a time span. Today the present speaks a new language, and a language which has been renewed again and again. Consequently the facts present a "how it was" which is mute; and our question, "How was it?" founders on facts which tell us little or nothing.

How did people live in the old days, how did they eat, how did they drink, how did they sleep?—these, taken together, mean, how were they related to us?—and we do not know. We need not go back very far to establish this. We have no idea how our parents lived. When they tell us about it, when they take us with them into the past, we are amazed; we hear of a world in which everything was different. Of course the facts were different as well; they sat in different chairs and they wore different clothes. But this is not the reason for our amazement, for there is not much mystery in those facts. How they lived with those facts—that is what remains a secret. How did mother live wearing a skirt that came to her knees and a waistline at her hips? How did the neighbours sit behind the blooming aspidistra? What sort of a conversation went on in the living room with the red plush? Even if we were present there ourselves as youngsters, it still remains strange and inaccessible.

What our grandparents tell us is even stranger, at least if we try to understand what their story contains. "There were no cars"; that is all right; but let us not have the idea that we understand what this simple information, this fact, implies. A city without cars is radically foreign to us, as foreign as a street full of playing children in the center of the city; as foreign as a wagon rumbling on the main street with the driver asleep in the back. Only a story can bring this strangeness to us—if we are inclined to listen.

Things were different then. That is why it is so hard for the past to penetrate to us; the past cannot come to us because there are no points of contact, no similarities. Discontinuity permits no communication.[26]

There were days when our present discontinuity was unknown. Eileen Power speaks of these times when she writes, with barely disguised nostalgia, "The hurrying, scattering generation of today can hardly imagine the immovable stability of the village of past centuries, when generation after generation grew from cradle to grave in the same houses, on the same cobbled streets, and folks of the same names were still friends, as their fathers and grandfathers had been before them." [27] What they passed on to each other has now been lost.

Consequences of discontinuity

What has been lost was indicated by Alfred de Musset. He writes:

> To give an idea of the state of mind I found myself in during the days of my youth, I cannot do better than compare it to an interior of a modern home; rooms with furniture from all times and from all countries. Our age has no style of its own. Homes lack the stamp of time. In the streets one meets people with beards from the times of Henry III, some are clean-shaven, some wear their hair like Raphael, others the way they did in the times of Christ. The homes of the rich are curio shops; in them there is to be found antique, Gothic, Renaissance, Louis XIII, all mixed up. All the ages are around us, except our age, which has no style of its own.[28]

This was written by de Musset in 1835. The dissolution of the stability continued to advance to less visible, but not less important, human institutions. De Musset conveys this when he says that he, himself, was like the confusion around him. He did not find the words which later flowed easily from Margaret Mead's pen. In her book, *Male and Female*, she points out that:

> Every home is different from every other home, every marriage, even within the same class, in the same clique, contains contrasts between the parents as superficially striking as the difference between one New Guinea tribe and another. . . . Side by side, next-door neighbours, children of first cousins, some-

times children of sisters or brothers, the ways of each household diverge, one family bringing up the children to prudery, privacy and strongly marked sex roles, another to such an open give-and-take that the girls seem tomboys. Then again comes marriage between the children with the different upbringings, and again the clash, the lack of timing, the lack of movement in step, of the new set of parents. Every home is different from every other home; no two parents, even though they were fed their cereal from silver porringers of the same design, were fed it in quite the same way.[29]

The multivalencies

Comparing these two quotations from de Musset and Margaret Mead, we see that there is a definite similarity; but there is also a difference. De Musset's complaint refers to the confusing effect of the simultaneous presence of all times; Margaret Mead's description shows that the dissolution of the stability now involves more essential spheres, that it has come nearer and has succeeded in affecting the inner reality of our existence. It is no longer accurate to state that the modern adult world is suffering from a universal anachronistic pluralism (although it is nonetheless true that our time still embraces a chaos of styles, while barely having one of its own); this world is also suffering from an increasing multivalency of all its institutions. Every action, every matter, every word has not one, but many, meanings. For some words this pluralism is so important that their meanings differ from person to person. The meaning of the word *work*, for instance, is different for each of us; nonetheless, this word is used extremely often. Words like *faith, disbelief, freedom, obligation* all have strictly personal meanings for each of us. Even words basic to our existence—*mother, father, child, husband, wife, birth, death, love* and *hate*—have lost their universal interpretations. When we read that the child has no enemies more dangerous than his parents,[30] the remark manages to startle us out of another, and as we thought, better opinion; but only a second afterward we have filed it under the subject of "parents," which was already very extensive anyway, being the harbor of our dearest memories as well as the stillwater of our obstinate desires to be mature at last.

And when even the word *parents* has become multivalent, is it not probable that the child is unsettled by an existence which makes words and things multivalent on such a scale?

The child and multivalencies

Growing toward this pluriform and multivalent maturity, the child encounters incredible difficulties. Every step it takes toward maturity is a step into a mist of multivalencies. This begins as soon as the child goes to kindergarten; his classmates are dressed differently, they have different manners, different habits, and different needs. They even talk differently; one has a Southern accent and another one rolls his *r*'s because he came from Scotland. When he goes to his friends' homes, he finds the most usual and familiar things absent or suspect. His friends have another religion or no religion at all; some of his friends fold their hands before meals, others make the sign of the cross with astonishing speed, others again are in the habit of thoughtfully touching their chests; at some homes one is supposed to wait until every one is seated; at other homes this is apparently considered highly unusual, and one is expected to attack the food as soon as it comes in sight. His friends' parents appear to have different political views, which he learns from their doubtful silence or constrained smiles; the teachers give evidence of ever-changing interpretations of the historical past and of the desirable, or fearful, future. The child encounters families in which, in the morning, the mother wanders around the house like a modern Eve, and other families where the least allusion to sex is taboo.

Adults can hardly imagine how hard it is for the child to find a way in all these diversities. Our very maturity means that we have put this diversity into shape, and that we live with a monovalent choice out of the multivalencies around us which is valid at least for ourselves, at the most also for a very few around us, so that everything outside this choice does not touch us. The multivalency does not assault us, it slips past us, it hardly affects us. We have succeeded in establishing a small and relatively simple domain in this complex society; to the rest we are blind, we do not see it, and so we can act as if it were not there. But the child cannot do this. That is exactly what being a child means—to be defenceless against this multivalency and to shrink back from it. The confrontation with maturity is the discovery of a threshold, a limit.

Thresholds on the way to maturity

No doubt the child learns of this threshold long before it goes to school. Adults' gestures are unsure, since they originate from a domain of maturity whose boundaries are determined by an inability. "The gestures of the feeding hands, whether of mother, grandmother, Irish cook, English nurse, Negro mammy, country-bred hired girl, are no longer the assured, the highly-patterned gestures of the member of a homogeneous society." [31] The mother's hand offering the nipple to the child's mouth is no longer only directed by an age-old code between mother and child—it also is moved by the insecurity which rules all our actions. The child is conscious of this insecurity—for besides drinking, it is also tasting maturity—and it is repulsed. The gesture which maturity should show, which should smooth the way to the other person, to the mother, to maturity—certainly this gesture still smooths the way, still creates trust and therefore creates a way—how could the child grow up otherwise?—but it repulses at the same time. It both invites and establishes a limit. And so the child is ever turned away. Like the famous pilgrim to Mecca, he goes one pace backward for every two paces forward. The journey takes a long time. The goal is reached late. The child is a child for a long time; it is late in reaching maturity.

The first reason for the child's increased childishness and for the origin, the lengthening, and the deepening of maturation thus originates in the multivalent pluralism peculiar to modern maturity.

The invisibility of the mature state

The second characteristic of modern maturity is its invisibility. To the eyes of the child, maturity is invisible. In the past, if a child walked through the streets of his town, he could see and hear around him how trades were practiced, one of which trades he would choose himself later on. The rope-maker, the smith, the brazier, the cooper, the carpenter, they all worked in places accessible to any child: in their houses, in workyards, or somewhere in the open. Today most trades are shut away in factories, where children are not allowed. How can a child know what happens there? His father, when he comes home from his work, brings with him at the most a story and a smell; no doubt these are important indications, but they are only indications: the reality itself remains invisible. Besides, more and more jobs are coming into existence that are invisible to the child even if he does witness what is being done. What sort of an idea can the child have of his father's work if the father is a superintendent, a social worker, a tax collector, or a psychotherapist? And as for the last, what does my child think of the work I do? People called "patients," who do not appear to be ill at all, come at appointed hours and stay in my room some time. This does not tell him anything but that he has to be quiet while they are there—and then they leave again. Can I expect my child to choose my profession? Obviously not; if he did, I should be justified in doubting the soundness of his choice, for he would be choosing an emptiness, a meaningless thing—a disappearance into a room, a silence, and a thoughtful reappearance. For this is what I show my children, nothing else. That is why I feel reassured when I find that none of my children wants to be a psychotherapist. And I think that a tax collector, a social worker, and a superintendent should have the same feeling of relief when they find that their children are in agreement about this one thing—that they will never follow in their father's footsteps.

Invisible occupations of former times

In the past, occupations absolutely invisible for the child doubtless existed. But they were scarce; and besides, what is more important, they were characterized by a very visible style of living peculiar to that occupation, and by a family tradition. If the father were a preacher, he strode through the town dressed in the clothes of his profession, wearing a dignity that went with his work. And when hats were taken off to him, he distributed his greetings in a way that fit every person. His child saw what he was; in the extension of the visible things lay the characteristic qualities of the profession, although those qualities were invisible themselves. Now the preacher drives a car in no way different from the car owned by his neighbor, the plumber; he does not wear different clothes, he has no greeting in a style of his own; he is like anybody else, just as uncharacteristic as anybody else. What does he do, this preacher? Even to us, adults, it is not quite clear, although he has much more work to do than his predecessors; for the child the matter is entirely obscure. That nonetheless preachers' children show a greater preference for becoming preachers than psychiatrists' children for becoming psychiatrists is the result of the fact that the preacher at least is visible in the pulpit once a week. Band and gown cause the child to decide to be like his father; the seaman's child discovers his future in the gold braids of cap and coat, and the soldier's child in the military insignia.

What makes the child decide?

Please do not think that the child makes a wrong choice if it is such external vanities which make him decide. Because the sort of choice we want him to make, the sort of choice that, according to the modern conception, really makes him decide on his future occupation, that sort of choice is impossible for the child—and has always been impossible. To make a choice that ideal way means to be able to judge the chosen occupation and all the other occupations as well, as many as possible—and even then, can the child ever be sure he had considered every possibility? No; the child cannot decide in this way.

Actually adults are not able to do it either. No person in the world can boast of having made one important and authentic decision on the basis of mature and thorough deliberation, in which every possibility was weighed. We do not marry that way, we have no hobbies that way, we do not join a political party that way, and we do not convert to a religion that way. To make a choice is to decide without rational foundation, to take a risk, to create the future.

What does a choice imply?

To make a choice is not to find a safe course between matters that are no longer dangerous because they have been examined; at the most that would be drifting with the current. To make a choice is to project a course into the unknown, into a road full of danger. The child who sees his father's white coat and says he wants to be a doctor is putting himself into the future with more conviction and readiness than the child who has no hold on a white coat but who is told by the psychologist that he would do well to become a doctor.

Since the future has become invisible to such an extent that the child cannot manage to throw a net over the reality which awaits him—since, in other words, hardly any adult provides the child with information by visibly showing his occupation so that he can make a choice, which means boldly project his existence into the future—somebody else will have to build, by artificial means, an emergency bridge to a destination which has become elusive. It is only to be expected that this artificial bridge will be built on columns other than the one the child used when he could visibly judge the mature state. The columns of this new bridge are called "function-analysis," which involves a knowledge of what is implied by occupation A, B, or C, and a knowledge of the child's structure—whether he is affective, manual, intellectual, communicative. The result is a well thought out (which means hesitating) signal, a gesture which threatens to rob the future of every charm. Regrettable; but is there another way?

An almost anachronistic entreaty

For very many children there is already no other way. Yet I should like to protect those youngsters, who will be very few as time goes on, who go to meet their future without a psychological examination. I wish to protect a boldness which in the near future will border on irresponsibility. But it can still be done. I would like to say to them: do not look too much at those who legalize the motives of their actions with pieces of paper. The paper replaced a choice. The motive replaced significant trifles.

Putting myself in the place of these children, I cannot resist saying: if the future is laid out before me as a result of an examination, then I do not want to step into it. If an examination is necessary to show me that I should marry this woman and not that woman, then let me have the second woman. Maybe it will result in a lot of inconveniences, but it has the invaluable advantage of being my own choice; I shall have made my own marriage with her, so that the inconveniences will be my (our) inconveniences—and not the risk the report did not cover—and the happiness will be our happiness—and not a praise of psychology. *Let me fail!* this cry I wish any one who is able to create a future of his own.

Invisibility makes choice impossible

But this sigh belongs to a dead past. It is easy enough for me to say: let the child be free, let it keep away, for as long as it lives, from anything called psychology, let it *live*. As long as I shut myself away in my office, I am negating what I have just said. I am invisible; there is no element of visibility, however small, which would allow my child to get an idea of my occupation. The same thing applies to the factory worker's son; when his father leaves, the door dividing home from the outside world closes behind him, the son cannot accompany him (he would be killed in the traffic) and another door, the factory entrance, closes behind his father. Relentlessly. The son is not permitted inside (he might be caught in the machinery), and he cannot see anything of what his father does during the day—his father who falls in his chair in the evening and gets out his newspaper, saying, "He was in a bloody temper," meaning the boss, or, "We've got a new radio in our department," meaning the music that gratified his ears when he was busy doing what his son will never see.

"What are you going to be?" asks this father, when his son leaves school; to this question he will get the almost stereotyped reply, "I don't know." "In my time," says the father—certainly, in his time children knew at least a little of that choice; a few things were still visible. But these fathers are getting scarce; they will die out.

Soon no father will be able to say, "In my time we knew what we were going to be," for nobody will remember ever having known, nobody will cherish the memory of an insecure, risky time in which a future was built on nothing, or rather on a few futile visibilities, on trifles—that is, on significant beacons. Today one's occupation is prescribed by institutions which have lately become necessary, which falsely suggest they are supplying an age-old deficiency. This deficiency was apparently embodied in the happy-go-lucky choice, the choice made on a few silly visibilities, the choice without motives—and yet such a choice was never unmotivated. For true motives are not to be found in what is available—in what has been yesterday and can be inspected as an inventory today—but in what will be tomorrow. To make a choice is to be invited; and that is what making a choice meant then.

Choosing after making an inventory

Soon, making a choice will mean choosing what appears as the most probable or the least impossible from an inventory. It is to be expected that making the inventory will be put off as long as possible, for something that might justify a choice does not exist. Nor did it exist in the past. The things which decided the choice then were not to be found in the person who was making the choice; they were outside of him, they were in the future. Today they have to be found in the person who is making the choice; the future is empty. But the person who makes the choice is just as empty; no one starts life with a program. So he will have to wait. "You'll have to wait a little longer," says the expert to the mother. "The child is still too immature. Let us put him through college first." And if he goes through college and he still does not know (this happens every day, even now) then the expert will have to say that the inventory is still deficient, the child is still not formed (how could he be?), he is still too playful (but how could he have acquired maturity?). "Can't he go through another year of college?" Ever putting it off: the children are empty, as they have always been, and their future is empty, but that is our work; the expert waits till the child has picked up a bit here and there.

The foggy present

If the future is empty, the present contains only trifles. Each kick against a football, each half-smoked and then discarded cigarette is the counterpart of a future in which nothing can be distinguished. The present is filled with matters that do not relate to anything. Could it be expected that the child, the youngster, the boy who, in the old days, "could do his share" will suddenly know what he wants in the middle of all this unrelating (which means not tuned into a future) atmosphere? If adulthood is invisible, youth lives in a fog.

Invisible marriage

Not only a person's occupation, but his marriage too, the attribute par excellence of maturity, has become invisible.

In the middle ages the *chevalier recréant* was known and feared —the knight who, once married, did not appear on social occasions anymore. He was at home, in his castle, enjoying himself with his young wife; so much did they enjoy themselves that they refused to appear socially. This state of dual seclusion was generally condemned. Marriage was expected to be what it was intended to be, a social institution, not a cell; a center of social activity, an open institution—which, however, can only be really open if the *secret à deux* is respected, if it is acknowledged. The middle ages rejected the swampy existence of a male and a female living snugly together, snugly but spongily.

In certain respects every modern married couple is an example of the *chevalier recréant*, but not in the sense of ours or somebody else's marriage being a more or less radical seclusion. That, certainly, is not the way we lead our lives; the husband is away from home most of the day, and the wife can walk on the street freely, and does. Besides, society comes to the family readily enough; there is rather too much reading matter than too little, and most of us are politically or socially aware and active in some kind of political, religious, entertainment, or scientific group.

In another sense, however, marriage is invisible: that is, the fact that marriage is a sexual union does not become clear to the child in any way. If the parents get along rather well, the child may see evidences of the harmony between them, and maybe even witness an embrace or some erotic teasing. In some families the child often witnesses these tendernesses; indeed, the modern child may observe his parents' love making much more frequently than did the child in earlier ages. In those days embraces occurred very seldom; parents did not sit on each other's laps. But the earlier child did see and hear more of the fundamental relationship between his parents—and that relationship is what nowadays is withdrawn entirely from the child's eyes and ears. In the past (and now I mean a long time ago), a child slept in his parents' bedroom until an age when little can be kept secret. Not infrequently a child slept in his parents' bed; but if he was not in their bed or even in their bedroom, he still was within hearing distance of the parents. The child witnessed their sexual contact, however vaguely. Even when the child only heard the noises, these noises still helped to give a certain visibility to sex—a visibility which although it remained locked up in sound and therefore without visualization, was still an impression. Later on, his observation could build on this experience.

The child of today does not see anything. He does not sleep in his parents' bedroom. Any psychologist and any psychiatrist can tell us why not, and why it would even be extremely dangerous (and yet, why was not it dangerous in the past?). The child has his own bedroom, the door of which is closed. When the parents go to bed, a second door is closed; they may even lock it. Should the parents notice that something of what happened during the night penetrated to the child, measures will be taken immediately. Any carelessness in this matter punishes itself; the child gets a tic, he starts to wet his bed, or he sleepwalks to his parents' bedroom door, searching for the spirit that haunts the house, searching for the absent sexuality of the parents, those parents who embrace each other and sit on each other's laps for nothing.

The closed bedroom

The door will not be opened, the child can be certain of that. The parents, perplexed by their child's symptoms, consult a child psychiatrist; and almost certainly, even at the first consultation, he will inquire about their sleeping habits. If he gets suspicious about the noises, he will advise removing the child to where he cannot hear. The result is astonishing. Tic, bedwetting, and sleepwalking disappear like snow before sunshine. The sexuality is covered up, the haunting spirit does not show itself anymore. The child is no longer afraid. But let us not fool ourselves: the spirit is not gone; its appearance is only put off. Soon—or rather, much later—it will reappear. The effect of the psychotherapist's advice (which was undoubtedly right) is primarily to postpone. The child has to wait. The invisibility of sexuality pushes the child into a strengthened puerility and into a late maturity.

CONTINUITY AND THE INCLINATION OF CHILDREN TO ASK QUESTIONS

Lyell's graduality

When Charles Darwin went on board the ship *Beagle* in 1831 to make a trip around the world as a naturalist, he had, packed in his luggage a book that had only just appeared. This book, which helped him greatly in the discovery of things that otherwise might have remained unobserved, was Charles Lyell's *The Principles of Geology*.

In this textbook of geology Lyell explained for the first time that the changes in the earth's crust, observed by the geologist where different layers are folded, creased, and upset, are not caused as had been thought, by abrupt catastrophes of earthquakes and volcanic eruptions, but by a gradual evolution, extremely slow and still going on. The changes we see, which so forcefully suggest extreme movement or cataclysms, are still occurring; and the speed of these changes at present is the same as it was in early times. These were the principal thoughts of Lyell's book.

Darwin in the Galapagos Islands

Darwin went ashore on the Galapagos Islands. Going from island to island, he found iguanas whose colors differed; and, it occurred to him that differences in color, like differences in the earth's crust, were not caused by an influence which had acted suddenly (such a sudden change was hard to imagine anyway), but by a very slow and still occurring process.[32] Thus his theory of evolution was born. The observation that the color of the iguanas appeared to harmonize with that of the rocks which also differed from island to island was not really important, however much it may have added to the theory. As it happened this idea was not unknown. Biologists before Darwin had expressed the opinion that animal and environment are both parts of the same process. What was new in Darwin's theory was the idea of a forever-lasting slow motion, that animal and environment are both being subjected to a change of a very slow nature, which is still going on. Those last words are important: *still going on.* The forces of those days are the forces of the present.

Then is now

To Lyell this was the crucial point. In a letter dated March 2, 1827, he writes, "I will write a book on the identity of causes in the past and in the present"; in 1828 he writes his father, "I want to prove the identity of the causes which act in the present and those which acted in the past"; and in a letter dated 1829, he formulates this idea in its complete form: ". . . that no causes whatever have, from the earliest time to which we can look back, to the present, ever acted, but those now acting, and that they never acted with different degrees of energy from which they now exert." And finally, in the subtitle of his textbook, he expresses his intention to prove that the early changes in the earth's crust have been caused by forces which are still acting at present.[33]

What is important is the identity of past and present. Darwin, too, stressed this point. However much the phrase, "the origin of species" may suggest that the idea of origin will be examined—that is, the newness of plant and animal at the moment of their appearance—the book merely ascribes this "newness" to what had been previously. The whole diversity of life is embodied in the first life on earth; what the present is, is an unabridged version of what the past was. The present is just a result, an adaptation of the past. And that is what the future will also be; there is nothing new under the sun. There are always the same materials (earth crust, living matter) and the same forces (geodynamic, and biological).

Continuity

It is the idea of continuity. Nature does not leap, *natura non facit saltus*. "*Tout va par degrés dans la nature et rien par saut.*" Leibniz [34] with these words formulated the law which he, himself, thought so important, the law of continuity: "*La loi de la continuité.*" It can easily be proved that this idea of continuity has not always been thought true. I shall go into this presently, but before doing so I have to point out that I do not merely wish to show that the idea of continuity has not always been there; it is not the idea that matters so much, as the continuity itself. Previously there had been no continuity of things, and now there is.

We adults effected this change. So intently have we turned this idea into reality, that now, if we should doubt it, we should be doubting reality. Consequently, we are able to say, "You see, reality is continuous." It would stop being continuous as soon as we retracted this idea, which affords children so many hardships. For the thoughts we think become real, if they are great thoughts. That is what thinking means, to make real. If thoughts do not become real, then they are not thoughts, certainly not great thoughts, but playful fantasies which, miraculously, sometimes also touch reality and hang on to it. "Have you noticed," wrote Oscar Wilde,[35] "that Nature has recently begun to look like Corot's landscapes?" Really, is not this a beautiful example? For Corot did not think, he only looked; he played with visions and put them down on his canvas. They flew off it and nestled in Nature.

The foundations of a miraculous science

When was the idea of continuity born? At the beginning of the seventeenth century? Perhaps the birthday of this thought can be identified now with great accuracy. In the beginning of the seventeenth century lived one of the greatest thinkers, a man who changed reality considerably by his thinking; he was involved in an adventure which enacted itself within the borders of a strictly personal existence, within the walls of a small study. The effects of this adventure have determined the existence of many (till now, of all) generations after him.

In November, 1619, Descartes, in the service of the Duke of Bavaria and out of work because there was nothing to do as far as military matters were concerned, rented a heated room in the neighbourhood of Ulm, where he "occupied himself with his own thoughts, in the happy circumstance of not being troubled by worries or passions." [36] On November 10, strange things occurred; thoughts arranged themselves, unknown prospects appeared before his eyes, prospects of a new scientific activity, still vague and not yet fully elaborated, but with fixed directives. *Mirabilis scientiae fundamenta*, the foundations of a miraculous science were born. What foundations? And of which science? Descartes never answered these questions, as far as we know. But there have been many conjectures. Probably Descartes' discovery (all of his work points to this) is concerned with the possibility of patterning every science after mathematics. What was the point of this discovery? Bréhier,[37] who formulates this question, answers by alluding to a passage in another of Descartes' essays, the *Géométrie*; in the last paragraph of the last chapter is to be found an observation of universal importance. "If the first two or three terms of any progression are known," writes Descartes, "it is not difficult to find the other terms.[38]

This is the idea of continuity. It had never before been formulated as a universal law, a law to which all things and all incidents had to conform. The concepts of continuity and its opposite, discontinuity, were known in the middle ages as well as in antiquity;

but the latter had never been rejected in favour of the exclusive validity of the former. Discontinuity, which means a nongradual transition, a leap, an unconnectedness, and which implies accidental or free occurrence, was accepted in every respect as possible and real. Now discontinuity seems almost inconceivable. We have become so used to connection and gradual transition that we cannot think of anything unconnected. We look for structures; driven by a quaint necessity, we desire connections, gradual transitions. That a thing could have structure without connection (without the connection of gradual transition) is unimaginable to us. And yet it is only possible to speak of the structure of things and incidents if there is no continuous connection. For continuity equalizes; it ultimately abolishes all structure. It produces homogeneity; and there is nothing so devoid of structure as homogeneous matter.

Descartes' principles

But I do not express myself correctly. It is not continuity that produces homogeneity, it is the other way round; homogeneity is a condition for continuity. The idea of gradual transition would not have occurred if the things, between which the transition was supposed to be made, had not previously been made equal.

I will try to prove this by citing Descartes' *Principes de la philosophie* (1644). The second part of these principles of philosophy is concerned with "*Les principes des choses matérielles,*" which is an elaboration of what Descartes wanted to express in his idea of continuity. His argument is based on a few cardinal observations. They are:

1. Neither its weight, nor its resistance to touch, nor its color is typical of an object; only its extensiveness is essential. [If a paperweight loses its weight it still remains an object; if it flows away between my touching fingers, and if it changes color, it is still an object. In spite of all these not unimportant changes, the objectiveness of the object remains untouched.]

2. What has extensiveness, is an object. [This conclusion follows immediately from the first thesis; if smell, taste, shape, weight, consistency, in short, if anything that is variable is not typical of

an object, then it can only be circumscribed by that which is invariable: extensiveness. The object occupies space.]

3. What has extensiveness can be divided; the parts necessarily still have extensiveness, and consequently can be divided again. This division goes on infinitely; there are no atoms. [This thesis also follows from the previous one; if matter is only extensiveness, then it can be divided infinitely, for every measure can be halved.]

4. Everything consists of the same matter. [That is clear; if matter is only extensiveness, then every matter is alike. As, obviously, there are differences between objects, the next thesis follows.]

5. The difference between objects is a nonmaterial difference, a difference in motion. [I shall return to this thesis presently. The question which this thesis invites is: Where does this motion come from?]

6. Motion is caused by another motion. [After this, the next thesis is inevitable.]

7. The first motion was initiated by God.

The final principle is the first thought

It is done, it cannot be denied: God has been eliminated. For, as a rule, in such closed lines of thought, the last thought is the thinker's starting point, the thought that matters. Descartes wanted to eliminate God; God who previously had literally been present in all things. This is all over now.

Let us see how Descartes takes God by the hand. He starts by saying: Only its extensiveness characterizes an object. The object occupies space; everything else is unimportant and can just as easily be dispensed with. Is it not true? A paperweight is just as much a paperweight, if it should flee from my fingers, if it has no *dureté*, no resistance to touch, or if it has no weight or colour. This idea seems plausible.

Yet it is not true. No one would need a paperweight without weight; its weight *is* what matters. The paperweight which flees before my pointing finger would be highly inconvenient, if not dangerous. If all things lost their *dureté*, their resistance to touch, no one could either use or enjoy them. It would not be possible to stick a potato on a fork; one would not even be able to pick up his fork. And finally, the paperweight whose color changes might well clash so much with the colors of other objects among which it has to occupy space that it would be wise to flee; for using its resistance to touch and its weight, its owner would certainly throw it in the wastepaper basket.

A *matter of being scientific*

The reader who might think that I do not mean this seriously is mistaken. I *am* serious. The way Descartes treats objects is not fair. If science wants to consider objects as they are, in the form they have as objects, then it is not permitted to speak of objects which consist of nothing but extensiveness. There is no such thing—and there was no such thing. But Descartes' ideas have penetrated so deeply into reality that nobody knows where the idea ends and reality (or, if preferred, another idea of reality) begins. We shall see this presently.

Descartes' arguments

Descartes' first assertion was: extensiveness is the only essential characteristic of an object. This assertion contains a reduction which is not scientifically justified. The second assertion restates the first: what has extensiveness is an object. The reduction is the matter itself. So as far as objects are concerned, nothing matters except length, width, and height. This assertion gives us a right to speak of nothing but extensiveness if we are discussing objects, which is exactly what Descartes does. Objects are infinitely dividable (which follows immediately from the thesis that extensiveness is infinitely dividable), and everything consists of the same matter (everything has extensiveness). The inevitable result of this is: objects are identical (a piece of bread is a brick), and the difference between objects (a piece of bread happens *not* to be a brick) is a trick of extensiveness. And the only trick extensiveness can play is one, which, like extensiveness itself, can be expressed in numbers, in length, in width, and in height: that is, motion. If things are only space, locations in space and no more, there is nothing to consider but going from one location to another. Motion, however, so argues Descartes, requires a reason, or (which is not the same thing) a cause. One motion causes another, resulting in an endless series of motions. Where is the beginning? But who can imagine infinity? any attempt would make us dizzy. Rather have a beginning somewhere, a first motion started by a first mover: God. God once gave our world a push and it has kept on moving since, one motion causing the next and so on; the total quantity of motion remains the same, nothing is added—for that would only confuse the issue. We also know, says Descartes to his own and our assurance, that God is perfect; not only is His nature unchangeable, neither will He undo what He initiated. Here Descartes surpasses Pangloss.[39]

Pascal saw through Descartes' intention: "He [Descartes] would have liked to do without God, but he could not avoid letting Him give a little push to set the world in motion; after that he is finished with God." [40] That was what it is all about. Descartes protested against an Aristotelian idea of causality, which is open to all sides, which leaves room for unknown causes, for *qualitates occultae* that can act anywhere at any time; an idea of causality that causes a breeze of insecurity to blow through incidents. Descartes wanted to invalidate this conception; how many times in *La Flèche* had not people boxed his ears with it? Now *that's* finished (one can almost hear him say it); he locked away reality from anything that does not conform to strict continuity. There is no room for God anymore, except in the beginning. But that is only a safety measure; if God were nowhere at all, if He were not ordered to stay somewhere, no one would know where He might suddenly reappear. That is the reason for Descartes' complicated argument, for his reduction to extensiveness. For only in this system are all things identical, and only through this homogeneity is there a strict causality. The way from now on is in one direction only, not to be averted, and predictable. It is dependable, this way; so much so, that it can be examined and laws derived to which incidents of tomorrow will conform. The experiment becomes possible. What is valid now will be valid forever.

The past character of the experiment

It must be stressed that the idea of continuity is a result of a homogeneity which was produced by reduction. If this reduction—objects are localized space, extensiveness—is valid, then, but only then, is the idea of continuity valid. If the reduction is accepted, the experiment has sense; but only if. The experiment is valid for a denuded world, a world of naked localisation, not for any other world. The experiment, according to Fechner, belongs to a "night view," not to a "daylight view." [41]

How can experiments discover laws which will be valid tomorrow and in a thousand years? (These laws make it very easy for us to believe in the "objective accuracy" of genetic continuity.) The answer is obvious. The experiment is part of a world which is reduced to extensiveness: the experiment *measures*. This reduced world is a homogeneous world; it only contains identical things (for every measure is measure), and therefore it is continuous. The present is like the past: measure then is measure now; the numbers may vary, but numbers are infinitely dividable. The present is an elaborated past, a consequence of the past. And so the present is made the past, insofar as it is what necessarily results from the past. In this sense the future is the past, too, it is also what necessarily results from the past. There is no doubt about it: the experiment, directed at a reality which had been carried back to the past, discovers laws which are valid in the future, for that future actually is the past from which these laws were collected. The entire predictability of science is based on the "past" character of its "nature." Science predicts nothing, it only seems to do so by laying expectations in the future—a future, however, which long before was made past. The expectations come true because the predicted incident is chained to the past. Only by relating incidents to the past do they become predictable.

To predict, to really foretell, is still a gift of those who own the future in the full unrestricted sense of the word, the sense of what is coming toward us, and not of what is the result of the past.

These remarks can be illustrated and made clear with a concrete example.

Foucault's pendulum

In the middle of the last century Foucault surprised Paris, and soon afterward the whole scientific world, by a simple and there-fore eloquent experiment. In the Pantheon he suspended a globe weighing twenty-eight kilograms on a thin metal string sixty-four meters long. When the pendulum was put in motion, it appeared that the plane in which it moved to and fro every sixteen seconds was rotating; a peripherally-fitted scale showed a displacement of two and one half millimeters at every swing of the pendulum. This experiment made visible for everybody what Galilei had explained two hundred years before: that the earth rotates. Today hardly anyone who considers this law, which was confirmed by experiment, will ask himself whether the earth's motion, so de-fined, really explains the forces which control the world we live in.

What happened when Foucault set up his experiment? In the first place, the Pantheon—this church which was finished in the year of the revolution, then became a temple, then a church again in Napoleon's time, and finally a mausoleum under Louis Philippe —this monument of French history, this often consecrated and desecrated building, was no longer something particular, something that invoked silence and thought; it was space. Just space, space that could be measured. The Pantheon is 110 meters long, 84 meters wide, and 83 meters high; and that is all that can be said of the Pantheon as far as Foucault was concerned. So much is Foucault's Pantheon just space that the natural inclination to be silent automatically disappeared; to call out and shout did not make one feel uneasy. On the contrary; by calling out, one perceives the pendulum.

"Is it all right like this?" Foucault must have shouted, a shout which transformed the entire Pantheon to its very foundations, which made it a cavity, a hollow space. "A little more to the front," some one shouted back at him—and the pillars became piled up bricks, supports for the heavy roof; the length stretched itself out to 110 meters, the height shrank to 83 meters, the colors of the paintings became paint, paint on bricks. "Be careful, don't hit the wall"—matter against matter, space against space. In this space was the pendulum.

It is the same sort of transformation that we experience if, let us say, in the middle of Mahler's *Kindertotenlieder* someone makes the remark: "That is a third." This may be true, but it is true in another reality, a reality not identical with Mahler's music, a reality that Mahler used, and which, because it was used, was absorbed into the totality of his creation. This reality cannot be peeled out of the totality without doing it irreparable damage. In the same way bricks are used by a church builder; they constitute a condition, but not the intention, of the church.

Who ever has seen a wellknown building or a house he has lived in being pulled down will have been surprised about the entirely different, essentially different, qualities and proportions which come to light. Was that the living room where he sat so often? Was that the staircase? It is unbelievable. But he need not believe it, for what he sees is the room reduced to space, the staircase reduced to width and height.

About a few reductions

Foucault caused this sort of transformation. The Pantheon became space; and he treated this space as extensiveness. He suspended a pendulum in it and he made it swing. The weight moved. The earth rotated. Which earth? The earth which conformed to the Pantheon of the pendulum. No other earth. Only the earth which was reduced to space, location in space. But is there another earth?

Is there indeed not another earth, so different that Foucault's earth disappears into nothingness in comparison? We meet this other earth when we open the window on a summer morning and see that it is daylight; the sun, coming up over the green horizon, is chasing the morning fog. "The earth rotates"—this is the same sort of truth here, as, "That is a third." Just as the third vanishes into the music that Mahler heard, and which we hear after him with his ears, because our ears are not up to it, just so does Foucault's rotation vanish in the summer morning, in everything that is happening outside, that is moving outside, moving in an entirely different way from the movement created by Foucault. Certainly, created!

When he wants us to hear the music he is hearing, the composer uses the assistance of intervals. In the same way the architect requires the co-operation of bricks and cement. He uses Foucault's space, he cannot do without it if he wants to build, just as Mahler cannot do without intervals if he wants us to hear his music. He implores them to help him, they are difficult enough to handle, these intervals; they are so ostentatiously measured, so very much interval, space; how hard it is to absorb them in music. The same difficulty is experienced by the architect; he only succeeds if the bricks disappear into his creation, if their heaviness becomes invisible and Foucault's measurements are absorbed into the proportions he saw when he started.

When Emma Bovary finds that her love is answered, everything around her moves "stronger than if mountains were shifted," as Flaubert said. Of this movement Foucault and his followers could never perceive anything. When, at another occasion, she is deeply affected with emotion, "the ground under her feet trembles"—but no seismograph could register this trembling. And yet this trembling is an effect of a shock more real and essential than all seismographic shocks put together. The earth rotates—certainly, if you are satisfied with a denuded, stripped, and dimmed world which has lost all human qualities; then, but only then, does it rotate. The seismographic shock may kill me; but the trembling Emma Bovary felt is still more real and more believable.[42] The earth shock is inflicted on me from the area where death resides anyway, from that part of our existence which is identical with Foucault's space, a part which makes us lifeless, which kills us, which drives life out of matter. The shock hits at that part of me that has been connected with death ever since I was born and even longer; the shock hits me in my past. From the moment of conception life flows on to disintegration with a relentless, continuous, causal, and necessary speed, and that shock has merely come too early. At the moment of the earthquake my continuity is intersected by another continuity. After all, both are discounted in the same past. My getting killed in the earthquake is happening in a far past. To die in the objective world is a matter of the past. But to die, to really die in our world, means dying now.

The law, attribute of the past

Foucault moves in the past. The very fact that he arranged his experiment with the greatest peace of mind, considering it of no importance at all whether the pendulum would swing now or later, in the year 1849 or in 1850, proves that he was concerned with a past matter. He measured what had always been, and forgot that he was measuring the result of a reduction which he applied himself. Is it surprising that the law is still valid, even now, a hundred years later?

Let us presume that Foucault's pendulum might have uncovered an irregularity which in the course of the experiment would have shown itself variable, and that mathematics would have made clear that these irregularities were phasic. Would it surprise us, then, if the experimenter predicted a deviation of a circumscribed magnitude exactly expressed in numbers, in—let us say—the year 1984? His prediction would place the past in the year 1984.

It might be called idealistic to say that the tremblings felt by Emma Bovary are more real than the earthquake which kills us. Yet they are a matter of the grimmest reality; a summer morning is more real and essential to the existence we call ours, than Foucault's experiment can ever be. Actually, those who call themselves realists are merely those who separate one aspect from the totality of man and world—the deadly aspect—and then extend it into an idea of totality. Is not life more than death?

Nineteenth-century homogeneities

There is no doubt that the idea of the obligate continuity made possible by Descartes, and formulated as a law by Leibniz, had its great chances in the nineteenth century—for instance, Lyell and Darwin.

In 1850 Robert von Mayer and James Joule, independently of each other and using entirely different methods, formulated the mechanical equivalent of a unit of heat, an achievement which originated from the concept that heat and action represent the same energy. They are equal, heat and action, as are Descartes' objects. Of course they are only equal as measurements (extensiveness); but since Descartes' time, measurement has become so important to us that we forget how many unequalities are ignored. For heat and action, unreduced—that is, essentially—are not equal. He who is cold will look for a stove, not a tractor. We have been told that shivering transforms action into heat; but this information does not make the relation between shivering and coldness more natural—rather, the reverse.

In 1894 Freud conceived the idea that the neurotic's symptoms can easily be explained if it is assumed that an energetic quality, transferable by nature, is used first for this, and next for that, thought or action.[43] This idea was expressed more accurately in 1905;[44] the cells of the human body, and particularly the cells of the sexual glands, produce a substance which, transported by the bloodstream, charge parts of the body with a potential. This potential is transferable; it can move from one organ to another, from one thought to another, from a thought to an organ, and from an organ to a thought. This (extensiveness-like) theory of libido soon came to explain not only everything in psychic pathology but also every manifestation of life in health. Ultimately this explanation is another equalization. Whether one writes poetry, dreams, works, fights, dies, produces neurotic symptoms, or has sexual intercourse, in all these activities the same energy is used; moreover, since this energy is related most closely to sexual intercourse, everything consequently can be referred to it. There is only one condition attached to this explanation, and that is, that the human existence must be understood as nothing but the effect produced by the activity of organs or groups of organs. The libido theory is at the bottom concerned with the cell and its products, that is with extensiveness, extensiveness in the sense of Descartes and Foucault. The libido theory assumes a homogeneity.

In 1884 Hughlings Jackson read his famous Croonian Lectures, in which he argued that the human existence can be understood as proceeding from simple to complex, from automatic to voluntary, from well-organized to less well-organized; in short, as an evolution. This evolution can only be intersected by another slow and inevitable motion, namely the one which is peculiar to a diseased central nervous system. Health is an evolution, disease is a dissolution. The diseased person has fallen back to a simpler state of existence, he is going through the phases of evolution in reverse. To hallucinate is to see at a lower level; hallucinations are degraded thoughts.[45] These conclusions are rather arbitrary, for the hallucinating person observes exactly as the sane person, and he distinguishes what he observes from his hallucinations. Besides, his hallucinations are not less complex, not less voluntary, and not better organized than are sane observations. They are different in every aspect, and no common standard can be applied.

In his hallucinations, a patient gives evidence of living in a world of his own, where incidents are taking place that are invisible to us, and where things exist which do not exist for us. That is his delusion. The man who is dominated by a hypothesis can always find evidence to prove it. Jackson enumerated many cases, and in doing so, did not omit showing what was essential to him: the equalization of sickness and health. The mentally diseased person is a sane man who has been pushed down a few steps in evolution. The sane and the diseased stand on the same stairs. The diseased person does not show anything "new," anything that the healthy do not have. That is the essence of the matter: a homogeneity, an equality. The lunatic must not be a stone of offence, a warning, or an enigma; he is only a cripple, a crippled sane person. Do not be alarmed, he has nothing to say to us—that was Jackson's point.

Jackson had read Spencer. It is Herbert Spencer who makes clear what, with all this, we are doing to the child.

Herbert Spencer's father

Spencer wrote an autobiography in which there is a remarkable, and it seems to me particularly valuable, note on his youth, in which he tells of the way his father treated him. It is a pity that Spencer did not mention how old he was; this paragraph is in the chapter on the years before he was thirteen. I shall quote it all:

Something remains to be named, however. I refer to the benefit derived from an unusual mental discipline. My father's method, as already intimated, was that of self-help carried out in all directions. Beyond such self-help as I have already exemplified, there was always a prompting to intellectual self-help. A constant question with him was "I wonder what is the cause of so and so," or again, putting it directly to me, "Can you tell me the cause of this?" Always the tendency in himself, and the tendency strengthened in me, was to regard everything as naturally caused; and I doubt not that while the notion of causation was thus rendered much more definite in me than in most of my age, there was established a habit of seeking for causes, as well as a tacit belief in the universality of causation. Along with this there went absence of all suggestion of the miraculous. I do not remember my father ever referring to anything as explicable by supernatural agency. I presume from other evidence that he must at that time have still accepted the current belief in miracles; but I never perceived any trace of it in his conversation. Certainly his remarks about the surrounding world gave no sign of any other thought than that of uniform law.[46]

We say again: this is the point. Was the idea that ruled Spencer's father's discussion that God had been eliminated? [47]

God in exile

I think it was. God had to leave. He left. God is absent; in 1900 Leon Bloy acknowledged this with tears in his eyes, with the cry that ends the nineteenth century. "No news from God," cries Bloy. "Just at the time that everything, even the merest irrelevance is mentioned, there is no one who can tell us any news from God." Newspapers are crammed with the most superfluous (but causal) futilities; but no paper carries a rubric, however small, reading "News from God." Any such news would be the purest nonsense, for no one would be able to write even one sensible word on the subject. The news does not reach us. The source is so far away that no correspondent can be sent out; and indeed, the most exceptional characteristic of this exceptional correspondent would be, that he would never write a word. For God is absent. He is there, at the beginning of things, but this is only a security measure; that He is there means that He is nowhere at all. Very probably He can no longer overlook the effects of His capricious first move. In response we speak of Him with great awe, with great distance. The largest capitals are not big enough to mention Him.

> God is absent in the towns, in the fields, in the mountains and in the plains. He is absent in law, in science, in education and in morals. He is even absent in the lives of the religious, for they, who still want to be called His friends, have no need for His presence. God is absent as never before. . . . To be absent has become one of the qualities of God.[48]

The absence of God: one of God's attributes

Bloy felt bad about it; in our day, everyone accepts God's absence as an accomplished fact. Even a religious man, like Dietrich Bonhoeffer, ascertains, in a moment in which it must have been impossible for him to write anything but that which constituted his most sacred convictions, that western European history since Macchiavelli and Descartes has been ruled by the idea of eliminating God. Bonhoeffer states this with a fatalism foreign to Bloy. There is no anxiety in his question, "Where is there any room left for God?" One misses the pain which characterizes Bloy's outcries. Bloy was still able to look back on a century that had manipulated everything into a homogeneous continuity. He belonged to that century. Bonhoeffer writes in the middle of the twentieth century. The years that divide him from Bloy render him immune to the alarming nature of God's dislocation, so he can make a virtue of necessity. "This is our religion: that we must live as people who can manage life without God. The God who is with us, is the God who leaves us. Without God we live for and with God." [49] It is a lost cause; we are left on our own, and things are left on their own; the things and we are executing the law of continuity, which was born out of homogeneity—which means out of God's absence.

Spencer and the children after him

In the quotation from Spencer's autobiography, the observation that Spencer's father gave evidence of an unusual mental dis-

cipline is the most striking. Unusual? We hardly do anything else
when we are conversing with our children.

When my child asks me, "Why are the leaves red?"—it is
autumn, we are taking a walk in the woods, the two of us; he is
asking why the leaves of the trees are red (Why does he want
to know?)—when he asks: "Why are the leaves red?" I say, "Because it is getting colder"—and I forget that I am giving him an
answer that he does not understand. For how can my eight-year-old
child see the connection between two so diverse, so entirely different realities, as temperature and color? And so he repeats the
question: "But why, Dad?" "Well," I say, "it is autumn, and then
it gets colder and then the leaves turn red."

Because now I notice myself that I have not been making things
very clear (nothing at all, in fact), I add, "The cold changes something in the leaves and the stuff into which it has been changed
happens to be red."

Happens to be! Do I notice that I am taking away from the
child a necessary charm of autumn? And yet, I am right. The
chemical reaction in the leaf could just as well produce emerald
green or sky blue. Of necessary charms I know nothing. That the
lips of a young girl are red is a result of a peculiarity of that part
of her skin; I hardly understand that a young girl must have red
lips to be a young girl. Just so has it long been lost to me that
autumn leaves are *necessarily* red, or *necessarily* yellow, or *necessarily* brown, and that they *necessarily* fall down and float through
the cold air. No, this thought is not worth anything to me.

The child is satisfied; the leaves could just as well be sky blue or
spotless white; the cold apparently makes such changes and the
effect happens to be red. But where does the cold come from? Any
father or mother knows that my son is going to ask now, "Why
does it get cold in the autumn?"

This is an inconvenient question. For I have to think about it
myself and when I have remembered I have to transform my
knowledge into child size. "Listen, son"—odd words, the child
is doing nothing else. But I pronounce them in order to take a
breath, and to warn the child that the answer is going to be
difficult. The first threshold.

What is wrong with us? Only a moment ago we were both happily kicking at the leaves and looking at the colors, my son and I, and now, all at once, I am complicating his enjoyable, easy autumn. But what can I do? So I say what every father and every mother would say: "It's because of the sun." "The sun," the child wonders. "Why did Dad jump from the cold to the sun?" To adults, nothing could be easier. But I do not leave it with this piece of information, which is only a prelude to a train of thought. "In summer the sun is high up in the sky, it's almost straight over your head then. You see where it is now—it's not very high at all." That was a clever answer, I did it! But the child still does not get it. How should he connect high up with warm, and low with cold? How does he get extensiveness into this idea, which has nothing to do with extensiveness? Was it not the cold we were talking about? Another threshold.

And so this discussion is full of thresholds. I do not really answer the child's questions; instead, I am pushing him from me. Not crudely, not with both hands, but in an extremely subtle way, with understanding words. Anybody who might see us would think, "Those two are getting along splendidly. Look at that father talk to his son!" But it is only an appearance.

Words between adult and child are necessary words, a few excepted. Words that have become necessary. Generally, it is true that the more people talk to each other, the worse their understanding is. Our time is a loquacious time; and seldom before have people understood each other so badly. Is not a happy marriage characterized by few words and by silence? Married couples who talk a lot usually use words to box each other's ears with. And just so do we slap the child with words, which make a less dangerous way to slap it superfluous. I am strongly convinced that fathers talked considerably less with their children in former times. It was not necessary; they understood each other. Now this understanding is violated, not least by those impossible answers we are always handing out.

Why are the leaves red? Because of the cold—how untrue. Why is it cold? Because of the sun's position—untrue. Why is the sun so low? Because of the earth's location in its orbit—equally untrue. Why its location in an orbit? Because of its motion. Untrue again. Why motion? Because of continuous motion. Untrue. Why continuous motion? Because of God. What blasphemy!

"Why are the leaves red, Dad?" "Because it is so beautiful, child. Don't you see how beautiful it is, all these autumn colors?"

There is no truer answer. That *is* how the leaves are red. An answer which does not invoke questions, which does not lead the child into an endless series of questions, to which each answer is a threshold. The child will hear later on that a chemical reaction occurs in those leaves. It is bad enough, then; let us not make the world uninhabitable for the child too soon.

Why does it snow?

"Daddy, why does it snow?" "Well, during the summer there are leaves on the trees and flowers on plants, but now it is so dark and barren outside, that the world needs a white blanket."

But no one believes in this answer. We do not believe in answers which locate the sense of incidents within the incidents themselves, and the sense of things within the things themselves. To us it is necessary for the sense to lie outside the things and incidents, outside the present. This is our first rule of life, that only what lies in the past has sense. The result is an endless regression. For every past has been present before and must have derived its sense from a still earlier past. This road of endless regression is the road on which we have sent the child.

The child asks questions

It is a wellknown fact that children ask endless questions. Sometimes it seems that they do not even hear our replies. Before an answer has been formulated, they have asked another question. Child psychology tells us that the child asks questions because he likes to ask questions; he is at an age when asking questions is normal. He comes to this age period naturally, and eventually will leave it just as naturally; his questions are born out of a predispositioned necessity. Just as teeth grow out of his jaws during a certain period of his life, so do questions grow out of his head.

I must admit that the alarming nature of a child's forever asking questions is removed by this explanation. No father needs to get anxious because of his child's endless chatter. It's in the book; it's all right, every child does it.

Whether this is true remains to be seen, though. Would the child come to this endless chatter, if our help did not put it on the road to endlessness? We are the cause of it; we send the child into an endless regression.

And so the child is taken away from us. He is also led away from the present, and soon believes only in the past. Every answer he gets from adults leads him further back to past incidents. We teach a child that only the past has sense, not the present—and even less the future. "What makes the bulb sprout?" the child asks; and we talk about seasons, substances, circulation, in short, about past things, while only one answer is right: the plant wants to bloom. The sense of the sprouting lies in what every one can see, if he wants to see. Watch how the bulb sprouts and observe how it is ruled by one intention. Observe the future: it is obvious. The present is the visible future. Observe the present and show it to the child, show him the intentions of the present. But no one since Descartes, Leibniz, Lyell, Darwin, Spencer, Jackson, and Freud dares to do that anymore.

An empty future

How can we be surprised when the child does not know what he wants to be? After having bent him backward toward the past for so many years, and after having made the future almost entirely inaccessible, we suddenly want him to say what he wants to be? The child does not know. We have only ourselves to thank for it. The child does know everything (in principle) of chemical reactions in autumn leaves, everything about the earth's rotation around the sun, about the corresponding cold in winter and about the snow which can be caused by this cold; the child is even exceptionally proficient in this mature causal train of thought. But he has lost the idea that the present shows the sense of things. No one can expect the present to provide directives for the future if the present is allowed one, and only one, aspect—the aspect of the most recent past.

MATURATION

It is clear now, why Rousseau pushes the child away from him. The assumption that his new understanding of the child is opposed by old misunderstandings has had to give way to the view that Rousseau's understanding acts as an emergency bridge over a far too broad fissure between the child's and the adult's world. Consequently, the passages of *Émile* which evidence a hard and a rejecting attitude acquire a different and even positive meaning. Let us turn to them again.

"What the child needs to know is that it is weak, and that you, adult, are strong; besides, that, because of this difference, it is under your authority. That is what the child needs to know, what it needs to be taught, what it needs to feel." It cannot be said that this passage is exceptionally pedagogic. We are not doing any better, though, when we answer the question of why autumn leaves are red by pouring a scientific explanation into the child's ears. Even more than Rousseau intended, we teach the child with this answer that he is weak and that we (who know) are strong. We make him feel that he is under our authority (the authority of knowledge), and we teach him to realize that his state is, above all, a childlike state.

Rousseau, however, meant another way of feeling. A few lines before those just quoted, he writes: "Use authority when dealing with children; to reason is for adults; that is the way it is." He does not mean: "Use punishment if the child does not want to listen." He means: "Do not try to make it listen, make it accept your authority naturally." Apparently the adult has become much more subtle since Rousseau. The idea remains the same though. It is: Stay away, child, do not come too close to us, for it is dangerous, if not fatal.

Maturation as evidence of the distance between young and old

Ever since Rousseau the child has been keeping its distance. This process of the child and adult growing away from each other began in the eighteenth century. It was then that the period of adolescence came into existence.

In 1808 the word *Flegeljahre* (awkward age) appeared for the first time in a German dictionary; it had been used as a title for a book by Jean Paul four years earlier.[50] It seems probable that the phase of life described by this expression had appeared only a short time before. Muchow, who mentions these facts, discovered, after examining biographies and autobiographies, that in none of these life stories was there even one word on the psychic symptoms of puberty or the years of adolescence.[51] We now know why: there was nothing to see then on the border between youth and maturity to ever induce comment. "Childhood is one of the great discoveries of the eighteenth century." [52] And Victor Hugo's remark, "Columbus only discovered America; it was I who discovered the child," [53] was not entirely untrue—he was only mistaken in the ownership of the copyright. The child had not existed before him, and he only came into being later on; he was created by us. Our adulthood has acquired such a peculiar shape that the child has to be childlike if he is ever to reach us; he has to get through a complicated period of psychic maturation before we adults can get the impression that he is really with us—that he really can take part in our complicated, inwardly contradictory but nonetheless, and even partly because of it, so delightful maturity.

Increasing distance

The process went on, the gap widened; to reach maturity became harder and harder. Around 1900 adolescence had become a period of exceptional complexity lasting a number of years; it is therefore understandable that during this time the first monographs on adolescence were published. In the last fifty years the maturing process has come to end less and less frequently (in certain cases even never at all) with the conclusion of this long-lasting period of adolescence; it now continues far into the next years of life, which until recently had been years of maturity in every respect. So a new phase has been added to the maturing process: the period of postadolescence.

The most recent addition to maturation

Postadolescence begins when the period of forced and voluntary isolation has been completed. It is difficult to state when this actually happens, not only because there are great differences in individuals, but also because the last years of adolescence may be characterized by a fight against isolation which often has every appearance of having been won, while actually the youth is still entirely confronted with isolation. In postadolescence, the isolation is over. The gap which divided the child from the adults, and which widened so enormously during adolescence that it broke almost every connection, is gone. The child belongs, it has stopped being a child; it is a young man or a young woman, twenty, twenty-two years old. Yet these two young people are not really mature, either of them. Being mature means having achieved the most necessary command of ourselves and of that which has been entrusted to us; and this young man and this young woman, who are out of their teens, and who have managed to live through their adolescence without too much damage, are still not mature. At that age the young man often has not yet got a job, particularly if he is one of the more intelligent. And neither has the girl. Marriage is impossible, as a rule; and the years of changing jobs and of broken engagements begin.

Adults are quite satisfied with this situation. Let him give notice, is our comment when the young man does not seem to be happy in his work; at his age one should be allowed to look around a bit. And as far as the engagements are concerned, we find comfort in the (right) thought that it is better to break off three (well-intended) engagements than live through the misery of one divorce. "You're lucky you didn't get married," is what the sad girl hears when she has had to break off an engagement which had been none too happy for some time. This is the time of trial and error, and if it is completed by the age of twenty-five, we are quite satisfied. Young people who conclude their postadolescence period at a later age are not at all scarce; and for quite a few maturity begins at thirty or even thirty-five.

It is clear that this process threatens to dislocate our very existence. The symptoms of this dislocation are becoming more and more apparent. At the same time, however, it appears that the ones growing up are forcing a solution which may embarrass us adults. We may even revolt against it; but without doubt, it indicates the only right way out of this hopeless impasse. Let us wait for a moment before discussing the solution. It seems to me that I should first show, with a few examples, how much the relationships between young and old are ruled by distance—even when they are on very good terms with each other. First, though, I shall review the meeting ground of old and young.

Adults who walk backward

Without knowing it, and surely without wanting it, the adult, because of his peculiar sort of maturity, keeps the child in a child-like and irresponsible, meaning immature, state as long as he can. Again and again the adult offers the child a pattern by which he can arrange his maturity; every pattern undoubtedly invites the child to grow up, but at the same time it forbids him to really and truly become an adult. As the child tries to come nearer, the adult, invitingly, steps backward; each time he offers the child a new life-phase, a new pattern, a new effort, and each time the child finds that he is not able to reach the adult. As soon as the child has mastered a new pattern, the adult has another one ready, with new, unknown, and sometimes enormous problems. Each time the adult puts a new phase between him and the child. The child never reaches maturity until the moment that society gives its permission, when at last it allows work and marriage. The relation between child and adult is characterized by the distance between them. The way they get along with each other and the way they talk to each other no longer evinces natural closeness and equality, as it did in the days of Montaigne and Locke. It shows a definite inequality, inevitably resulting in distance. Here are a few examples which illustrate this distance.

The mysterious hour

In *Psychoanalysis of the Fire*, Bachelard tells the story of how his father lighted a *"brûlot"* on special occasions.

When there was a big party during the winter, when I was very young, a special beverage was prepared, the *brûlot.* My father poured brandy, a product of our own vineyard, into a large bowl. In the center he put sugar lumps, the largest he could find. As the match touched the heap of sugar lumps, a blue flame descended with a small sound over the poured-out brandy. My mother turned out the light. The mysterious hour of ceremonious festivity had begun. At that moment the grown-ups started to theorize; if the flame burned itself out too late, the *brûlot* had been too weak; did it go out too soon, then not enough fire had been concentrated, which would affect its effectiveness against the flu. Somebody told of a *brûlot* which had burned to the last drop, and another knew of a fire in a distillery in which barrels of rum had exploded as if they contained gunpowder. Of course, no one had witnessed this explosion, yet everybody tried to find an objective and universal explanation for this extraordinary incident. . . . At last the *brûlot* was in my glass, hot and thick and really substantial.

At first this passage does not seem to contain anything remarkable. We all have memories like that, memories that are wrapped in a mysterious veil. We recall how the living room looked when the Christmas tree had been lighted. We remember New Year's Eve as a very special occasion, with candlelight creating an entirely new atmosphere. We have memories of evenings in the park in the autumn, and of the cosy mess of spring cleaning. There seems to be nothing extraordinary in these memories, which is why psychology (except for a very few instances) does not mention them. From a pedagogic point of view Bachelard's story is even less important, for the father does not say much. But—it is just the fact that he does not speak at all during the time that he is doing all those things that is remarkable. He does not moralize, he shows no admonishing or encouraging tendencies, he does not warn, although there is fire on the table. He does not even forbid. And when people are talking while the brandy is burning, what they say can hardly be called pedagogical. To our taste, it is not directed enough to the child. No educative words are said, the child is not even spoken to. The adults decide among themselves how long the brandy should burn; and they tell half-serious and unchildlike stories which are taken seriously by the child.

How does the child participate?

And yet it would be difficult to find a more typical example of the modern relationships between old and young. For what is happening? The child is participating in the adult world, he is sitting at the table with the adults, he is drinking *brûlot*, and he is listening. He is even listening with great attention. The adults are aware of it. They never forget him, although they are talking among themselves. They emphatically include him in their story, but entirely unnoticeably. Actually, they are addressing themselves to the child continuously, although they neither look at him nor speak to him. He is supposed to understand part of the story, but not too much. It is an elaborate story and partly incomprehensible to the child. And this incomprehensibility must remain—the adults take care of that. At the same time, they take care that it is incomprehensible to the child only because he still *is* a child. He has to go on being interested, he has to be fascinated by these events, which, ultimately, are inaccessible to him. The adults are leading the child to incomprehensibility.

In this way does the child participate in maturity. He does not play an active part in it, but rather the contrary: it is the father who lights the *brûlot*. No child would ever be permitted to perform this solemn and mature act. And afterward, when they are discussing how long the brandy should burn, it is the adults who discuss, on the basis of their experience—that is, their maturity—the most subtle differences. And the child listens. Perhaps he asks a question; but his questions do not mean that he and the adults are talking together on the same level. His questions can only touch this strange world, which is not entirely comprehensible and therefore ultimately inaccessible. When the anecdote of the exploding barrels of rum is told, he hears of a world which is unlike his own, he hears of the world of the adults, in which, apparently, the most amazing things occur.

Actually, many things are happening in this incident. The child makes his acquaintance with a way of life which one day will be his. He meets adults, he sits at their table, he observes the gestures of maturity, and he hears their conversation. It is not at all by accident that he is there; the *brûlot* would not be complete without him, and would even lose its meaning if he were not there. The charm of burning candles on New Year's Eve is almost entirely lost when there are no children to enjoy it. How dislocated and false do they seem burning in restaurants and cafés. There is no sense in a Christmas tree without children. Christmas trees in homes for the aged only have meaning insofar as their light recalls those little faces of long ago, and for the old people, the children come back again.

Everything in the mature world—*everything*, a fact we are inclined to forget—derives its attraction and its meaning from the child, who is always present in one way or another. Everything! Purely mature events are dislocated events, superfluous events.

> *Tout ce que l'on fait on le fait pour les enfants*
> *Et ce sont, les enfants qui font tout faire.*[54]

The child who participates in the *brûlot*, like the child who sits at the supper table on New Year's Eve, or who is present in the gathering around the Christmas tree, that child who is participating in adult life, is conscious of the fact that this hour is his own. Yet this hour is taken away from him minute by minute. His elders are distant from him, and perhaps they are never so distant as during this hour when they are coming toward him, this hour in which they show him so much of maturity—that is, the future, which means distance. "*C'était l'heure du mystère et de la fête un peu grave,*" says Bachelard, remembering this hour. The adults are mysterious when they present themselves to the child. The mature world is another world; that is what the child realizes when his elders come toward him. For that matter, the elders are not trying to belittle the different qualities of their world. When they tell their stories, they are inclined to make their world even more extraordinary; if possible, they add a few miracles. No adult believes in exploding barrels of rum; but if he tells this story to his children, he has to take care not to fall victim to his own persuasive powers. The point I wish to make is not that anecdotes must be adapted to the child's level, but that these stories accentuate our own maturity. In the life of the child there are no exploding barrels of rum; but these barrels do occur in his breathless conjectures about the adult's existence, in which everything, and particularly everything else, appears to happen. And the child is right.

Fairy tales

It is doubtful whether exaggerated stories were told to children in former days, for instance, in the days of Montaigne. Fairy tales, exaggerated stories indeed, had not been invented. They came into existence when adult and child parted. Romanticism's great interest in fairy tales is connected with the increasing distance between mature and immature in those days. Fairy tales meant for children are only told in times that know maturation.

It is not a coincidence that fairy tales are cruel. By their cruelty they show how unattainable maturity is, and how repelling—and that is what they were invented to do. Modern fairy tales are not so cruel. To read the fairy tales of the previous century, those of the Brothers Grimm, for instance, to a modern child, would certainly be to lead it into difficulties. The reason for this change is easy to see. The cruelty of the fairy tale was able to keep the child away from a too-near maturity; but today the distance between adult and child has increased to such an extent that the cruelty is no longer effective, it is too crude. In earlier days the cruelty gently pushed the child back; today it drives him into fear.

During a war there is sense in warning the child about the danger; when a warning is as real as the danger, it does not frighten the child. In times of peace, however, there is no sense in warning children about the dangers and atrocities of war; war is far away, and its distance lends fear to the warning. The same is true for the warning aspect of the cruel fairy tales. In the vacuum which lies between young and old today it causes fear and anxiety. That is why our stories have become more prudent. They are no longer meant to prolong a short and undivided maturation. Instead they have been adapted to deal with an extensive maturation with many phases. They have to guarantee a certain relation—and preserve the distance that goes with it—for a long time, maybe ten, maybe twenty, maybe even twenty-five years. This period in the Grimms' time, that is, the first half of the nineteenth century, cannot have been much longer than in Rousseau's day, and he described it as "rather short."

There is one element which our stories have in common with the older ones, the element of impossibility. In the old fairy tale of "The Sparrow and the Dog," a wife is requested by her husband to kill a little bird which he is holding between his teeth; when she swings an ax, she misses the bird and cuts off her husband's head. In Dorothy Kunhardt's modern story, the dog Peewee [55] grows from a very, very small dog into the largest animal in the circus. These two stories do have one thing in common: both are absolutely impossible. And both are meant to do the same thing: to prohibit, or at least to impede, the child's approach to maturity.

Strange maturity

A second example. André Gide, in his autobiography, *Si le grain ne meurt* (1928) says that when he was a child he enjoyed the privilege of once in a while accompanying his father on a walk. On these walks his father would ask him riddles; or they would amuse themselves listing words which sound alike but have different meanings. We get the impression of a very good understanding between these two. And while they walked like that, it got dark. The lanterns were lighted—oh, the mysteries of gaslight— and Gide remembers that the light in the cafés invited him to peep inside, where he saw a strange mysterious world of adults. After such a walk, says Gide, I went to sleep drunk with darkness and with strangeness.

We are inclined to linger over these words: drunk with strangeness, "*ivre d'étrangeté.*" They do not seem to tell us more than we all knew when we were children. In the youthful years of almost any autobiography, we find this sort of description. And yet, these words, which seem so natural, are exclusively modern. *Ivre d'étrangeté*, drunk with strangeness. The child is drunk with strangeness when it learns of the world of maturity.

The conversation with his father, the riddles and the homonyms, was not in the least superfluous to this experience. Certainly, a preadolescent child can get intoxicated all by himself on the strangeness of the adult world, which seems so large and so deceptively accessible to him. An adolescent child must even *be* alone while exploring this strangeness, although he almost gets ruined doing it. But the young child, the not-yet-ten-years-old, needs the adult to learn about this strangeness, this distance, this maturity. If young Gide had lost his father on the way and had had to find his way home alone, he would not have been so eager to observe the strangeness of the city in the dark, the city of the adults. We can be sure that he would not have peeped in at those rooms filled with smoke and laughter. He would only have thought of home, and he would have pushed this strange mature world from him in his helpless and nervous search. And in response, this world would have assaulted him with pure hostility. He would have gone to sleep not drunk with strangeness, but upset by fear. To explore this strangeness, to know what maturity is—and to realize what being a child means—the young child needs the trusted adult, the adult who is with him, to whom he can cling, who holds his hand. It is true, this adult speaks to him in words which descend from the same strange maturity; but the sound of his voice is so trusted that he can bring the world of maturity closer without fear, at least without too much fear. While Gide was peering, his father may have said, "They're having a drink"; or "They're dancing"; or "It's their day off"; words which by themselves belonged to the world he was looking at, but which, since they were spoken by his father, helped to bring this distant world closer, so that it became possible to observe it. These words were able to resolve the absolute paradox of near and far which is so characteristic of the modern relation between adult and child. The riddles they told one another were a medium by which the child was freed to look around at all the unattainable peculiarities of a city by night.

The child's world

The adult is inclined to think that he can put himself in the child's existence. As a rule, he is not conscious of the fact that the modern child lives in an entirely different reality. For the adult, life has assumed a definite shape, and it never occurs to him that the child lacks the experience to see it in that shape. Without thinking about it he assumes that his child lives in the same house as he does, not realizing that while every nook and cranny is familiar to him, to the child it is foreign territory, even if the child has his own room to play in, and his own swing, and even his own cupboard. When he takes his child for a walk along the streets of the town, he assumes that the child is treading the same streets, seeing the same houses, and observing the same traffic. The distance which divides maturity from childhood makes it hard to remember how he himself experienced his home and the things around it when he was a child. His memories are vague; and besides, they are so intertwined with mature interpretations that they have lost almost all of their childhood qualities. The adult is inclined to think that his own childhood gradually merged into maturity (although the smell of an old book immediately proves how different things really were then, in that vague past which looms up so suddenly), and he presupposes the same gradual transition for his child. If he digs in a sandbox, he assumes that it has a more childlike, but apart from that an entirely identical, meaning for the child. When he takes his child to the playground, it does not occur to him that a swing or a slide might have a different meaning for the child, that it might have another shape, that it might be an entirely different thing. Maybe he is surprised for a moment when his child seems to be delighted with the swing, but emphatically refuses to set foot on the merry-go-round; or when he finds that his child has no eye for any of these diversions, but enjoys himself hugely endlessly opening and closing the gate. He will reason away his surprise by remembering that children do have whims. It does not occur to him for a moment that the sandbox looks entirely different—I should say *is* entirely different—to the child, and that the playground, besides being a place of bliss, can be no less a place of fears. And these playthings are *meant* for children. The sensations of a child when he walks down the street, or when, with his parents, he pays someone a visit, or when he helps to put flowers on grandmother's grave, or when the family crosses the river by ferry—all his sensations of the adult world are even more radically different from those of adults.

Captured maturity

The child lives in a world different from his parents' world within the house he shares with them. At first the child stays near his mother, who remains the center of all his living space as long as he is a child. A little later islands of trusted space appear in different places, secret places surrounded by foreign matters that determine their limits. The attic, the space under the table, the corner in the livingroom, the cupboard under the kitchen sink—these are all reconnoitered and occupied. Then the immediate surroundings of the house are reconnoitered—the doorsteps, the neighbor's front door, the light pole, the window around the corner. Everything outside these places remains foreign, if not hostile, for the time being. The street is owned by all sorts of traffic, by unfamiliarity and danger, by adults. Not before adolescence does the child enlarge his familiar space into the whole world, but this world is still so marked off from the adults' world that it can be the field for a long risky adventure. This world is unlimitedly confronted with that other world, the world of adults, the "second reality," which Gide mentions when he remembers that once, when he was awakened by an unfamiliar sound in the house, he sneaked downstairs and saw that his parents and many other people were having a party. The adolescent sees through the pseudo victory of his preadolescence period; and for the first time he puts himself on the threshold of the "second reality." [56] His discussions with adults assume another character. His parents, who before his adolescence had, in a trusted way, been bringing distrusted maturity closer, are repudiated, as for the first time all by himself he probes the almost fatal dangers of this distrustedness. His parents are too much part of his own childhood; and since it is precisely his childhood which he is trying to get rid of, he begins controversial discussions with his parents.

He has to push himself off from the bank which divides childhood from maturity; and he finds the right resistance to push against in his parents, for it was they who tried to be close to him despite their maturity when he was a child. Unlucky the child whose parents have so much understanding of adolescence that they give him no opportunity to push himself off. The complaint of the adolescent youngster that his parents—*his* parents—do not understand him shows that they talk to him in the right way— as parents, not as pseudo pedagogists. When the youngster complains that *nobody* understands him, this complaint shows that he still sees adults as people who treat him as a child, and only as a child. As long as adults mean this to him, it is to be desired that he remains convinced he will not find understanding anywhere.

Anxious parents

It is difficult to be a parent. The distance which divides parents from their children compels them to treat their offspring with subtlety and understanding, which actually means with anxiety. The harmful effects of a lack of understanding are too obvious to refuse parents the right to be anxious about avoiding it. But at the same time, parents have to be careful they don't decrease the distance separating them from their children. For too much understanding is equally disastrous: too easily the child gets caught in a tie which may keep him a child for life. In every association between parents and their children there is evidence of these two rules of conduct: the rule of understanding, and the rule of not understanding; evidence of the parents' two ideas, evidence that their child grows up by the grace of their understanding and of their not-understanding, or, in other words, by the grace of their anxiety and of their courage. Most parents do not know how to act; they fear their children because experience, and especially books, makes it clear that the most obvious way of treating them is the wrong way. Every pedagogical book contains advice which at first seems quite unexpected, but which, on second thought, appears to be very sensible. If the child puts his fingers in the sugar bowl, the father can read in every book that rapping its fingers, which he did instinctively, was wrong, wrong because of several good reasons—and the next time the father will not do it again. When the mother notices that her little daughter is enjoying herself hugely playing with the contents of her potty, she will be inclined to look disapproving (if only because of the laundry); yet she will be sure to find a serious warning against showing this very disapproval. That was exactly what she should not have done. If she is interested enough, she no doubt can find out why this disapproval was wrong and why the right thing to do, one she would never have thought of herself, was right.

Is the right procedure the least obvious?

It is not particularly surprising that pedagogical, like psychological—not to mention psychotherapeutical—advice so very often should be the advice which is the least expected. As a rule psychology recommends a way of doing things which is different from what seems most likely according to the daily and uncomplicated way of thinking. It is not impossible to feel, that we would make fewest pedagogical and psychological mistakes if we suppressed every spontaneous impulse and substituted its opposite. Are we so extremely unintelligent today? And if we are, how did our grandparents manage? For they had no book to explain the logic of raising children. Or didn't they need those books?

To me there is no doubt about it; they did not. They did not need enlightenment, they knew how to act because they acted in a continuity; the child was right next to them, he was part of their mature world. There was nothing wrong with a rap on his fingers or with a disapproving look. This and similar measures from adults could not harm the child; he was mature in the first place. But all this belongs to the past. The tie which binds the child to his parents today is a dubious one. A little too much kindness and the child is caught in a mother or father fixation. A little too much unkindness and the child gets another sort of neurosis. A little too much kindness and a little too much unkindness at the same time whirls it into an oedipus complex, either positive or negative. It is a miracle if the child manages to avoid all these dangers. And it is admirable that parents, in spite of the fact that they are frightened on every side, still manage to find a way so that not every child, without exception, ends up at the psychiatrist's.

Children's questions

The two passages from Bachelard and from Gide are examples
of the right way to treat children: neither parent tried to diminish
the distance between him and his child which is the condition for
ultimate maturity. However difficult it has become for parents,
many of them still show the same ability to do the right thing:
they let the distance remain. Not seldom, however, even these
parents take an entirely different course when the child starts to
ask the questions which are awaited anxiously by every father and
mother: the questions about birth and sex, and about life and
death. As far as the first two subjects are concerned, many parents
are of the opinion that children ought not to ask them at all. They
are right. Since the distance between adult and child has become
so wide that the child remains absolutely estranged from what is
really mature, he has no right to ask a question which leaps over
this distance.

The questions about birth

"Where do babies come from?" is still the most innocent of
the questions. The answer that the child grows in the mother's
tummy is accepted by the child willingly; this answer does not
touch maturity. The adult may think it does. When he gives this
correct answer he may see before him the distended abdomen
and the marks on the loins, he may hear the woman in labor
groan or cry out, he may smell the newborn baby—and of all
these things he says, "My child must not know this." And he is
right. The child should not know. Since we have made maturity
invisible, it is not right to confront the child suddenly with crude
maturity. The child does not want this, either. He is quite satisfied
with an entirely childlike interpretation of this information—how
else can he think? It is debatable whether the child interprets at
all. The information is meant to muse on, to be stored, to be
thought out later on. If this were not true, how explain the
fact that the child does not ask further? For the slightest interpretation of the information that the child grows in the mother's

tummy leads to the question: "But how does it get out?" To us, adults—who do interpret, who know that "tummy" means an abdomen with intestines, with a uterus, with holes—to us there is no question more obvious. But it does not occur to the child, unless the answer that the child grows in the mother's tummy is ostentatiously loaded with maturity—if, for instance, the father shows the child a picture of a pregnant woman. Then, in that sense, in the sense of maturity, the child will go further with his questions. If he does ask this next question (which is evidence of a wrong sort of enlightenment), the child will be satisfied with the reply, "The same way a pee-pee does." Quite uncomprehensive. But not on the child's level. The child does not know any physiology. That is what some parents do not realize—and some psychologists. Only when a physiological insight is forced upon it will the child continue with, "But how can a baby get through such a small hole?" A second, more serious, evidence of the wrong sort of enlightenment; the child has to be led to a question like that. He does not want this information when he asks the simple and innocent question, which does not mean anything, "Where do babies come from?"

If the adult has tempted the child into this dangerous question, he has arrived at an impasse. How can he ever explain how a full-grown baby passes through such a small hole? The little girl must grow very suspicious of her own body as she considers this problem. And the boy will get the impression, at a very early age, that the female's construction underneath must be highly mysterious. Perhaps both of them think that the baby is squeezed out in an oblong ribbon, like toothpaste. No adult can make it clear, not even if he tells a necessarily complicated story about widening and narrowing, a story that will not do without illustrations. It is well-known how certain books meet this requirement.

What answer is given when the child asks, "How does the music come out of the radio?" "The aerial catches it out of the air," says the father, "and the set turns it to music." "Oh," says the child, and the father turns back to his newspaper. But when the child asks, "But *how?*" this same father, who so diligently answered the question about birth, replies, "Don't bother me,

I'm reading the paper." A very sensible answer. The child is not able to understand it, is he? No matter how much trouble the father goes to, he will not be able to make the child understand; a radio set is a thing so mature by nature, that its working can not be explained to the child.

Well, no adult can explain to a child how a baby is born. He can only do it by permitting the child to be present at a delivery. But he will not permit that, and rightly so. One way or another it is clear to him that, after making maturity invisible, it would be inconsequent and therefore dangerous to suddenly confront the child with extreme maturity. The child is not allowed to see the delivery of a calf—the farmer's child is, but then he does not ask where babies come from—and the child is certainly not allowed to watch his mother deliver a baby. But then, consequently, no stories about birth! The simple information is enough; the child will not ask further—unless the parents lead him to ask more with words loaded with causality.

Questions about sex

"Will auntie get a baby, too?" asks the boy who has just got a new little sister. "No," says his mother, "auntie will not get any more babies." "Why not?" he asks then. "Because," she says, after a slight hesitation (which is noticed by the child), "because uncle is not alive anymore." "Silly!" says the child, not imagining in the least into what strange thoughts he is leading his mother. For she, forewarned by the books on sexual enlightenment, knows that this is going to be it. The child wants to know about sexual intercourse, she thinks—but nothing is less true. Continuing this faulty reasoning, she asks herself, "How am I to tell him? What was it the book said? It was so neat." Of course, the answer was neat because the author of the book thought it over for days and days, and also got another chance to polish when correcting the proofs of the book. The mother cannot think of this pat answer. One cannot blame her. But she blames herself. She says, "I shall tell you later"—and immediately remembers that that is exactly what the book called the most dangerous and contemptible answer.

"Silly!" says the child. "No, it isn't," says the mother. "A baby has to have a father and a mother, hasn't it?" Wouldn't this be her answer if she had never consulted a book? I think it would. No answer is more obvious. The child understands immediately; he knows for himself that father and mother are both necessary. Mother prepares the meals and father builds a sled, isn't that obvious? The child does not ask more than this obviousness, and nothing gives us a right to suppose that he is asking for more when he says: "Silly!" The books think he is. And the result is that mothers and fathers develop a line of conduct which must be amazing to the child. For whereas the parents put him off with a few words when he inquires about mature matters (at the most he is pushed back with a few causal jumps into a nebulous past), this question evokes suddenly a saintly fervor in them; they tell and tell, and what they say gets crazier all the time.

"Look here," they say, "you have a tiddy and your little sister has not." The child cannot deny this, but he will wonder what this has got to do with it. "Your sister has a little hole there." The boy knows that well enough; the fact that his sister urinates too is no news to him. "Now, before the baby comes, the father's tiddy goes into the mother's little hole."

Dear adult, this is simply not true. These words may make sense to adults because of their extensive entourage of experiences and considerations; for the child who lacks these experiences and who is not ripe enough for these considerations, these words are misleading. What sense can they make to him? Nobody will be able to block the wrong ideas to which these words give rise.—"And when the tiddy is in the hole, the father lays a little egg in the mother."

Not only does this information contain a harmful uniting of sexuality and excretion, it also contains a serious misstatement. What man has sexual intercourse with his wife in this way? Is not sexual intercourse essentially different from this placid story about egg-laying? It is absolutely impossible to explain to the child in what way it is different. The essential intention of sexual intercourse—that even to adults hardly mentionable drive which gives sense to every separate sexual fact and incident, but which has no sense in itself—this is beyond the child's understanding. And the more one tries to explain, the less the child will understand. Every word leads the child away from a real understanding. The child is not able to comprehend it. A real comprehension lies in the simple, correct, and complete information that a child needs a father and a mother; he should not be told more than this.

No sexual enlightenment before pre-adolescence

When the child is eleven, twelve, thirteen years old, which means when he has reached the age when he notices sex as a quality of his own contacts, then, but *only* if the child asks for it,[57] a discussion cannot be avoided. But this discussion will have a different, a more mature, aspect. Words like "hole" and "laying eggs" are not necessary any more. The boy will suspect what it is about; he will interpret, he will draw maturity closer, even if years will pass before it can really be with him. The girl, too; it will give sense and content to the unmentionable thing when her mother tells her about that which in itself has no sense or content. For the younger child this information is foolish and misleading. It acts to abolish the distance which adults are continually creating, and which they increase at every opportunity. This cannot be done; an adult cannot give with one hand and then take back with the other. Sexual enlightenment needs to be true to what the child observes of sex at home, that shadow of sexuality which appears in the usual, daily, friendly relationship between father and mother, in their harmony, in the distribution of tasks, and in the few embraces they show their children.— "Why doesn't auntie get a baby?" "Because a baby needs a father and a mother." And so it does. The child can see that for himself.

Absent death

Beside sexuality, death has also become incommunicable. In the past, in the middle ages, death was accessible and therefore communicable. Death was there. The sick were sitting at the roadsides, and their loud presence confronted every passerby with a *momento mori*. Epidemics raged over Europe and allowed no one any doubt as to the reality of an unexpected and abrupt end.

The diseased man died in his own home; if in his dying hour he was conscious, and bade farewell to those dear to him, he did not omit the children. The children saw death, they understood its signs. They heard the death bells, and they were in the procession when the body was carried to the grave. The grave was in the center of the town or village, visible to anyone; no one tried to hide the gaping pit.

How secretly we bury now. A few hardly noticeable limousines, a glimpse of the coffin, camouflaged with shrouds and flowers, and finally the graveyard, not unintentionally transformed into a garden of green and flowers. Death is invisible. Like a thief it steals through the hospital wards. When it has found its prey, it is requested to digest it in secret, in a separate room, in seclusion. No one is allowed to see it, especially not the child. Even the dying patient is not allowed to greet his own death; until the very end the doctor comforts him with a recovery in which even the furniture in his room does not believe; and in extremis the dying man is given morphine so he will not see.

All these grim modernities have only one reason: death should not show itself. So obscure is death that its appearance is more obscene than the nakedness of a shameless gesture. The doorway which divides death from life has been closed; only on its threshold is there a faint glimmer of the light behind it. *"La mort est une grande porte noire sous laquelle passent des rayons."* [58] It cannot be doubted that in the past the light was clearly visible for everybody. The door was kept open by the dead relatives, and by the many, many, dead children.

The dead children

"Antoine Arnaud was born in 1560." That is, in the days of Montaigne. "In 1585 he married the daughter of a government official in Paris. She was twelve or thirteen years old when she was married. During the first two years of their marriage there were no children."—Hardly surprising, considering that the young Madame Arnaud was still awaiting her first menstruation. He who feels indignant about this does not realize the state of mind of a woman of those days and the nature of her marriage. Husband, wife, and marriage itself are changing concepts. Nothing gives us a right to assume that Madame Arnaud was miserable. She very probably was not. But a twelve- or thirteen-year-old girl who married an adult husband today would probably escape to her parents in desperation on the first night.

"When Madame Arnaud was fifteen, her first child was born; it lived five days. After that she bore a child every year: Robert, Catherine, Jaqueline, Anne, Jeanne, a lifeless daughter, Antoine, who lived three years, Simon, who did not live long, Henri, a son who died young, Marie, Madeleine, who died after a few years, and Simon. By 1603, Madame Arnaud had born fourteen children over a period of fifteen years; eight were alive. She was thirty years old. Then the children came at longer intervals. First twins, who died young; then three more children, of whom one remained alive. The last child brought her own death. She was thirty-nine years old." [59] In twenty-four years she had born nineteen children, of whom ten had died. The doorway of death was kept open for every child by its brothers and sisters—and by its mother. When a child reached maturity, it married. And then its own children would see to it that the door remained open. Death was everywhere, visibly.

Who wants these times to return? Who wants plague and cholera to come out from their hiding places and resume their travels? Who would like to recover the child's affinity to death? Who would desire mothers to run after their newborn babies through the doorway which permits no return?

Happiness

These questions hurt. Who would want those things? Of course nobody does. Who does not want death and insecurity removed from our existence even further? We all want that.

Yet no one can say why. No one knows why a human life should be long and healthy. We think we know, certainly; it does not even occur to us to doubt this knowledge. But as soon as we permit doubt to enter our thoughts, however, we see that this knowledge lacks all foundation. We have to die once—it does not seem likely that death will let itself be driven beyond this final line—and if so, what is more important? to look back on a long and healthy life, or on a single moment of happiness, a moment of extreme meaning, painful perhaps, but nonetheless delightful? We want both, a long life and a life rich in happiness; but it is questionable whether the latter is greatly helped by our attention and concern for the former. Probably not. But if not, there is no compensation: how can we give attention and concern to "happiness"? We ought to be able to go and meet it when it suddenly appears, this thing called happiness. We ought to know it better than anything else, we ought to be able to say: This is happiness, this is what it looks like and these are its properties—but when it does appear, it is always so new, so unlike its previous occurrence, that if we had had to create it, we would not have dared to give it this shape. No, we can only give attention to nonessential matters, for these can be known, these can be looked for, these can be pursued. Attention to the body is possible; attention to the happiness of this body is absolutely impossible.

Even the attention to the body easily misses its object. The body which shapes itself in the extension of this attention stops being the body that we are. The doctor who taps on the chest, who palpates the abdomen, who raps under the patella, does not touch the same body that demanded its owner's attention. He only touches the conditions, the instruments, of that of which the owner can dispose. Before the doctor begins his examination, the owner has left his body, he has abolished his incarnation; that is why he can offer his body as an object for examination, as "chest with caverns," as "abdomen with probable abscess," as "knee without normal reflexes." The help offered by the doctor concerns the body, this unanimated, disincarnated body, this instrument. An aspect, although perhaps a very important aspect, of the body which in daily life constitutes the owner. This is also true for almost any concern or attention. The attention to housing conditions, to nutrition, to hygiene, concerns nonessential matters, attributes of happiness; necessary, perhaps indispensable, attributes, but still attributes, no more. No one could formulate the concern to which life, which uses these attributes toward happiness or unhappiness, is entitled. Maybe this concern could be formulated; but it is very doubtful whether the formula would penetrate to us, the formula of a concern characterized by so little interest in the attribute that we lose faith in it.

Happiness is an odd thing. The person who is seeking it does not find it; but the one who is not might have it. He who is close to it gets no permission to enter; but he who roams aimlessly walks in freely. He who settles down to enjoy happiness once found will discover an emptiness; but he who does not expect anything will keep it. Happiness may cause our fidelity to be met by infidelity; sometimes happiness even greets the most glaring unfaithfulness. If we try to make happiness stronger, it crumbles in our hands; but these same hands are too small to enfold it if we only want to hold it. He who wants to purify it, who wants to remove everything from it that is not purely happiness, will not be able to hold on to it; before the first stain is removed, happiness will have gone.

The last observation makes us think. Happiness exists by the grace of a certain amount of unhappiness. Happiness is the crown on a life that knows sadness and trouble. Although our most beloved memories give the appearance of pureness—which they do—we discover on a closer examination that the pureness is a varnish whose composition is built upon less happy, or even unhappy, times. The souvenir which embodies our dearest memory is so precious to us because it contains the negation of that moment, its perishing, its end.

Perishability

Things are dear to us, because they perish. The slightest breeze could blow away the lock of hair which the mother has saved as a remembrance of her child—it is very dear to her. All significant moments are locked up in perishable trifles: youth in the ticking of the clock in an old couple's bedroom, for instance—and what is more perishable than this ticking? The honeymoon is caught in the raindrops sliding down the window of the train compartment, passing each other, and then suddenly leaving their previous paths; the happy couple watch the rain, fascinated—now it is a memory. Until the last minute the broken love is embodied in the spilled ash on the floor; the next morning the ash is gone, and so, perhaps, is the room, the house, the town.

The child knows that the little things deserve attention; he picks up our adult shreds and scraps and hands them to us—we do not know what to do with them, we smile about it and brush them from our trousers, suspecting vaguely that this gesture compromises the ordination of things. But what else can we do? We have directed our gaze at the big things, the seemingly imperishable things. And yet these things do not touch us; they just impress us, and they try to mislead us. What really touches us are the little, the futile, the very perishable things.[60] Man is a creature of trifles; [61] things that slip between his fingers are valuable to him, they will stay with him. What is perishable appears to enfold everything. Things are valuable to us—our things, things of our existence—because they are caught in a fast and radical deterioration. They need our nearness, and so they are near to us. And the people we love, those few who are with us for a while, how could we love them if they did not grow old and die? It is the light of death that makes them dear to us.

Can we today still explain this to our children? We have closed the door which divides life from death—softly, but with determination. Eventually even the glimmer on the threshold will disappear. And children will grow up thinking that death is the one jarring note in life. Even now the signs which prove that this is going to happen are apparent. The child is being led away from everything that is mature. Sexuality has been an ineffable subject between old and young for a long time; soon death will be also.

We have said that the child lives in a separate world often enough. But perhaps these words are still too cautious—and too theoretical—to portray with enough clarity how separate this world really is. He who wants to see with his own eyes the separateness of the child's world, who wants to observe how the child is put down (lovingly) in a space of its own, cannot do better than visit a playground. He will have to adjust his eyes to the observation of certain peculiarities. Or rather, he must take off the glasses which make all inevitabilities seem acts of love. What he will then observe is what I have described in this book: a fenced-in space, an island in the middle of the mature world, an island of comparative safety in a fatal maturity, an island of (necessary) exile.

When the child ventures on the street—he must go to school and come home again—he has to be armed against the dangers he will meet. The grownups have given him a crossing guard. The children wait on the pavement until their group has grown big enough, then the guard puts up his hand, the traffic stops, and the group of exiles hurry to the other side of the street. No sooner is the last child off the street than the waiting traffic accelerates and hurries on.

A group of exiles? The thought that we are good for the children is more agreeable; so good are we that we lend them the attributes of maturity to defend themselves. Look, there they go; everybody stops; the businessman, whose time is money, the large truck, whose delay can be expressed in hard cash—everybody stops for the children. Are not we good to them? Doubtless we are, but it is the least we can do; we are obliged to be good to them, because of the great amount of irreparable evil we have done. Our goodness pays for a great injustice.

Understanding as the smallest compensation

Our understanding of children has become necessary because of a loss of understanding of a different kind, a natural understanding. The psychology of the child, which means scientifically-phrased understanding, is the smallest compensation for the lost natural understanding in the relationship between old and young. In Montaigne's day no one needed a psychology of the child; he was permitted to enter the adult's world early and unhampered, and there was no gap which necessitated a scientific bridge of understanding. There were no playgrounds then; the child played in the streets, among the adults, he was part of their life. When, in 1901, Ellen Key exclaimed that the century of the child had commenced, the children might have exulted over the fact that, at last, somebody had seen what a sad state the youngsters were in because of the growing complexity of maturity; [62] but they might just as well have burst into tears because this had become necessary. When adults are interested in the child, there is something wrong with the child—and with the adults. Growing children were never as secure as when there was no child psychology. This psychology is the result of a state of emergency.

THE FORCED WAY OUT

Primary school difficulties

Our children are late in everything. They no longer fit the institutions founded for them. In particular they have difficulties in adjusting themselves to school; they have become too immature for it. We usually blame the school, which we are inclined to consider an oldfashioned institution. But the way school now functions is additional evidence of the misunderstanding between young and old. School is in need of a renovation; not a change of nonessentials or of parts, but a renewal of the whole thing. Education as a whole has to be revised; and if the revision is to be effective, it must be nothing less than a total renewal of educational methods, which—as the recent serious attempts at renewal indicate—will be so radical that the slightly older teachers will observe these changes with wonder and will not feel at home with them, even if they do not doubt their necessity and agree as to their effectiveness. For it is clear to anyone who has anything to do with children and with education that something has to happen. Ever more children are experiencing serious difficulties during the first few years of primary school. Ever more children remain apart from what is being taught during a good part of the years they go to primary school. Schools are haunted by the ghost called alexia, one of the family of ghosts to which infantile autism also belongs. It is quite clear that this situation cannot be allowed to continue.

The previous pages have made clear why. The child is more infantile than it has ever been, and that is why it is not able to keep up with an educational program geared to the previous generation. Yet educational programs of the last century, and particularly of the last fifty years, have been adapted considerably to the changes in the child. Compared with past programs, modern education is characterized by a definite infantilism; and every change in educational methods will undoubtedly evidence an ever-increasing infantilism. Compare the instruction books of twenty to thirty years ago with those of the present; the older texts are examples of sturdy maturity: the child was supposed to understand those matters, and he did. One does not get the impression that the authors were very concerned about the child, and this is certainly true of still older instruction books. The teachers were equally little concerned about whether the child was "ripe" or not; they took it for granted that the child could digest reasonably formulated, but in every respect mature, knowledge. Why should they be concerned? the child understood what he was being taught and what he was reading.

Those days are gone. Today the child often does not understand what he is hearing or what he is reading, with the result that today's teachers do worry about the nature of their teaching. The effect of their considerations consists in the first place of a great compliance; one can always talk things over with the teacher, which could very seldom be done in earlier days. The books, too, have become more compliant. It is clear that the authors have tried to find the most agreeable and the most comprehensive way of presenting knowledge. The child is "invited" to follow the argument; there is no "must" any longer. The child is requested to absorb matters only after they have been packed in the most attractive wrappings and put within his reach.

Secondary school difficulties

Secondary school has to cope with the same problems. Here, too, the child appears to be too young for his age, and to keep him interested the teaching has also been made more infantile.

The complaint of teachers that books given to pupils to read must be replaced by works of ever simpler scope has been voiced so often that it seems unnecessary to list any titles for comparison. When I turn over the leaves of my old schoolbooks, it becomes clear to me that important changes have occurred in the really not too many years that have passed since I studied them. With amazement I establish the fact that my class, with understanding and admiration, read:

> *Suis-je chez dona Sol? fiancée au vieux duc*
> *De Pastrana, son oncle, un bon seigneur, caduc,*
> *Vénérable et jaloux? Dites! La belle adore*
> *Un cavalier sans barbe et sans moustache encore*
> *Et reçoit tous les soirs, malgré les envieux,*
> *Le jeune amant sans barbe à la barbe du vieux.*
> *Suis-je bien informé?*

We were sixteen, seventeen at the most. And that was only Victor Hugo. And we also read Goethe, Shakespeare, Corneille, and Shaw. I really cannot remember ever, in one way or another, not having understood what they were saying. The whole class understood. The opening words of *Faust* were listened to with suspense; some of my classmates recited parts of texts with an inspiration which could hardly have originated only in the inspiration of the teacher. I remember clearly that once there was a discussion about the artistic value of *Das Lied von der Glocke* which went on and on and was continued in the teacher's study.

It seems likely that these texts are going to be scrapped from the list one by one. Even now, in some secondary schools, the *Albums du père Castor* are read:

> Un petit coq
> au jardin
> ouvre le mais
> pique les grains.

Soon a daring student will put on his list of books something like *Dennis the Menace*. From a psychological point of view he will have performed an important deed; school will have been infiltrated by the separateness of a world in which to be naughty—to be antiadult—has become an unchallengeable privilege, the school which in former days was intended to be the last step toward a total and unconditional maturity.

Difficulties in higher education

If secondary education does become more infantile, the university will have to take over semimature tasks, for which it was never meant. The difficulties which will be caused by this are clearly apparent. Until recently, higher education was a pure, or almost pure, monologue. The professor taught, the student listened and took notes; he worked out his notes without assistance from anybody. Now students are complaining about not being able to follow this sort of instruction. A lecture should be a discussion; the student should be able to ask questions, he should be able to make proposals. Apparently the student has been separated from the lecturer to such an extent that the latter must leave his platform (which, in any case, has lost much of its majesty in the course of the years); the lecturer must move among his students, if he at all cherishes the hope of coming across a student who is willing to listen to him and who understands him.

Every university teacher who acknowledges this invitation and who leaves his platform comes to an almost stereotyped conclusion that the student knows even less than he had thought possible. The student lacks what seems to him the most elementary knowledge. The student has not read any books. About authors, by whom the lecturer and his contemporaries can recite entire paragraphs, only the names appear to be known. But what can he expect? The student did not read these authors in high school; how could he have provided himself with the texts? The lecturer finds himself obliged to start his course by having the students read what previous generations read in their high school days, and even earlier generations enjoyed in their highchairs. And this is just what the lecturer is not able to do, there is no time for it. And besides, he adheres, and rightly, to the task—circumscribed by custom—of presenting mature knowledge. Consequently he provides himself with assistants, who do the dirty work—which means the group discussions, the practical courses, the personal tutoring, the course aids. The government is very accommodating; it provides the money for the assistants with an openhandedness which would be surprising if one did not know how necessary it was. Sooner or later the lecturer will discover that the real work, the teaching, is being done by his assistants. What he had called, rather disdainfully, the "dirty work" appears to be the thing that matters; the assistants are the real teachers, the professor is an ornament, a name, a relic; a man, probably, of amazing erudition, but just because of this erudition a man who is absent, only to be reached by his assistants. They are the only people who can follow his arguments.

It will not come down as far as this. For every lecturer sees for himself that the dirty work does not deserve the name. He will lead the group discussions himself, he will answer questions, he will invite criticism. He will be more and more inclined to replace monologues by dialogues, eloquence by understanding, and presentation of knowledge by co-operation; a co-operation which will guide him in his teaching, and which will even provide him with the words of the language he must use in order to be understood by his students. And if the student still remains alienated from what he is being taught, there is always the government official for student affairs, who will be glad to listen to his sighs and who will do his utmost to improve or re-establish the contact between teacher and student. Perhaps soon this official will be able to refer the student to an institution where he can recuperate from his derangement and get back on the right track again.

Difficulties in society

The student who passes his last examination (which has lost more and more of the solemnity it had in earlier times) discovers he is not at all ready for society. Nothing else can be expected. If university education is to be more infantile, then the leap toward maturity must come afterward. Even now there are several occupations in which nothing is expected from the newly-appointed employee during the first few years; he is supposed to get acquainted with his work, he is moved to different departments once or twice to see whether, perhaps, they would be more suitable, and he is forgiven his worthlessness—despite his diploma, which is the visible certificate of his all-round competence. And if he becomes adjusted at last, his minority is still not completely over, because in the time he had been adjusting, the work to which this adjustment was necessary has changed, and by the time he is ready his work has evolved into other, newer forms. His knowledge is antiquated by the time he is ready to use it. His instruction goes on; and he is subject to a never-ceasing demand for "occupational flexibility." [63] What does this beautiful expression mean except that maturity is never reached? *Flexibility*—the word means only that the worker has no general view or control over his work; it implies that the worker must let the work come toward him; that he has to face new tricks of ever-newer forms of work, and that when these tricks become clearer to him, he must carefully maneuver around them in order to achieve some security. Occupational flexibility is a quality necessary for those who do not have the deciding say in the relationship between a worker and his work. Work, this anonymous and self-ruling thing,[64] forces the worker into a never-ending minority.

Persisting immaturity

One who is a minor is called immature. Immaturity penetrates all life's phases. With a disturbing naturalness, experts explain that education belongs to every phase of life, from the cradle to the grave. "The process of education must be regarded as continuous throughout life." [65] Without hesitating one speaks of "adult education," forgetting that these words contain a contradiction. Education is only possible in a relationship of teacher and pupil, a relationship inevitably characterized by authority. And the one who is under this authority is immature. There is no getting away from it; the—in itself correct, in any case, necessary—desideratum of "adult education" makes children of us all. And when the adult becomes infantile, the most natural acts and attitudes must be learned. "Marriage also needs to be seen as a skilled occupation, for which the preparation should not stop short at a course in domestic economy." Husband and wife must learn how to get along with each other "so that man and wife can be a team." Nor should a wife be deprived of a course which teaches her the needs of her baby and how a good mother can meet those needs: "There is a need for a practical introduction to the intellectual, emotional, and spiritual needs of the early years and of the ways in which the mother—natural or adopted—can help to meet them." [66] Soon there will be no act that is not learned; even the suckling of a baby will become a difficult artificial manipulation.

The desideratum of adjustment

The quality by which modern maturity proves its immaturity is adjustment. In the textbooks of adult psychology one can read that adjustment is maturity's most important attribute, its criterion. He who is adjusted can call himself mature. But it should be kept in mind that this so-called maturity is a modern maturity. True maturity, and by this I mean a maturity which is not diminished by adult education to a semimaturity, is much more characterized by nonadjustment—nonadjustment in the sense of independence. The true adult is master of his work; his work does not make *his* existence insignificant. The adult acts—which means that he gives evidence of a freedom which, if necessary, gives him a right, a total and unlimited right, to act on his own, to carry all responsibility alone. Today, acting as an adult means acting in a team. The plea is made that the team is an improvement—as any loss is praised as an improvement—the team is said to create cooperation, harmony, and integration. The peculiarity of all work done in teams, however, is primarily the lack of responsibility of each of the participants. No one is responsible. No one is wholly mature.

In the relationship of a worker to his work, the worker is moved to the second place. Work done on an assembly line is a perfect example. The work comes toward the worker. Not only work: everything that is a "task," or can be transformed into a task— marriage, fatherhood, motherhood, the difficult period around forty, climacteric, old age, grandfatherhood, grandmotherhood, dying. Everything comes toward us in a shape which we do not recognize any more and which we will never know, not only because this shape is liable to change—and is therefore unpredictable —but mainly because the task, by virtue of its coming toward us, makes us secondary, and being secondary, we cannot know, we can have no awareness, we cannot act. Action, awareness, knowledge imply being first.

What ought to conform can be tested

The task moves toward us, it penetrates us, it destroys what does not fit, and polishes what does fit. It makes us an extension of the task. Every behavior becomes codified; no one dares to withdraw from the codified way of doing things. A person who is ill is suffering from a textbook disease; if the disease diverges from its known course, it is personal and consequently not real. He who makes his dying an individual act is leaving the path which leads to the conclusion of all medical help, a trespassing for which the penalty is morphine. If a car can do a hundred miles an hour, then we will drive it a hundred miles an hour; the machine compels us to grip its steering wheel, strain our legs, and get the "passing" expression on our face. If a new way of registering or classifying appears to have sense, then we register or classify in the new way, taking it as a model for our future action. The second quality of modern maturity (which is closely related to the first) is its conformity.

The task moves toward us. Between the terminal moraines of this unmovable, irresistible glacier, there, where the ice is melting and the melting water permits a not too hard but rather cold approach, is found the psychological test, the psychotechnique, the thing that above everything else pressures us to adjust. Indeed, this test is greeted as a very humane help by which the institutions of labor, with their natural complexity, make themselves known for the benefit of the newcomer. Yet the test means, "Not yet, but pretty soon"; or, "Not in this way but in that way"; or, "Not here, but there." In all these decisions is incorporated the tendency to make the person who is being examined conform to a certain sort of work, which serves as a standard value. The tendency is to adjust him to this work.

There is no doubt that the applicant can benefit greatly from this examination. Does it not guard him against making false steps, does it not save him time, does it not show him the way? By this test one learns to know him, so that it becomes clear which direction he should follow and which direction he should avoid. Thus the expectation.

Yet, the supposition on which this examination is based is doubtful. The examination takes for granted that the person who is examined can be known in such a way that he can be described as if he were a lifeless object. He is like this and like that—this is the conclusion—therefore he is, or he is not suitable for this sort of work. This sounds acceptable. But it only sounds acceptable because we have gradually learned to believe in the objectlike nature of our being, in the possibility of the judgment, "He is like this." This belief appeared for very good reasons. Our existence imposed on us a certain objectivity; and we more or less became objects.

What is the goal of a test? Does it examine an "objectivity" which remains the same before and after the examination—the way the moon apparently does not change if she is observed by telescope? Or is the test, primarily, a concrete evidence of the task, or conglomeration of tasks, behind it, of which the fast-approaching character consists in equalization, equalization with the task? If we are an objectivity, then we may be expected to behave according to the same pattern (our own) in all circumstances. The man who is irritable here will be irritable somewhere else. The ascertained manual ability would be apparent in every concrete action, just as the manual inability could never change into its opposite. Anyone who asks himself the question whether the life he has lived so far confirms this equality of behaviour, and consequently the identity of his own qualities under different circumstances, must see that this is not true. That is the reason why two people can have so different an opinion about a third person whom they both know well. With each one, this third person acts differently. In the same way, a person might be different in Amsterdam from the way he is in New York. He could be different in factory A from the way he is in factory B. But then—what is there to be tested?

This last remark is not justified. The examination given in order to accept or reject an applicant for a certain function is not aimed at knowing him; it only tries to equate the applicant with the work, to the function for which the applicant applied. If he is successful, he can be accepted. If he is not, he is worthless. The examination—this is another way of putting it—tries to exclude all those applicants who might react differently in factory A and factory B. Such applicants are too unstable. The test aims to find people who are equal to themselves in all circumstances—people who can be tested. The test tries to make a person "testable"—that is its first aim. If the person appears to be testable, then the test can decide whether he is suitable for the job or not. In practice these two procedures are intertwined. If a person appears to be not suitable for a certain form of activity, it still is not at all impossible that only his untestableness was demonstrated—maybe he was extremely suitable. It is worth considering whether or not the exceptionally suitable person often is one of these untestables. I doubt whether Einstein was testable; yet for a certain function he was extremely suitable.

We are not testable, we are made testable. Made testable by the conglomeration of tasks which have acquired a commanding position, and of which the test is an essential part. The test is the spearhead of an army coming toward us. That, at least, is what it seems. Actually the spearhead has penetrated much further. The applicant has passed it a long time before he presents himself for the test. Before he learns of the test he has been educated; and he has talked with his parents, the parents who made his future inaccessible, who made him believe in the genetic character of his existence, who made his existence a logical conclusion. A logical conclusion can be measured. Before he enters the testing bureau, he has passed through spaces which made him measurable, testable. "And all the while he himself had been handed over as a pass at the entrance." [67]

When does comparative maturity begin?

If a doctor decides to become a surgeon, he will have to go through a special training period of five years. If he was eighteen when he began his medical studies, and twenty-five when he qualified as a doctor, he will be thirty by the time he finishes his education. He can then start to work as an independent person. Unless, of course—which is the rule—he spends two years in military service. He is thirty-two then. Unless he works in a hospital abroad for a few years—which is usually recommended. Then he will be thirty-four. Unless at that moment he chooses a superspeciality; in that case, he will be expected to subject himself to another few years of training, so that when his education is entirely finished, he will be over thirty-five. Will he be mature then? This question hardly makes sense. And yet his maturity can still be doubted, he still cannot assume complete responsibility for himself and for those entrusted to him. For he has to start a practice; in order to buy all the things he needs, he has to borrow money. If possible he will borrow it from his father. Will he feel free toward his father? Will he not have certain obligations toward him? It can hardly be doubted. These obligations, however lightly they may weigh on his conscience, will still keep him immature in a way. Never before has the encouraging, consoling remark that life begins at forty been more true.

Not for everybody; certainly not. The example, no doubt, is extreme. There are still occupations which permit a rather fast maturation. In every country there are still areas where maturity is so visible and inviting that the child leaves his childhood quickly and easily.

City and country

Those who live in a city do not know what to do with these matured young adults. What can we do with the farmer's boy, who is surly and stiff and does not say a word; or with the farmer's girl, who answers our questions with a few barely audible words. They give the impression of being highly immature. And yet the same boy knows what he is expected to do when his father asks him to put the horse in the stable or to bring round the tractor. And the girl who stands before us so timidly does not hesitate to act when her mother is in childbed. Both are definitely more mature, more able to carry responsibility for themselves and for others, than the city boy, whose ready wit suggests maturity, but who would not know what to do if his father said, "You'd better do the work today, I don't feel very well." Even more mature seems the city girl, with her smartness and her female adroitness; yet she does not know how to carry a child on her arm and she does not feel sure about the right amount of salt in the potatoes. Their smartness, shrewdness, adroitness, their manliness and femininity, are nothing but drawn swords; so dangerous is the big city's maturity, that the child has to arm itself, with the weapons of maturity itself, at an early age. The smartness and shrewdness guarantee the last possibility of contacting the adults, and so the possibility of a final assimilation. In the country maturation is often still a simple task. Not infrequently it is no task at all.

The western world and Samoa

It is easy to understand that maturation is unknown in Samoa. "Nor are they permitted a period of lack of responsibility such as our children are allowed. From the time they are four or five years old they perform definite tasks, graded to their strength and intelligence, but still tasks which have a meaning in the structure of the whole society." [68]

If the children in Samoa participate in the adults' society from the time they are four or five years old, then there is no reason at all for them to go through a period of maturation. There is nothing which divides them from the adults; consequently there is no bridge needed to join them. And if there is no bridge, no one can fall from it: in Samoa neuroses are unknown.[69] If there is no bridge, there can be no acrobatics on the railing: in Samoa there are no great love affairs.

But in our world, the bridge—constructed in the days of Rousseau—has increased in length and is still growing. The result is that the chances of falling off are great, and will be ever greater. So easily does one stray from those who are hurrying forward on this almost endless bridge, which is so dangerously haphazard at so many places, that it is almost too risky not to grudge oneself a moment of leisure with a loved one, assuming a posture at the railing which is beautiful for those who have eyes for it, delightful for the two who are silently holding on to each other, but so close to the fate of those who fall off that the postures are held ever more shortly; after a few moments one resumes the wearisome journey, that is, if one is not dragged down to the depths of a dubious inwardness. I trust the reader will forgive me this strange metaphor. What I want to say is that neuroses are not at all unknown in our society, and that being "passionately" in love, which means deriving a certain satisfaction from the misery this condition often induces, is a state of life which particularly belongs to our civilization. But if I put it like this, it lacks, wrongly, the Kafka-like perspective in which these interludes occur.

An endless process

Where will this end? There are two aspects to this question,[70] one of which will be discussed below in another chapter. The question which I would like to answer here is, Will this process go on indefinitely?

Is our society, the society of the adults, to become even more complicated and even more multivalent in the future? It can hardly be doubted. Will the adults' society consequently put still more obstacles in the way of those who are growing up? It can hardly be avoided. But when will they be mature, then? When will they be able to practise their occupation with (comparative) independence? Is it not to be feared that maturity will be postponed such a long time, for certain groups, that the girl (woman) will have barely a few years before her climacteric to have a few children?

There is evidence that it will not come to that. Lately we are seeing that those who are growing up are themselves forcing a solution. These youngsters appropriate maturity, before the adult society is inclined to grant them its permission. Before society acknowledges them as mature, they are married. The ultimately fatal process of protracting their minority is being stranded on sexuality.

A biological necessity

Biological sexuality begins its maturity at a fixed time of life, which lies in the same age period for every race on earth. Psychosexual maturity begins later. There is a great variability in the time elapsing between these two forms of maturity. There are societies where it is short, almost absent; in our culture it lasts a long time. If biological and psychical maturity follow one another closely, the child who is growing up can be expected to resign himself to wait; to be able to wait is a desirable human quality. But if the time between them is longer, the chances will increase that those waiting will look for forms of sexuality which can fill up the waiting period. Falling in love is one example; masturbation is another. In masturbation the waiting person retains access to the other sex, but the other sex is not present, its presence is only imagined; there is no contact. This absence of contact is the intention. But if the time lag is too long, there comes a moment when all emergency solutions fail. Those who have to wait have affairs; marital-like relationships without children, relationships in which, as a rule, the marital-like arrangements are kept secret. But if the period of time between the biological maturity and the psychical maturity permitted by society becomes too long, the young are not inclined to fill this period with a compromise. They marry. And with this act they bring the process to an end. Society protests, but its protest is unjustified; is it not protesting against the hard, ethically neutral, facts of biology?

To rebut this biological argument, the following can be said. The supposition is that psychosexual maturity would announce itself immediately after biological maturity, if society did not object. Or, in other words, that every postponement is a result of a frustration imposed by society. An honest observation of the youngsters who are living in this supposed frustration and of their behavior makes the correctness of this supposition extremely doubtful. As a rule there are no signs of pressure in their existence, nor of their being depressed in consequence. The young people who are living a life of continence, correlating with their age, evidence a freedom and an enjoyment of life which contradicts the pinch which this biological theory implies. A young man can enter his third decennial in complete asexuality, an asexuality that gives not the least impression of being an effect of pressure on the individual. If no sexual appeal ever reached a youngster, his sexuality would not come into existence; perhaps, at the most, as a vague restlessness, but even this is doubtful. Evidence for this is hard to provide, since a child would have to grow up in an environment in which no sexual appeal—not even the slightest—could occur. Apart from being undesirable, this would be impossible. For our society is so soaked with a never-ending sexual appeal, disguised in thousands of ways, that an isolated youth probably could be isolated from anything except sexual appeal. One has to fall back on experiences of association with the young, and with autobiographical notes. Neither the experiences nor the notes justify this theory of frustration, which is repudiated anyway by the existence of those who live in a mental celibacy. The man who (rightly) lives in celibacy has made another appeal predominate over the sexual appeal. He has molded his life in such a way—or received life molded in such a way—that it is possible for him to be unmarried without feeling the unrest which seems so inevitable to married people if they imagine a life of absolute continence.

A *sociological cause*

Not for reasons of a biological nature, therefore, is the youngster inclined to end the period of asexual biological maturity. The reasons are to be found on a sociological level. Our society has become so genitalized, particularly during the last few decades, that hardly any young person can manage to be biologically mature in an asexual way for longer than, let us say, five years—and that is a short time considering what is expected of him.

When the youngster is biologically mature, he encounters many and frequent sexual appeals, which often excite his sexuality forcibly and which always stimulate it; at the same time he is requested to show little or nothing of this sexuality and certainly not to draw from it the logical conclusion of a sexual contact. Out of the combination of these two diametrically opposed stimulants originate the sexual difficulties so typical of our western world; and the same combination is responsible for the forced solution.

The youngster in our society is supposed to prepare himself for a wholly physical and very genital sexuality; at the same time he is pushed in to a complete sexual minority. He reacts to this situation logically: he prepares himself for a genital sexuality—that is, his own genitality and that of the other sex becomes clear, even abundantly clear, to him—and he keeps himself away from concrete sexuality—that is, the other person's desired and enticing genitality is an absolutely denied and forbidden territory. In practice this means either that he is in love, or he masturbates. As is known, the one is incompatible with the other, not because they are at variance with each other—although they are that, too—but primarily because they are essentially identical. The young person in love is in contact with the other sex, but his being in love forbids almost every word, every touch, every physical contact with the loved one. Masturbation implies intercourse with an absent genitally opposite person. Masturbation and being in love are adequate responses to the contradiction with which the youngster is confronted. The youngster in love is not frustrated, and neither is the sexually solitary youngster. They cannot act in any other way; they are responding faultlessly to what society is requiring from them.

Frustration and response

Yet it is clear that request and response easily lead to frustrations. The situation can last too long, for instance. It did last too long for the students of previous generations. And as that older society positively condemned marriage among students, the only solution for these students was to frequent prostitutes, a solution which suited the radically immature and exaggerated pseudo maturity of the student of those days perfectly. The student swore and drank—and still behaved like a child. He was pardoned for everything.

Times have changed. Today's student barely swears and he does not drink much. His behavior is far less uncouth; he is only a bit wild when he is indoors, and even during these moments his wildness does not come as easily as before. He doubts the genuineness of his student existence. In the eyes of the nihilist—frequently a person who has lost all faith in a student's peculiar existence—he reads a criticism which he cannot entirely ignore. His studentlike behaviour is an affectation, it has no meaning any longer. Nor does he frequent prostitutes anymore. There is a particular reason for this. In the days when the student was happily nestling in a state of studentlike uncouthness, his future life partner was guarded in the safe harbor of family life. The fathers (who had been students themselves; did they remember?) saw to it that no sexual, and certainly no genital appeal, ever reached their daughters. It was easy for these fathers. The newspapers and periodicals still looked innocent, and their daughters were like the papers. They could feel that life had always been like that, and always would be. The newspapers changed; and so did the daughters. The nylons pictured in those papers are on the daughters' legs. The student is aware of this. Looking at the newspapers, he sees his chances. He chooses a girl from the group to which his future wife belongs; and he has an affair with her. This pseudo marriage (for they will prevent children) with her is the response to a new appeal.

This new appeal may be expressed as follows: 1. Marriage is a sexual, not in the least even a genital affair; 2. Here are our daughters. See how they are dressed and observe how they possess, undiminished, the genitality so essential to marriage; 3. Choose one; they want to be chosen; 4. But do not marry.

Do not marry! The first three injunctions drive the daughters into the arms of the young men; the fourth postpones their marriage. Isn't an affair the logical conclusion: the petting to climax, the secret marriage without children?

The end of the compromise

But the solution of the secret marriage cannot be kept up for long. The absence of children makes the relationship monotonous; not enough happens. Apart from the comradeship, what happens is that the sexual relationship finds its fixed form and norm after a few months, a few years at the most; and not in the least because there are no children, it does not renew itself and becomes dull. The more so, because this sexual relationship, considering the secrecy and the need to prevent children, is often incomplete. It is not easy to be satisfied for many years with a fragmentary sexual intercourse which leads to nothing, and still remain fresh-looking and attractive to the partner. Besides, getting entangled in a temporary attachment like this makes it easy to switch over to another attachment, just as temporary. Partnerships are broken up, the game is continued with some one else. Very soon the game lasts too long, and nowadays it lasts too long for many. Who could expect a future surgeon to go on playing this game until he is thirty-five? Let us suppose that he has met his future wife when he is twenty-three. An affair, which is to last twelve years! And the girl? She is twenty-one; does she have to wait twelve years? She will be thirty-three by then.

So they marry, and by so doing, stop this fatal development. The postadolescents are interrupting the process of a forever postponed maturation; they are appropriating maturity and are creating a new status, soon, probably, a new life-phase: the phase of the married postadolescent.[71]

Youth refuses to compromise; they want to be married, they want a room in which they can live, acknowledged in their married state. If necessary they are satisfied with a one-room apartment, as long as they are allowed to live in it together and to have a child in it. If they are "allowed"; that is the word still used by the adults who observe all this with anxiety. They consider this an impossible situation, these adults; they see how their children are rooming together, how they are leading a *vie de bohème*,[72] how they are leading a life which is in complete disagreement with the puritan life at home, where everything has its accustomed place, where no one needs to doubt whether he is in the living-room or in a bedroom, and where there is never a book on the sink, nor a package of butter on a book. They are stupefied, these parents, when, on top of all this, there is going to be a baby in this mess; and even a second one. And they cannot understand how these youngsters can keep their tempers in spite of all these irregularities. "When I married," the father will say, "I was earning enough money to rent a house and to buy the furniture. And I was able to keep my wife and children." For many those days are gone. But he has himself to blame, this father; together with all other fathers and mothers he has seen to it that society has assumed such an unfriendly, repulsive, inaccessible, and dangerous character, that the youngsters have become confused. Now they have had enough. They economize and live in one room, married. The parents can hardly protest.

As it is, parents are protesting less every day. They do have the feeling that what is happening is good rather than bad. Some of them are even sure of it, and are openly saying so. Those are the few who are pleading for salaries for students, and for bungalows for the married student couples. The few who see that the working studentship not only meets a need for money, but quite often includes the desired certificate of majority as well. Those who realize that the state of being a student has basically changed; those who see that it cannot be a coincidence that there are so many nihilists among students or that so many student societies became "democratic" (as it is called). In short, all those (for maybe there are more of them than I, in a disappointed moment, dare to hope) who have eyes for this new phase of life—which today is still reserved for one social class only—the phase of the married postadolescent.

This phase runs from the age of about twenty to about thirty-five, and potentially involves the next phase, the phase of productivity; therefore, it is of such importance that there is every reason to observe closely what they are doing, these postadolescents; and there is sense in providing them with money, now, for what they need for their design. We need not provide them with the design; they will do that all by themselves. Is not what they are doing capturing maturity?

CHAPTER 3

Neurosis or Sociosis

THE MEANING OF SYMPTOMS

The year in which the theory of the neuroses and the theory of psychotherapy came into existence out of nowhere [1] can be identified with particular exactness. Both theories appeared in the summer of 1882.

It is a well-known story. In the two years between 1880 and 1882, a Viennese doctor, Josef Breuer, had been trying to gain insight into a disease which had been known since antiquity, but whose symptoms were so capricious and so unstable, and whose physical basis, even after accurate physical examination, appeared so entirely lacking, that nobody knew the outlines of the disease nor the meaning of its symptoms. A young woman—she was twenty-one years old—whom Breuer had been visiting regularly was suffering from this disease. She had a paralysis of the right arm, a disturbance of her eyesight, an annoying cough, and many more symptoms; these symptoms, however, without exception, were characterized by the amazing and in those days entirely unaccountable fact that they were not caused by a defect of a physical nature. Her arm was neurologically sound, even in a state of complete paralysis; the ophthalmologist found no signs of disease in her—nonetheless faulty—eyes; and the throat specialist could not find anything wrong with her throat, in spite of the fact that her cough continued to suggest a physical defect. In addition, she exhibited a remarkable disturbance: she had a tendency to go into a sort of unconsciousness, now and then, for no apparent reason. In such a fit she was not completely unconscious; she answered questions and she was able to take part in conversation. That she had a certain degree of wakefulness was proved by the fact that she made sure that it was Breuer who was with her and nobody else. She felt his hands until she was certain it was he who was by her side. That is to say, all the functions of her waking life had ceased, with this one exception; she could still make contact with her doctor. And as this condition of partial wakefulness was well-known in hypnosis, Breuer named this last symptom "spontaneous hypnosis."

As a result of the talks Breuer had with his patient, he acquired an increasing understanding of the nature of the disturbances, which (and this cannot be emphasized strongly enough) had never before been understood by anyone. His understanding remained fragmentary and vague, however, until, in the summer of 1882, the patient suddenly complained of an entirely new symptom and after a few weeks got rid of it just as suddenly.

This symptom was a sudden inability to drink. Even when eventually she was tortured by a bad thirst, she could not succeed in taking one sip from the glass Breuer offered her. She did bring the glass to her lips; but at the moment they were about to touch the liquid, she fell into a condition very similar to spontaneous hypnosis; and then, apparently horrified, she would put the glass back on the table. Again there were no physical defects.

The explanation of this extraordinary behavior came a few weeks later. Breuer was talking to her while she was in a spontaneous hypnosis; and she suddenly told him, showing evidence of an intense nausea, how she had seen a dog drinking from a glass of a lady, who, ignorant of what had happened, had afterward drunk what was left. She had barely finished her story when she wanted a drink—still in a state of spontaneous hypnosis. Breuer handed her a glass of water; she took it from him, brought it to her lips—and woke up drinking. From that moment the symptom disappeared, and never reoccurred. Breuer's famous note reads, "After she had forcefully expressed her pent-up anger, she wanted to drink and woke up from the hypnosis with the glass at her lips. After this the disturbance disappeared forever." [2]

This sentence indicates the birth of the theories of psychotherapy and of the neuroses, since it embodies the entire explanation of the causes and therapy of neurotic symptoms. And even more: this sentence, which seems so innocent, in any case so very simple, implies a philosophy which is the prevailing philosophy of our society today. Let us see how things developed and what actually happened.

The first publication

In 1893, eleven years after the great discovery, Breuer and his assistant, Sigmund Freud, published a provisional survey of the results of their research. It may be summarized as follows.

1. Every hysteria is the result of an injuring experience—a trauma. An experience like the one Breuer's patient had: seeing a dog drink from a glass of a lady, who afterward drinks from it herself. An unbearable experience.

2. This experience (of which the hysteria is the result) must be so unbearable that it cannot be included in the totality of life, it cannot be digested. As a result the experience becomes nonparticipating; it becomes subconscious, or rather, it is pushed into a subconscious state; the experience is pushed out of consciousness.

3. What has been pushed aside, however, does not cease to exist. The experience existed intensely; it was loaded with emotion. And it is just because so much emotion was involved, just because this experience was so intense, it could not be fitted in with the totality and had to be put aside. Can what is repressed protest, but not make itself known? This seems to contain a contradiction. If one harbors a revolting memory, sooner or later he will be reminded of it. But that reminder is exactly what should not happen, since he would get ill from the emotion attached. Consequently the revolting memory makes itself known in another

way, so different in appearance that it is not recognized. It appears as a symptom. It is better not to drink than to remember by drinking, and remembering, die emotionally. Rather the symptom than the emotion.

4. The symptom disappears "immediately and definitely" [3] if the emotion can be made to express itself.

Breuer's presence

Breuer and Freud soon had to take back the words "immediately and definitely." Apparently it was not as easy as all that to cure these symptoms. Still, the statement was never taken back completely, simply because there was truth in it. Many symptoms did disappear (in the long run and for a certain length of time), if a patient succeeded in recalling the memory and in making the emotion attached to it express itself.

This brings up one question immediately: if it were only a matter of expressing this emotion, why couldn't the patient do it herself? Why didn't she get a few spells of crying and vomiting? Why did she need another person? And not just anybody, either; she needed Breuer. Why did she need Breuer? For it is quite clear that Breuer's presence was a *conditio sine qua non*; the patient felt his hands until she knew it was he, and only then did she start to talk. "She only started to talk, when she had convinced herself of my identity by feeling my hands," writes Breuer; [4] it is obvious that this fact impressed him. Breuer did not know what to do with this observation, however. Neither did Freud. Especially not Freud; his whole work can be read as one great duel with this observation, which was repeated thousands of times later on—the observation that the patient needs somebody, not just anybody, but one particular person. In this sentence of Breuer's is embodied another theory of the neuroses. But it is better not to digress now; this will be discussed more extensively later on.

The theory and the therapy

Using the above four statements, we can temporarily define the theory of the neuroses and the theory of psychotherapy: every neurosis,—for it soon appeared that not only hysteria was involved

—every neurosis is a traumatic neurosis; that was Breuer's theory of the neuroses. And the therapy: find the trauma, make the patient remember it, and let the emotion be expressed as forcibly as possible.

Symptoms have a meaning

The fact is, that this simple, undeniably psychiatric, that is, medical, scheme very soon led to a general theory of human existence which appeared to be extremely viable and which was accepted by a great many people. We must examine the first three conclusions and think over what they actually mean.

They look innocent enough, these suppositions of Breuer's: every neurosis is a traumatic neurosis; the trauma is subconscious; the result is a symptom. This last assumption solved the secret which had guarded the symptom for ages. The patient who, with sound legs, cannot walk because his legs are paralyzed, is unable to walk because his legs are filled with an emotion which was not permitted adequate expression. He had, for instance, walked to a fatal spot with these legs, a place where he had to hear some extremely unfortunate information. He let the information submerge into his subconscious, and the walk as well; from then on, for the very reason that he no longer knows about this walk, his legs are "the legs of the walk," they refuse to work; the emotion is in them, and the patient cannot walk on emotion. Besides, the chances that he can still hear are slight; for with his ears he heard the bad tidings, and to hear might make him remember them again; he is trying to prevent that, consequently he is deaf— even if the otologist finds nothing to indicate this deafness. And so on. Every symptom has a meaning. What had been a mystery began to make sense.

Everything has a meaning

The conclusion that symptoms have a meaning leads easily to the thesis that *everything* has a meaning. Of course, it is a leap from the strictly psychiatric to the generally human; but who could object to that, once that it was known that there is hardly a border-line dividing the normal from the neurotic? Besides, there is another reason why this formula that everything has a meaning was accepted so eagerly.

Everything has a meaning. When, before Breuer and Freud, if a man moved his leg up and down while he was talking to his wife, and an onlooker asked what the meaning of this leg movement could be, no one would have taken the question seriously. The movement was something that just happened. We have different ideas now. Not much imagination is needed to suspect that the man with the moving leg has a grudge against his wife; he is kicking her out of the room, even if he reduces his kicks to very modest, and, to the uninitiated (are there any left?), innocent dimensions. If a person today finds delight in sucking his pipe long after the tobacco in it has gone out, it is clear even to a layman that he never really left his mother's breast, he is still sucking the nipple. Or rather, he did not suck it enough then, and it is still bothering him; he made the frustrated desire submerge because it was too disagreeable, and it is coming to the surface when he gnaws his pipe, when he lets saliva run into it and then sucks it back. In the past the question whether this sucking and gnawing might have a meaning was simply never raised. Everyone had his peculiarities, and that was all there was to it.[5] If someone then happened to be visually inclined, no one would have wondered why; now it is quite apparent that he is out to see something else in the things over which his eyes so eagerly rove—his mother, for example, who never, in his youth, appeared naked before him.

I could give scores of examples of trivial, so seemingly unintentional, until recently so apparently innocent inclinations, acts, and habits, which, on closer examination, all appear to have a meaning—which is to say, they are guilty. They can be found in every textbook of psychology. Everything has a meaning: the man who forgets something means something by it; the man who makes a mistake in writing is expressing his most secret thoughts; if he arrives at an appointment too early, there is some reason for it; if he arrives too late, that, too, has its deeper meaning.

The meaning is always located in the past

The fact that in each example the meaning is to be found *in the past*, is of particular significance. The man kicks his wife because of incidents already past, and also because of earlier thoughts about these incidents; the pipesmoker sucks his pipe because of his skirmish with his mother's breast which turned out so fatally. The visuality of the eidetically-gifted descends from frustrations of an earlier desire to peek.

Threatened innocence

Who can feel at ease with all this? Life is full of trivialities— which appear always to have a meaning. And what a meaning! This meaning always escapes *us*; it almost seems a law that it is always somebody else who discovers the apparent meaning of our actions. What he discovers is honorable only by exception. And he is always right. To deny it does not help, for the meaning is essentially unknown, it is subconscious. We cannot possibly feel at ease with it. And yet—I am convinced—we accept the idea that everything has a meaning so eagerly because more than almost any other formula, it makes us feel at ease.

Dorian Gray's lilacs

The spray of lilac fell from his hand upon the gravel. A furry bee came and buzzed round it for a moment. Then it began to scramble all over the oval stellated globe of the tiny blossoms. He watched it with that strange interest in trivial things that we try to develop when things of high import make us afraid, or when we are stirred by some new emotion for which we can not find expression, or when some thought that terrified us lays sudden siege to the brain and calls on us to yield.

The words were written by Oscar Wilde in 1891, two years before the work of the two Viennese doctors. We may presume that they express the thoughts of a man who had never heard that the meaning of all things was to be found in the past. Still, these are the thoughts of a man sensitive enough to hear and understand the language of trivialities.

I cannot know the meaning behind Dorian Gray's interest in lilacs and in the scrambling bee if I remain true to the idea that everything has a meaning, true to the opinion that only incidents in the past, and especially incidents that were broken off in the past, are the bearers of occurrences. Shall I take it that Dorian's interest has the same meaning as Jonathan Swift's delight in Lilliput's small creatures and in their crawling movements? that in this way, he is expressing his own, once frustrated, exhibitionism, and is also softening a too painful memory of his own birth? (The reader who wishes more information on this subject is referred to Ferenczi's article on Gulliver fantasies.[6])

Trivialities

Lest the reader feel I am leading him on a false track, it may be necessary to point out that this quotation from *Dorian Gray* is of exactly the same caliber as the examples I mentioned before. Dorian Gray is looking at the lilacs the same way that the man who is having a discussion with his wife moves his leg up and down. If we imagine ourselves present at their discussion, we might hear her make a few less than agreeable remarks; the man, who might very well have incited these remarks, is thinking; he is moving his leg up and down, and in this movement he locates his thinking. In the same way Dorian is looking at the bee in this important moment; he locates himself in the bee, and in the bee the significance of the moment becomes concrete. Later on, when he thinks back to this moment, he will say, "I can still see the lilacs and the bee scrambling over them; it was that moment." Just so will the man say, a long time afterward, "I can still see my leg go up and down; I was trying to touch the tablecloth with the tip of my shoe." And if he won't say it, his wife will: ". . . and just as I had said that, you started moving your leg up and down. I had to keep looking at it. I can still see you do it, when I think of that awful moment."

Is it not this trivial moment itself that is significant? The moving leg does contain a meaning, but it does not seem probable that the leg is moved because of what had been in the past. If its meaning must be located some time ago, in the past, the moving leg might embody the sad story of a marriage resulting in mitigated kicks; a more recent meaning behind the moving leg, though still in the past, could be located in the unfriendly remarks the wife might just have been making. It is so easy to assume; the past contains hundreds of incidents, and there are always a few that can carry the task of being the cause. The past so eagerly sucks us away from the present; yet it is the present in our examples that is significant. If it were not the present, then why would the man be observing his foot with so much interest? Why would he be measuring the distance to the tablecloth as if the future of his marriage depended on it? And why would she be inclined to think, "If he touches the tablecloth, it will be all over between us. He did not touch it. Not now either. He did not touch the tablecloth, thank God." The moving leg contains something by itself, a present actuality, *now*—however much the activity may be connected with the past at the same time, however much it may recall the past.

And the same is true for the pipe. I am reading and I am smoking my pipe. It goes out; I go on reading. Suddenly my attention is caught by a sentence in the book. I look up and gaze at nothing. I am repeating the sentence to myself, I am tasting the meaning of the words, and at the same time I am sucking my pipe; I let saliva get into it and I suck it back, little by little, just as if I were pouring a little meaning into the words, and then sucking it back again, sharper, more biting, closer to the author's intention.

It seems as if I have extracted the meaning of the words out of my pipe. And exactly in the same way did Dorian Gray look at the bee—fascinated, curious, frightened. And yet every movement of the bee in itself can only be good; the bee has no knowledge of Dorian Gray. The bee is grappling with its own idiosyncrasies.

Bee and lilacs: a closed unity

The bee is grappling with its own idiosyncrasies. There is no doubt about that. The bee and the lilacs, and the sun, and Dorian Gray's shadow constitute a closed unity, ruled by laws of its own. An ethologist could tell us all about it; no doubt he could make it clear that the bee acts the way it does because of a number of causes, all originating from the closed unity, bee-and-lilacs. And since this unity is closed, the observer, as observer, is entirely out of it.

Is not the last statement a tautology, though? When I say that the scheme bee-and-lilacs is a closed unity, and then I say that the observer—in this case, Dorian Gray—is not in it, am I not using a condition to the former statement as a conclusion in the latter? Worded like this, it is hardly noticeable. But if I were to say, the incidents of the bee and the lilacs can be explained with the laws contained in the unity bee-and-lilacs; and consequently the observer, as observer (not as shadow) is out of it —then the tautology becomes obvious. It is possible to prove a lot of things in this way. For instance, that Achilles never passes the turtle. First, the time is circumscribed in such a way that for Achilles to pass the turtle is impossible; and from this it is inferred that it is impossible. The conclusion is flawless—yet Achilles still passes the turtle. The demonstration is based on a tautology. And we are not proving anything when we say that bee-and-lilacs are a closed unity, and therefore Dorian Gray is not in it. The latter is a condition, not a conclusion of the observation that bee-and-lilacs are a closed unity.

What are we doing, actually, when we say that bee-and-lilacs are a closed unity? Are we constructing a trap, like the case of Achilles and the turtle? But of course we are setting a trap. It is just as ridiculous to say that Achilles cannot pass the turtle as to say that Dorian Gray is not in it. And just as no one doubts that Achilles does pass the turtle, within a few strides and without the exertion suggested by the infinitesimal calculus, one should not doubt that Dorian Gray is included in the totality by which he was fascinated. In the case of Achilles we say, "We can see with our own eyes that Achilles passes the turtle." In Dorian Gray's case we should say, "Let us use our eyes and see."

Bee and lilacs: an open unity

What we will then see is this: Dorian Gray has just heard a torrent of eloquent, passionate words. Bewildered, he drops the twig. He sees a bee flying over the flowers; it alights and nervously finds its way over the violet blossoms. He watches it spellbound. The route the bee seeks materializes his own search; every movement of the bee is his movement, every stumbling his stumbling. Soon it will fly away; and its flight may be a visible sign of his own failure. Is it not obvious that Dorian Gray is implicated in what he is seeing? Is not his fascination evidence enough for it? The bee, the lilacs, *and* Dorian Gray are a totality (we only need to look at it)—a totality, however, in which the laws of ethology are not valid. For if they were valid, it would not be necessary for Dorian to look at the bee so expectantly, with such a compelling, wheedling, demanding, imploring expectancy; all this would have been unnecessary. But this is the way he does look at it, and this would be the way we also would look at it in the same circumstances. When we see things this way, we are demonstrating another unity, one of which we are a part. If we should withdraw from it, then the laws of ethology (of biology, of geology, of astronomy, of physics, of chemistry) would certainly again be valid. But our withdrawal is the very condition of these laws.

The laws of nature

Withdrawing from the things means dehumanizing them. Only if we withdraw, can we find the "laws of nature." These exist, however, only in a closed unity, one which does not include us. As a rule, this condition of withdrawal is not mentioned, and therefore it seems that the laws of nature are always valid. But they are only valid in an artificial reality, a reality from which we are excluded. Only tautologies can make them seem valid in our world.

Angels, good and evil

As Dorian watches the bee, strangely fascinated, these laws are absent. At this moment, there are no laws at all. And it is precisely the absence of any laws that is so peculiar to this moment. Nothing is fixed, everything is in suspension, the moment is undecided. (Isn't he holding his breath? Even physiology is suspended; he doesn't even get out of breath.) The bee, however, muddles through this uncertainty and fills the moment—while Dorian Gray holds his breath; in vain, for the bee scrambles on. The eloquent and passionate words have been launched during a gap in time. The bee fills this gap; its industrious search shows Dorian a structure to cover this gap; in the bee he finds his own structure. That is the meaning of this futile occurrence: something guards the secret of the moment, not just a past frustration. A gap appears in reality, and instantly an insignificant incident fills this gap. What does it mean? Nobody knows. This knowledge does not rest with us; isn't that why we expectantly observe this trivial incident? The knowledge lies within the incident. These trivial occurrences decide for us; they contain a secret, if we only wish to see it. They are our angels, our good angels, and our evil angels. "*Dans chaque petite chose il y a un ange.*" [7]

Expelled angels

Now it is easy to see what happens to trivial incidents when they are provided with a meaning—*with a past:* the angels have to leave. And they went. Since I know that my pipesucking habit is the result of my frustration over a nipple, I do not feel any need to explore the bitter liquid for understanding; instead of extracting understanding, I would discover a nipple-complex. Do not think that this discovery would cause me anxiety. That only happened in the beginning, about 1900. Since then we have come to know that we all suffer from this complex, more or less, and any shame has been removed. If Dorian Gray had known that his interest in the bee on the lilac blossoms could be reduced to a frustrated craving for a crawling exhibitionism, his interest too would have died. The gap struck in reality by those passionate words would have closed itself. He could have felt at ease, the way we all feel at ease, nowadays, in this gapless, angel-stripped world; there is no place where the secret can possibly show itself. Everything has a meaning, an additional special meaning, a meaning in the past.

The discovery that the symptoms of a neurotic have a past could be so readily converted into a foundation for a general, eagerly accepted, philosophy because it brought us peace of mind. The idea that every human act has a past did, for humanity in general, what the statement that symptoms have a past did for psychiatry. Any symptoms which can be explained are not disturbing. The neurotic who proves, with his paralyzed legs, that he is clinging to a past incident is not disturbing to us; his legs have no story to tell; they function exclusively in the closed unity of the neurotic and his past.

A *subconscious meaning*

In psychiatry, and afterward in everyday philosophy, the conclusion that human phenomena have a meaning which is located in the past came to have another, an exceptional and far-reaching, significance. The past soon was regarded as a past of long ago, and then a past of very long ago; this past originated so long ago, that its owner could not be expected to know it. As far as the owner was concerned, the meaning of the phenomena was unknown or subconscious.

The word *or* here is misleading; it suggests a natural identity, which is lacking. If we conclude first of all—and rightly—that another person (the observer—the psychotherapist, for instance) knows the meaning, and the patient does not, the only possible inference is that the meaning lies within the other person and not within the patient. The subconscious of the neurotic is to be found within the other person. It would be a perfectly justified conclusion: the subconscious is a faculty of the other person. The name "subconscious" would have to be changed, though. But precisely this conclusion had to be avoided. The meaning had to lie within the patient; only then would the symptoms stop being disturbing to us. But how could this be explained? The meaning is within the patient, and yet it cannot be found within the patient. This contradiction has never ceased to defy us. The neurotic is not able to find the meaning of his symptoms, a meaning which to us is so obvious, not even when it is reasonably pointed out to him what the meaning is and where in the past he can find it. He does not know. And yet he must have this knowledge; if not in the customary way, then in a shape of "not-having" it; that is, subconsciously. The discovery that every symptom has a meaning appears to lead irresistibly to a second discovery, certainly not less significant: the discovery that the patient, apart from having a conscious reason, also and especially has a subconscious reason for his illness. The discovery that every symptom has a meaning leads to the separation of conscious and subconscious.

No sexuality

In their "Provisional Survey" of 1893, Breuer and Freud do not discuss the patient's sexuality.[8] This fact is the more remarkable because it is well-known how just this sexuality was accentuated later on. In 1896, three years after the initial publication, Freud writes that with *every* patient, or even with *every* symptom of *every* patient, one inevitably arrives in the sphere of sexual experiences.[9] Experiences of no pleasant nature, for that matter; the patients told how they were sexually approached by adults when they were children. Without exception they remembered scenes of being seduced by an adult.

The sexual trauma

The theory of neurotic disturbances was rounded off by this discovery. In childhood—not infrequently in even very early childhood—the neurotic experienced a sexual contact. For obvious reasons this contact could not be digested. Consequently it became submerged in the subconscious and remained there, because it had not been digested. But it did not remain quiet. The sexual contact haunted the patient's subconscious until at last it found a disguise: it appeared as a symptom. In accordance with this theory, the therapeutic advice was: unmask the symptom, make the unmasked memory, with the emotion attached to it, beat a retreat, and—the patient will be cured.

Four questions

Presently we shall see that this logical theory was soon hit by a catastrophe from which it never recovered. In the meanwhile, so many peculiarities have accumulated, that it seems sensible to disentangle them and examine them more closely. The following questions will have to be answered:

1. Why is it that the theory of the neuroses was discovered in 1882 and not earlier? According to Ferenczi, the theory of psycho-analysis was "the shared discovery of an ingenious neurotic and a clever doctor." [10] But that it should be solely the result of a coincidence, in which an exceptionally ingenious neurotic was

treated by an exceptionally clever doctor, can hardly be accepted. Especially considering that the discovery was then assimilated not only by experts but by almost every educated layman within a space of twenty or thirty years, which is very quickly indeed. The wisdom of ages would scarcely have failed to notice something which very soon became a matter of course for a great many people, since a rapid assimilation implies knowledge which must be rather simple and obvious. The question of why this knowledge appeared at the end of the nineteenth century and not earlier is an essential one. Discussing it will make it clear at the same time why this discovery did not come later, either; why not in 1925, for instance.

2. Why is it that the discovery of 1882 immediately resulted in the discovery of the two levels on which an incident can affect a person: the conscious and the subconscious? In other words, why was the discovery of 1882 also the discovery of the subconscious—at first only the patient's subconscious (Breuer's hypnoid theory); then, very soon, everybody's (Freud's theories).

The answer to this question has already been prepared: this discovery gives us peace of mind. If everything that concerns us is placed in a certain order, which is forever directed back into the past, the present ceases to be frightening. There had been danger in the present; but since the present has been given a meaning in the past, it has been allocated to a definite place and is no longer floating around us. Demons and friendly spirits become monuments of the past; they freeze and become mile stones.

But this not the whole story. The duality of conscious and subconscious was not forced on the patient; she came to meet it halfway. The first patient brought it into Breuer's office with her. She passed from her usual state into another existence, which quite rightly could be called subconscious, and which, on first sight, was certainly not more reassuring. It was the patients who demonstrated the subconscious; they started to remember things out of this subconscious; they managed to remember amazing events which were inaccessible until the moment they were treated. And then sane, perfectly normal people showed, with similar abandonment, that they were split in the same way. They acted and dreamt in the scheme of consciousness and subconsciousness. They made mistakes and slips of the tongue, they forgot appointments, and they remembered concealed symbols the next morning. Their existence was like walking and sleepwalking at the same time. It had never been like this before—at least, history does not mention it. But no one accepts this as evidence that the subconscious had not existed before. The usual argument is that it had been there all the time, this subconscious, but nobody noticed. Which elicits the questions: Why did nobody see it? Why, as soon as the first person saw it, did everybody [11] see it? Everybody saw it so clearly that the conscious seemed rather insignificant by comparison.

3. Why was sexuality not mentioned in the first publication, which was, after all, the result of many years of research and of many more years of deliberation? This question is closely related to the next:

4. Why was everything related to sexuality soon afterward? Neuroses, said Freud, are derangements caused exclusively by sexual difficulties.[12] "With a normal sex life, neuroses are impossible," [13] is the thesis in its reverse, just as absolute, form. When, during the last years of his life, Freud pessimistically considered the possibilities of psychoanalysis, he repeated this opinion. The motive which makes a neurotic woman seek medical treatment, he wrote, is ultimately that she has no penis and that she wants to have one.[14] But then, how can she get well? How can a man get well, for that matter; for although he has a penis, he must lose it in order to get well. For is he not obliged to accept his cure from a man (the therapist), and is not this prostration actually a sort of castration? [15]

The question of why everything became related to sexuality concerns us all. For it became apparent, that not only the neurotics, but also the non-neurotics, were determined to a great extent by sexuality. So much so that the new theory was called "pansexualism," an epithet which was repudiated so passionately, that perhaps it might have been well to give a thought to the cause of this passion. What hid behind it, in any case, was a sardonic grin, a grin which meant: Yes, you normal people, you too. It is no good giving yourself airs; even your elevated, spiritual existence is based on whether you have, or do not have, an unimpaired penis.

A *fifth question*

Before trying to answer these four questions, I must draw the reader's attention to a fifth question, a very simple one. The answer to this will lead us straight to the other four answers. The question is: The discovery occurred in 1882, but the first publication was made only in 1893, eleven years later. Why this long interval? Does the fact that the first publication was called "provisional" perhaps imply there were fundamental motives for this waiting?

Freud answered this last question himself. He waited till 1925 to do so, though, the year that Breuer died. The reason for the delay had been Breuer; he was opposed to publication. His reasons seem naive to us now: the patient fell in love with him and told people in Vienna that she was pregnant by him. No modern psychotherapist would be worried by such a story, but in those days, psychotherapists were much more sensitive. We are thus brought back to the question, what was wrong with sexuality in those days? Why was Breuer so upset when this subject was broached? Why was everybody so horrified, so indignant, so angry, when Freud confronted people with it? The whole civilized world pounced upon him, tried to annihilate him, to shut his mouth, to prevent him crying out so loudly what had to be kept silent at all cost.

Breuer knew that their publication of 1893 had been misleading. The patient was in love with him; he must have noticed. She told him that she was pregnant; he should have mentioned it in an objective scientific report. He even knew that every neurosis was a struggle with sex. "It is always bedroom secrets," he had whispered to Freud, when the latter once asked him what he thought was the cause of a neurosis. Later on he could not remember that he had said it; making use of his own invention, he submerged the experience and the statement in his subconscious. But Freud did not forget. He even added another expert's opinion, Charcot's: *"C'est toujours la chose génitale, toujours, toujours,"* noting, at the same time, that Charcot had very little interest in these genital matters.[16]

Something was wrong with sexuality in those days. Things that had to do with sex were not supposed to show themselves, they had to be kept a secret, they had to be kept in the dark; sexuality had come to a dead end. This is apparent in the lapsed eleven years between 1882 and 1893; it is apparent from Breuer's fright and reluctance, which soon turned into his not being interested; it is apparent from the absence of every trace of sexuality in the first publication; and finally it is apparent from the general passionate indignation when Freud brought it into the limelight. Evidently this was not supposed to happen. Sexuality was a masked, enveloped sexuality; one could not permit it to be uncovered. Everyone feared that irrevocable evil would come of it, and each man tried to protect the child, the woman, and finally himself against this evil.

The other questions

The conclusion that sexuality had come to a dead end implies the answers to nearly all our other questions. It explains why nothing of an erotic or sexual nature was allowed to appear. But it also makes plain what happened soon afterward: the discovery that every patient was struggling with sexual difficulties, so that sexuality was mentioned in every publication, and not just mentioned but even discussed at some length is explained—temporarily —by the nineteenth century's derangement of sexuality.

This is no small matter. Sexuality is an essential quality of our human existence, as has been proved beyond doubt by analytical psychology. Moreover, sex is concerned with a contact which, more than any other contact, requires an involvement of the whole personality. Isn't this true? In friendship, for instance, not all our faculties are involved; physical and sexual faculties do not play a prominent part. But in the sexual relationship, all our faculties are involved—at least as long as the sexual relationship fulfills the commonly accepted desiderata. The sexual contact is a complete contact; it fills the days and the years, and it makes the highest demands. Is it not logical that the neurotic—he or she who does not know what to do with life, who makes a Gordian knot of his or her relationships—that such a person runs aground on sexuality? It is almost unavoidable that he will get into difficulties in this area.

But it is still doubtful whether the neurotics of those days would all have landed in sexual difficulties, so completely without exception, and with such general abandonment, if sexuality itself had not been deranged. For everybody: for the entire western civilization. I shall provide evidence for this statement later; now it is more important to point out that a society which permits a derangement of sexuality is in danger.

How can a child grow up sexually if sexuality is kept a complete secret, if it is not allowed to show itself, if it is vehemently forbidden? How can a young adult reach an understanding with the other sex, if its sexuality is absent, and if he, himself, is sexless by social definition? Moreover, how can he be married and beget children, if, at the same time, he has to maintain stubbornly—not only toward society but also toward his partner—that, in a way, there is no such thing as sex? If on anything, the neurotic had to run aground on sexuality. Everyone had more or less run aground on it.

The question why the birthdate of the theory of the neuroses coincided with the discovery of the subconscious can now be answered. The subconscious, in those days, meant sexuality. Sexuality had arrived at a dead end, it was out of the picture, it was not participating, it was—or rather, it had become—subconscious. The neurotic who became entangled with life became entangled, above all, with sexuality. Every observation of the neurotic had to result in a confrontation with sexuality; and as this was exactly what had been put aside, what had been removed from (conscious) life, the discovery of neurosis meant the discovery of the subconscious.

Only one question remains: Why was this discovery made in 1882, that is, at the end of the nineteenth century? Or, in other words, what had happened to sexuality in the nineteenth century? In my opinion this is the most essential question on the theory of the neuroses. Before discussing it, though, it might clarify matters first to proceed with the historical review we left a moment ago.

A *disconcerting discovery*

By about 1900, the theory of the neuroses was well defined. In short, it was this: The neurotic had been subjected to a sexual approach by an adult when he was a child. The psychical injury sustained by this experience was made subconscious, for safety's sake. After a while, this produced a tension. The injury remained; when the child grew up, it started to hurt. The result was a symptom.

It is obvious: everything depends on the sexual trauma. It is therefore easy to understand why Freud became confused when it appeared that these sexual traumata, described so emotionally by his patients, had also occurred to every non-neurotic known to him with same frequency and gravity. At about the same time, he made another discovery which made him doubt the validity of his theory even more. His words at that moment are mentioned so rarely—and they have such significance—that I will quote them here.

In 1925, when Freud looked back at the many events in his life, he lingered over the year 1900. Commenting upon it, he writes, "When I realized that these sexual approaches had never actually occurred, that they were just fantasies made up by my patients, or perhaps even suggested by myself, I was at my wit's end for some time." [17]

The psychic traumata, which the patient, with the assiduous help of the psychotherapist, managed to remember, and whose remembering effected a vanishing of the symptoms, *had actually never happened*. One really cannot be surprised enough at it. And when normal people started to confess the same sexual traumata, and these stories, too, appeared invariably and with undoubtable clarity never to have been true—then something very extraordinary must have been going on. The sane and the neurotic both complained about nonexistent matters; the neurotic was even ill because of them, suffering from what never happened. What did this mean?

What was happening becomes clear if we take the last remark literally. The neurotic was suffering from what never happened—was he not suffering from a sexuality which had been made absent? To indicate this absence he had to resort to fantasy. "My father touched my genitals"; that was the only way in which the grown girl could say that her father had been an entirely sexless person. She could not say this with these words. What does not exist in any way cannot be expressed. She had to show its absence by a made-up—an absent—presence. But this was not the answer Freud formulated.

The forbidden solution

His correct considerations at this moment should have been these: If every patient and every normal person relates events, and even serious, very serious, events from his past which actually never happened, then something is wrong with that past. The past has become talkative, but it is talking nonsense, it is just playing the fool. For each fact in the present, the past is giving history, but a history which never was, which evidently was made up quickly; the past is fabricating history, it is making up astounding events and indelible experiences. The past would not do this if it had not been forced to do it. Yet, is that not the case, exactly? Is the past not obliged to talk and talk and talk, if the idea that everything has a past is allowed no exception? Apparently there was every reason to make this rule absolute; nineteenth-century man was afraid, he found safety if the "meaning" of things was located in the past. But the past was not yet ready for this task, it was just being built; nonetheless it had to produce a "meaning" for everything. Is it surprising that at the end of the nineteenth century the past started to make up stories?

Eventually the past learned its task. In our day it no longer produces hastily fabricated fantasies. The modern fantasies are much better constructed; so well constructed, in fact, that it is hardly possible to unmask them, if at all. The modern fantasies like "lack of maternal care," "affective disintegration of the family," and so on, have become "true." For the past which learned its task did not learn it just for the fun of it, but out of necessity, the necessity embodied in the irresistible idea that everything has a meaning. Everything is "past"; nothing is "present." Since the present was made uninhabitable by the signs pointing to the past, the past had to take over the task which had been entrusted to the present for as long as man could remember. The past did take over the task; and now we are all living in the past.

Perhaps it would not have been too late to stop this development, at the last moment, about 1900. Freud could have said: "My patients are apparently not ill in the past, they are ill in the present, for it is the present that induces the past to tell lies. Perhaps their stories are meant to take us away from the present, away from where it hurts most." But it was Adler who was the first to express this idea. The neurotic, he wrote in 1912, is not suffering from his past; he is creating it.[18] Jung was the second to say this. In 1913 he wrote, "If we are searching in the past, we are walking into the trap, set for us by the patient. The patient wants to take us away as far as possible from the painful present."[19] It was this statement, among others, which made Jung disappear from the analytical firmament.

Thus, the present was not allowed to remain significant. For the significance of the present—the conflicts, tensions, and fears of life in around 1900—was what made patients ill and normal people not quite normal. The past—after some delay—offered them shelter.

The solution

And so Freud's solution to the impasse of 1900 becomes easier to understand. Not in the present did he locate the causes of the symptoms, but always further in the past. He who, on principle, resorts to the past is obliged to retreat ever deeper there. For the past has once been present, and for that reason was part of the dangers which exist in the present. Only when the past loses itself in primeval ages, in other words, only when the character of the present has been substantially erased from the past—only when the past has been made entirely imaginary and so unreal—only then is the regression halted.[20]

That is the reason why Freud, when he removed the pathogenic conflict from the childhood years and looked for another time when it could be accommodated more satisfactorily, did not consider the time between ovulation and delivery.

There *are* psychotherapists who think that this time period is important. One needs only to realize what happens during this period to see how easily things can go wrong, especially during these months. First, the future subject as ovum—as half a subject, actually—is thrown out of the secure and cosy ovary. He enters the free abdominal cavity, dangerous because of extrauterine pregnancies. Then an octopus-like tentacle catches the poor wanderer and carries him to an extremely small opening, through which he has to pass. After that comes the journey through the uterine tube, a tight passage, the more anxious because the half-pilgrim never knows whether the army of spermatozoa is approaching or not. If it is not, a scornful death awaits him. But if it is approaching, alarming things will happen. For one of the army is admitted, even though it costs him his tail—castration number one—while the others remain outside, swearing, and the two half-subjects, filled with love, become one.[21]

The primeval scene

This postovular and prenatal theory is not Freud's; some of his followers created it. Although his bound-to-the-past doctrine made this theory, and others like it, possible, he would not have accepted it. Not because it is not true; for what is "true" in these matters? The patients of the psychotherapists who believe in this theory certainly provide enough evidence to support it. They dream of volcanic eruptions, octopi, exhausting journeys over lakes and through narrow passages; they dream about a clash, with themselves, in a guilt-laden atmosphere. No; as far as the *truth* of this theory is concerned, Freud could easily have placed the pathogenic moment in this period.[22] However, this theory would have been too near the present for him. His regression went back much further. This was also the reason why he could not accept Rank's idea that neurotic troubles reverted to the trauma of birth.

Freud put the psychotraumatic moment long before the moment of conception, even before the generation which preceded the conception, so that the connection with the present was entirely lost. He went back to primeval times, when, according to his view, mature sons turned against their fathers, who possessed the women too exclusively. Horrible things happened. Some fathers were killed and eaten; but other fathers managed to avoid this fate, and instead robbed their sons of their genitals. The girls who witnessed these scenes thought, in the confusion of the moment, that they had been castrated at an earlier occasion, which they did not remember. And since those days fathers have been full of suspicion, sons full of fear, and daughters full of shame and envy. And thus children arrive in this world entangled in a heritage of love and hate for their parents. Is it not amazing that not everybody is a neurotic?

By 1912 the principle of this theory of the *Totemmahlzeit* was already present. Freud never abandoned it, not even when ethnological research made it clear that these were untenable fantasies. "The relevant publications are well known to me," he wrote in 1937, "but they have not convinced me. The totem-meal has served me well, and I have never met those who reject it." [23] A haughty answer, but easy to understand if one realizes what it was that led Freud to this theory, which he borrowed from Robertson Smith. This theory, so wrongly called the theory of transference, and the rupture between him and Ferenczi, who had been more faithful than most others, show that above all Freud avoided the present. He did not desire to ascribe any meaning to it.

The consequences of the primeval scene

Patients thus are ill because of the totem-meal; the normal barely escape being ill. The childhood of every child is the evidence. Hardly does the baby have his first tooth than he bites his mother's breast with it; the adults are his enemies from the start. Soon afterward he messes with his feces, teasing his parents and warning his father; for aren't feces a pseudo penis? The father's subconscious does not miss the child's gesture. If the child is a boy, he is sure to touch his genitals sooner or later. Then the father hurls his taboo; the knife is on the way, so to speak. The father need not say a word, his presence is enough; for doesn't the child have a lively memory—even if it is subconscious—of the days when fathers had been less inhibited in their aggression? The girl has nothing to play with; she would like to have it, but all she finds is an absence. And exactly because she discovers that she does lack something, the memory of the primeval scene, of which she had been a witness, awakens in her—subconsciously. She made one mistake then, and she makes another now; she thinks that she has had a penis, but that her father took it from her. From that moment on her whole life is one hopeless struggle to recapture it. At first she finds it again in her feces; knowing her duty she hands it over to her father. Later on she will have a child; but this penis, too, she will give to the man. The poor girl; she struggles with her anatomy in vain.

How easily does the child slip. The first years of life are full of traps; many a child gets caught in them. The girls, especially, have a hard time. More women are neurotics than men—at least this was true in Freud's day.

The second theory of the neuroses

The theory of the neuroses was changed considerably by these ideas. Previously a neurosis was ascribed to a psychotrauma, an injury sustained in childhood. In the new theory, the child is born with an almost hopeless prognosis. It possesses a sexuality which is constitutionally defective; its relationships are corrupted by the totem-meal. Even if there is no trace of a psychotrauma, the child will inevitably get into difficulties. There are many barriers over which it must pass, the most important of which are the "oral phase," the "anal phase," the "phallic phase," the "oedipus complex," and the "castration complex" (the last two in reversed order for the girl); the neurotic is the adult who did not manage to pass all these barriers as a child. If he got stuck in the oral phase, he is "orally aggressive": he has a big mouth, he eats a lot with gusto, and he loves to smoke. Did he get stuck in the anal phase? then he is stingy and conservative, and he is often to be found in the toilet. Some fail to get beyond the oedipus complex; they cannot get away from their parents, they do not marry, or if they do, they find themselves constantly in situations which oddly resemble their childhood. Then there is the neurosis from which every woman suffers (occasionally, men suffer from it too): the castration complex, which expresses itself in a persistent grudge against the male, and in a paralyzing self-disgust. If the neurotic happens not to recognize himself in one of these types, he will benefit from the knowledge that the qualities are often expressed by their opposites; and also, the subconscious commonly shifts a quality from one group to another as a method of camouflage.

It is clear that in this theory the psychotrauma has disappeared; it was too near the present. Now—we should say that this "now," the "now" of the second theory of the neuroses, lies between 1905 and 1920; for a small group of psychotherapists it lasted until 1945; for an extremely small group it is still valid today—now the neurosis originates from a very distant past, secure and inaccessible. The neurotic is repeating this past; his illness is an unfortunate variation on an old theme. The normal person, too—if there is such a person—is repeating this past; the neurotic only differs from him in that he got stuck in what the normal person succeeded (more or less) in conquering. These barriers, constructed in primeval times, provide the "meaning" of his and our existence.

THE VICTORIAN WOMAN

Le deuxième sexe

According to Freud's theory, it is safer to be a man than to be a woman. For although the woman is born as a woman, the part she has to play immediately after birth is a masculine one: she sucks a woman's breast, in other words, she has a sexual relation with a woman. She lies in bed with her, and she has a physical contact with her which is not lacking in lust. Nevertheless, she remains a woman; no one can doubt her anatomy. She, herself, however, only discovers this anatomy when it is too late; when she has become used to the masculine (active) part she plays in her relation with her mother. This means that she discovers she is not a man. How much easier it is for the boy. The discovery of his genitals is the confirmation of his experience: he is a man, complete in every respect. The girl discovers a lack: she is the castrated, the mutilated, man. In her every monthly period, the blood of the primeval scene flows again; that's what she thinks, anyway (subconsciously). So how can she ever forget that she was castrated? She can never get away from it. Nor will she be able to get away from hopeless attempts to undo this castration. She must cope with the state of the *deuxième sexe*. The attempt which comes nearest to solving this problem is marriage. Then she has a penis, and in two ways: by her child and by sexual intercourse. But this possession is just an appearance. She is compelled by vague reminiscences of primeval times to give up her child to her husband, and so she does. The penis entrusted to her in sexual intercourse she also has to give back again every time. What torments her most is that the lust which is guaranteed by the penis is something she misses almost entirely. Her corresponding organ is too small. Actually she has nothing, the woman, less than nothing; there, where the man can boast of a convincing possession, she has only a hole.

The small truth

In this way—even if, usually, it is palliated and smoothed over—is woman described in numerous publications. Her critics are unanimous in their friendliness. If one of them protests occasionally, his words are mild and careful. For no one would want to burden himself with the odium of being irresponsibly old-fashioned —although everyone is aware that this theory is antique from the first to the last letter. This awareness is hardly put into words, it has to bow to the conviction that, somehow, the theory must be true. Man has a penis, woman has not—does anyone doubt this? The one who has is better off than the one who has not—can anyone deny this simple rule? The intuition that the theory cannot be true must bow to anatomy. Anatomy has the last word; the difference between man and woman can be measured with a tape. Numbers are convincing. Who can protest against numbers? They provide the ultimate truth.

However, the truth of numbers is a small (the smallest) truth. If it is true that woman is inferior to man, sexually, she is only inferior if one standard is applied to all things: the standard of measurability, of size, of extensiveness. As long as we recognize this only one standard, the standard of size, no one can deny that woman is defined by a deficiency; hers is the sex of nothingness. But *only* as long as we do that. The acceptance of another standard—a standard which seems almost forgotten, which nonetheless had proved its worth for more than three hundred years—the acceptance of this standard makes this theory the most peculiar statement ever made about the difference between man and woman.

The other truth

Hear how François Villon, born in 1431, sings of this female "nothingness," this absence:

> . . . *ce sadinet*
> *Assis sur grosses fermes cuisses*
> *Dedans son petit jardinet.*[24]

This was before Descartes. But even Voltaire wrote poetry in this vein, in spite of being a contemporary of Diderot, in whose *Bijoux indiscrets* he had learned in Diderot's words, of a "geometric sexology." He must have been aware even more of the other truth. The need to compare the sexes dimensionally was small. It was even possible to disapprove of man sexually. According to Erasmus, no part of the human body is so ridiculous, so droll, so foolish, as the male sexual organ. The nineteenth century thought different. It forced an opinion upon us, which now, in the middle of the twentieth century, has lost all its meaning. Although we cannot get rid of the idea that man has and woman has not, nevertheless, this idea is something out of the past. It *has been* true. At the end of the previous century, and during the first years of this one, man *was* the one who had. In those days woman was indeed the one who did not have. She did not have what the man had, and there was nothing she could put against man's possession.

Is this true? What sort of a woman actually was she, the woman of the last century?

"The" woman of a certain era

There is no answer to this question, because "the" woman of the nineteenth century did not exist any more than "the" woman of the twentieth century does. In the first place, woman is not different from century to century, but from year to year (at the least); one need only consider fashion, which is not just a creation of a few extravagant salons in Paris, inflicted on women every year. The leaders of fashion are experts in femininity; they are able to predict what sort of dress women are going to need, how long the skirt has to be, how deep the décolleté. But this is also why they can fail; women decide their own courses.

There is a second reason why the phrase "the" woman of the nineteenth century is somewhat vague. Even if a certain fashion in clothing is characteristic for a certain period, this characteristicness is certainly not valid for every woman in this period. Perhaps it is only valid for a small group, although this small group can be typical for the era, as has been proved by history, and can lead everyone of that era in a certain direction. And thus a certain fashion, worn by only a few, can be a guiding principle for every woman, even for those women who do not participate. Immediately after the second world war, for instance, a few women adorned themselves with the "new look"; it was these few who understood what was needed by all. Soon afterward every woman realized that this old style was new, brand new and highly desirable. The few who started the fashion were typical of the whole new era.

Taking all this into account, it may nonetheless still be accurate to speak of "the" woman of the nineteenth century. What did she look like?

The Victorian woman

She looked like the woman in one of William Holman Hunt's paintings, a pre-Raphaelite picture painted in 1853. The reader should look at as many paintings and drawings done by the pre-Raphaelites as he can; for in them the woman of the nineteenth century shows herself, the woman who lived not only in England (although there she was represented liberally), but also in France, in Germany, and in Austria—though there she may have appeared a bit later. This woman still possessed the rather strange, but still great, glory of past ages; but she showed at the same time that this glory was on the wane. She indicated the arrival of another era, an era in which she was going to be a negation in relation to the man. She already was this negation.

The awakening conscience

Although his contemporaries found Hunt's painting difficult to understand,[25] to us the scene is clear enough. Two young people have been making some music; he apparently has been accompanying her on the piano. She must have been singing in all innocence; for as he pulls her toward him, an unfeigned, entirely new, feeling has descended on her. This is the moment the painter has captured.

How different are the expressions on their faces. He knows what he is doing, he is a connoisseur; his fingers are not trembling, his lewd eyes are delighted by what he knows is coming; he is all desiring sureness. For him there are no secrets. As for her, she is flabbergasted; apparently she has had no thought of this moment; she does not know about it, for she knows nothing; she is not delighted, for he has taken her by surprise; she is not prepared. She has no desire; for what she might be able to desire is foreign to her existence, her girlish, childlike, innocent existence. She is just about to find out at this moment and at the same time, she begins to feel guilty. This painting is called *The Awakening Conscience*. We are inclined to call it *The Awakening Consciousness*.

From the way she is depicted, we might expect her to fall in a dead faint at any moment. Is it not remarkable? As the woman awakens, she begins to faint; she goes into a spontaneous hypnosis, she loses consciousness.

The prudish ladies

Could it be that the subconscious is born out of this "awakening"? Of a hesitating awakening, it is true; of an awakening which halts at the border of clarity. Yet, nonetheless, an awakening, a movement toward clarity. Could the discovery of the subconscious actually have been the discovery of the conscious? of more clearness, of openness, of light? It did not seem so to the nineteenth-century observer. What he seemed to discover was darkness, an unconsciousness, a state into which the patient slid out of her conscious and which could not be anything but subconscious. He saw it happen again and again; never have women fainted so readily.

Of course, she could permit herself to faint, the Victorian lady; for she fell on soft carpets, and not infrequently she fell into the arms of a gallant man, either a lover or a scoundrel. She could not know that, however; all she knew was that it was soft, and she fell. Today she would fall on concrete, the poor girl, so she does not fall anymore—nor did the Victorian lady's maid fall; [26] she would have cracked her head on the kitchen floor, or lost her job because of broken crockery.

The young woman in the painting wrings her hands in desperation. Is she not the sort of person Freud had in mind when he spoke of "the prudish ladies of my practice to whom all natural functions appear outrageously horrible"? [27]

The late nineteenth-century lap

It is not by coincidence that the painter has drawn this woman's desperate hands in her lap; her belly has been touched. When the young man moved away from the piano and pulled her close to him, he touched her belly—although his hand never reached its mark. He touched a belly that was not there. For the Victorian Lady's dress was one immense covering, with an extra shawl around the hips. Her belly was hidden, covered; her sexuality was absent. Was Freud wrong when he said that man was the "have" and woman was the "have not"? Sexuality had been hidden; how many skirts did the woman of those days wear? Can one imagine a healthy atmosphere under those skirts? Did the air penetrate under those crinolines? Was there anything there at all? or had everything melted in the airless heat? What else could there be under those tenfold coverings than an absence? A soft mollusk at the most, says Simone de Beauvoir.[28]

"Woman is a shell around an emptiness." [29] One cannot doubt it, particularly because this remark was made by Laura Marholm, herself a woman of those days, and a woman who could not have read Breuer or Freud. These words were written in 1894, only one year after the two doctors' first publication; and it can be taken for granted that their work, which appeared in a professional periodical, would not have been read by this woman. And even if she had read the article, the wisdom of her words would not have been due to reading it. Years afterward, Freud made a similar statement.

A *shell around an emptiness*

Woman was a shell around an emptiness; this is shown by William Holman Hunt's picture. From her neck to her feet, almost over her feet, she is covered; what is underneath is an emptiness. It was not empty for the man. The prostitutes he so regularly visited had disclosed all the secrets of this space to him. But she had no knowledge of her body; she was nothing more than a small, innocent, staring head on top of the shell. Eventually she falls out of it, out of her little head and into the shell. That is what her faint was: a fall into the shell, into an emptiness, into a nothingness. But why put it off? It was a fall into the subconscious. How true were Freud's words: Consciousness, he said, [the little head] is a surface phenomenon [of the immense sea underneath], consciousness [the little head] is an incident. Is it not true? A word, a little cough, a smile and a sweet little wink. Fleeting, innocent matters; ruffles on a massive, compact—yet hidden and therefore absent—primeval sea. "Woman is the one who runs away." [30] She could not do anything else; she wanted to stay, to stay in that innocence on top, but her innocence was too small, she was pushed out of it and she tumbled into the bottom, in the direction of the carpet or the gallant arms; into the id.

"Woman was ill because of an inner cleavage," said Laura Marholm in 1894, "a cleavage between what her mind wanted and the dark basis of her nature." One really need not read Freud.

Filling the shell

In the last year of the previous century, a Dutch author, Gerard van Eckeren, published a book which had the, in those days, very attractive title, *Defilement*. The modern reader would never guess that this title alludes to the very decent marriage of Eve, the heroine. When she has reached marriageable age, the author states with an honesty of which Freud deprived us—this is acknowledged with gratitude—"that she is a very pure, very innocent girl, who grew up in an absolute ignorance of the world. Her father [who, in those days, knew nothing about oedipal matters] has educated her himself; he has taught her everything he thought necessary for her education. She has observed the fertilizing of plants and trees, and the mating of animals. And with all this she has had no other thoughts." She had no other thoughts indeed, *o sancta simplicitas*. But she must have filled her nights with dreams, and made hundreds of "mistakes."

For you, dear reader, this is true. For you there is something inside the shell. For her the shell was empty. I wish this could be realized. She did *not* dream, and she did *not* make "mistakes"; the only thing she did was to fall into the empty shell occasionally.

Her fallings were repeated attempts, ever in vain, to fill the shell. This is why the hysterics of the last century made an arc on their beds, resting on their heels and head; at the culmination of this arc was the—absent—sex. As if they wanted to show, ostentatiously, what was lacking, what was needed badly. Please see, they were saying, see that we have nothing, nothing at all. And so much is required from us. Today this *arc de cercle* is hardly ever seen. The symptom ended its existence without being understood.

In vain did the Victorian woman fall until she fell at the same time into emptiness and onto the psychiatrist's couch. Then the first contents of the shell started to collect. And soon the whole shell was full, full to the brim, full of the strangest ingredients, which Freud and his followers catalogued extensively. The most extraordinary things—which today no psychiatrist sees anymore.

A hopelessly fatal desire

One day, van Eckeren's Eve, on a daydreaming excursion through the woods, meets a painter; he sees her, puts down his palette, and starts considering other ways of occupying himself. She is as bewildered as the lady in Hunt's painting. "Suddenly," writes van Eckeren, "clearly and cruelly, as a fatal consequence, consciousness awoke in her; it beat her down, as if paralysed. All the artlessness of her childhood and simple life now seemed faded artificiality, which did not protect her against the hopelessly fatal desire of her awakened femininity; not only to find the artist, but above all to find the man, the stronger creature, whom she could follow as a woman." [31] It is clear; Eve has awakened into a consciousness which beats her down into the shell, which paralyzes her as Breuer's patient was paralyzed; the consciousness which confronts her with an emptiness, with a task for which she is not prepared, the task of being a woman.

"A female, not just a lady, but a female in such a different, shocking, indecent way—a female that is running through the woods plaintively calling out for the male." [32] Come, come, one is inclined to say, no need to go to the other extreme. Today, indeed, there is no need to go to the other extreme. But then, it was unavoidable; to be woman in that way is the opposite of being ignorant. Either an empty shell or a full one. One can look it up in Freud's books; at first sexuality was absent, and then suddenly, woman was one great maze of sexuality. [33]

This contradiction is illustrated beautifully by the history of Hunt's painting. Hunt originally painted a woman who obviously had a doubtful past. His patron was scandalized, and asked him to change the painting. Hunt removed the "obviousness" from her expression, so that the young woman looked shocked as well as charmed; the correction resulted in a reversal of her condition. There was nothing in between these two extremes.

The same thing happened to Rossetti. In a painting called *Found*, he meant to portray a fallen woman; to his friends' desperation, he kept on changing it, until the final result was a sexually irreproachable canvas. He even symbolized the fate of the fallen, guilty woman by putting in a newly-born calf, which, as even his contemporaries said, does not suggest guilt as much as innocence. It simply could not be done; to be Freudian in those days was impossible. Woman in the nineteenth century was by definition innocent *and* unknowing, regardless of how guilty she felt. Her guilt even embodied her innocence. Hunt portrayed this innocence, but he really had no choice; there was nothing else to portray.

A *terrible occurrence*

"A hopelessly fatal desire," wrote van Eckeren. Hunt expresses this by painting the young woman wringing her hands in desperation. What will happen when she marries, this young woman? She has no knowledge, and her ghostlike, enamored feelings guarantee the continuation of her ignorance. Being in love does not mean anything else to her. The man's thoughts are of a different nature; and so were the father's thoughts. That is why, when Eve tells her father about the meeting in the woods, he says, "I meant to spare you this, my dear, dear child, by keeping you secluded from people, by making you find happiness in Nature, the highest expression of God's goodness on earth. I wanted happiness for you, my child, pure happiness without pain. But I see now that I have been a fool. Pain knows how to find every child of man, no one can evade its grasping claws." [34]

Pain. When Eve is married and the happy painter draws her toward him in the night, he is surprised at her aloofness. And when he still wants a sexual contact, she fights him "with a wild, almost insane stare in her wide-opened, frightened eyes." The foundation for a visit to the psychiatrist is laid.

The women of those days behaved like that quite often. They had every reason for it; did they not exist in a state of permanent anxiety? When Balzac, in his *Mémoires de deux jeunes mariées*, speaks of preparing the girl for marriage, he says, with grave compassion, "Dear girl, you will be going through a terrible time." [35] The wedding night was a lamentable story for many. For the man, because he could not understand why his wife was so prudish and so reluctant in these obviously pleasant matters. For the woman, because she could not reconcile her husband's aggressive sexuality with his gallant behaviour and the careful odor of his pomaded moustache. Back from the honeymoon, more than one woman started to pine. The doctors who were consulted understood much, but said nothing. They recommended a cure at a watering place, where (this was common knowledge) it was neither the water, nor the salts in it, that were effective, but the numerous men of dubious character who swarmed around the ailing women like wasps, and who made them immune to masculine stares, to masculine words, and finally to masculine deeds. They returned refreshed. The shell had been filled.

The change

Since those days much has changed. The old watering places lost their prosperity during the twentieth century. Every publication of Freud's made them lose more customers. We cannot be too grateful to him for that. The women of the nineteenth century died out, and the men, and a new breed appeared. One need not tell the young girl who today is about to marry that a terrible time awaits her. She would laugh in your face. Not only has she passed this experience long ago, she felt it had nothing terrible about it. On the contrary. The modern young woman is no longer the overgrown innocent; her sexuality is no longer "somebody else's possession" or "male knowledge"; [36] she knows how to be a woman, she knows the emotions of her sex, and just as the man knows about her (still, though, in a different way), she knows about him, knows how many ways the man may be different. This difference is not unknown to her. The first intercourse is no longer a meeting of complete knowledge and total ignorance. And the extensions of this knowledge, which both possess, are equal and uncomplicated orgasms.

A great change, and a very favorable one. Perhaps no change during the last fifty years has been so far-reaching and deserves so much appraisal. Certainly no change has been so important. For the sexual relationship is more than just sexual intercourse, it is even more than marriage. In being together sexually, each brings to the other what he or she possesses—not only their sexual properties, but everything each has. Youth, relationships with parents, expectations of the future, honor and disgrace, faith and disbelief. Only after man and wife have pooled everything that is inalienably theirs does it become clear in what ways the two of them will be rich or poor. The woman before 1900 brought a sexual incompetency with her; that was her "property." And what the man brought with him at the same level made evident the poverty from which both would suffer. This poverty was not only restricted to sexual matters; it first penetrated into allied matters and ultimately infiltrated everything.

The importance of the change

For the woman who during the night resigns herself to a sexual intercourse which is not wholly accepted or which is perhaps even endured with loathing, the day begins differently from the day of the woman who wakes in the morning full of the memory of a physical happiness which still envelops her. For the man, too, it is one thing to wake up moodily thinking about his wife's nightly resistance, and another to be able to tease his wife about her eagerness. The two appear at the breakfast table in a different way, they pray, if they pray, in a different way, they speak to the children in a different way, and they feel differently about their work.

In almost every relationship in life we can withhold something. In friendship, for instance, certain areas are not discussed; indeed, friendship can be defined as the relationship in which we leave the other person his property, yet willingly associate with him. In our work we keep back even more; in modern mentally (and physically) drained jobs particularly, we use only a part of our personality. But in the sexual relationship, and in religion, nothing can be held back; in every sense we uncover ourselves; both men and women show themselves as they are without reserve. The sexual relationship is a test for many things, perhaps for all things. The structure of the existence of a certain society at a certain time is clear as soon as it is known how the sexes related to each other. We can learn a great deal about life in the nineteenth century by looking at pre-Raphaelite painting, and by reading the periodicals and books of those days. Much of our own time can be understood by observing how men and women treat each other, and inferring from their behavior what their sexual relationship is. Comparing our century with the nineteenth, we can conclude that very much has been gained; life has become far more livable. Not that our lives have no evil; far from it. They have. Much evil, of no little importance; yet our lives are without a doubt less dangerous and less depressing than those lived fifty years ago.

The third theory of the neuroses

With all this, it becomes quite apparent that the theory of the neuroses had to drift into serious difficulties. For a theory which is based on a temporary malaise must reflect the characteristics of that malaise; and consequently, it is obsolete from the moment the malaise ceases to exist. That is why the theories today are different from those of Breuer's and Freud's time; not because therapeutic methods have changed. Analysis, which is still the primary method of psychotherapy, and rightly so, has not changed essentially since 1899. The change has been in the people who use the method; in the patients and in the psychotherapists.

The therapist has come down from his pedestal, he has become a normal person. He is no longer the man who knows everything, who understands everything, and who foresees everything; he is a fallible mortal. And no longer is the patient the completely ignorant person, a fearful moment between a dark past and an unknown future. Today the patient knows a good deal about what the therapist is doing and thinking. Of course, he is often wrong; but when he is, he is making a mistake in a matter which is accessible to him in principle. It was different earlier. The therapist knew everything and said nothing; the patient knew nothing and said everything. That is, he was expected to say everything, and that was just the trouble. She came in timidly; unpleasant things had to be said, things about which the therapist knew in any case. The conversation was always rather peculiar. The patient did not give up the secret; she showed a glimpse of it and then fenced about what was left. She exhibited it, and yet she was shocked and unhappy. The therapeutic conversation was a duel fought with amazing subtlety; the patient lay on the couch, the notorious chaise longue, and the psychotherapist made himself at ease in an armchair behind the patient's head, so that he could see every movement and every expression while the patient had to stare at the ceiling. Freud smoked one cigar after another with no conscience, while the patient writhed and wriggled. Quite openly he advised his colleagues to remain cold and insensitive; in his opinion, the good psychotherapist was characterized by "emotionlessness." [37]

Many things have changed in this scene. Even if modern psychotherapists are still careful to avoid displaying too much sympathy, their attitude toward a complete lack of emotion is not favorable. It is still true that the patient lies on the couch without having too many opportunities to observe the therapist; but at least the therapist has moved his chair so that he no longer keeps the patient captive in his stare; he allows the patient to rise from the couch, if he wants to, and to walk around the room, so that the patient can get a good look at him. The patient can thus make sure of the situation; and after his inspection tour, he can lie down again on the couch with the certainty that he is a free person, exactly as free as the therapist.[38]

The modern patient visits the psychotherapist because he wants to, and not only because he has to. He wants to discuss his problems. The conversation is frequently held in an atmosphere of deliberation; the therapist listens, asks questions now and then, and reaches a certain conclusion which he explains to the patient; and then the therapy is discussed. He keeps in touch with the patient, as the patient does with him. When the proper treatment does begin, the case is frequently "open" for both of them. The patient knows where he is going, although he can be wrong about the details of getting there; and the therapist sees to it that the patient does not grope in the dark too long for the goals of the treatment.

With all this, the piquancy, which more than anything else was once so characteristic of psychotherapy, has been mostly, or entirely, lost. When the modern psychotherapist reads the works of Freud, Stekel, Ferenczi, and the others, he goes from one breathtaking story (and from one surprise) to another. Who would not be interested in an article beginning with the words: "A buoyant woman of twenty-three consulted me when she had been married for a year to a man of forty, who had always treated her with great tenderness, but whom she had never loved with that abandonment so natural to her sex." One cannot stop reading. And no more could the psychotherapist stop listening; for what he heard was as enthralling as a good novel.

The piquant story

Parts of these stories were true; there *was* immense misery, after all, which, as I explained above, mostly materialized in the sexual sphere. Other parts were not true. Freud himself discovered even before 1900 that piquant facts were dubious, if not nonexistent facts. It is quite clear why. The patients had to explain why they were miserable if they wanted to be freed from their complaints. But that was exactly what they could not do. The words were lacking. They searched for ways to express themselves; and because adequate words were not available, they expressed themselves in terms which, it is true, did not really describe the actual misery, but which were at least related to it. Words, moreover, which were understood, for they were meeting the expectations of the psychotherapist. The cause of the problem had to be found in the past, because the nineteenth-century therapist believed only in the past. Therefore the patient told him the past. And he was interested in facts of a particular kind; as a right-minded positivist, he believed only in sharply-defined events, in incidents which would have been visible to anyone, if only anyone had been present. He believed in facts—consequently he was presented with fantasies. Every fact in psychology is a fantasy.

The real facts in psychology are outside the official empiricism. They belong to an empiricism of another order, the everyday empiricism, unchanged, unreduced by reflection, unchilled by distance. The empiricism which is characterized by the annoying quality that it can barely, if at all, be repeated. That which is closest to us; which provides the matter of which our life is composed from hour to hour, is farthest away from science. Science (and I mean especially anthropological science) begins at the wrong end; it begins with the skeleton. Until recently anatomy has been considered the anthropological science par excellence. First the bones, then the muscles, then the glands, and finally the gland which secretes thoughts. This is the sequence of the subjects the medical student has to make himself familiar with: first the bones, then the muscles; only after he has mastered the facts of anatomy and physiology is he ready to study human existence as it is (hardly a word of which is ever mentioned to him). And yet it is in this existence that illness exists, and in which health must receive some consideration. No, Freud cannot be blamed, really, for understanding only the "facts."

As far as the stories told by the patients are concerned, very much has changed. Only if the psychotherapist stubbornly expects anachronistic piquant stories—facts—will the patient tell him such stories. He will make them up and then strongly believe in them himself—for has he not created them out of real misery? The matter out of which he creates his stories is authentic enough. As time passed, more and more psychotherapists have come to be disappointed in their faith in the facts, however. On the one hand, the facts became ever more subtle, which had the result that the therapists nonetheless held on to their conception of causality; and on the other hand, more and more patients left the facts of the past to set out for the arena in which the problems that had necessitated the treatment were to be found: the present. And this meant that the therapist and the patient came nearer to each other. For a conversation which moves in the present is only possible in a more or less equal relationship; only if the partners in conversation are beside one another can they speak of what is actual. What is actual, then, appears not to contain anything out of the ordinary. No extraordinary events fit with a nonextraordinary contact. If it happens that the relation between the patient and the therapist regains its extraordinary character, then the facts—the piquant stories—will also reappear. There is a small chance.

Amazing insight and prompt cure

The amazing therapeutic insights and the prompt cures disappeared with the piquant stories. How much these go together can be illustrated by one of Wilhelm Stekel's case histories.

"Once I was consulted by a lady," he reports, in his *Nervous Fears*,[39] "who was suffering from attacks of trembling, during which she fell into a state of lowered consciousness. The first attack had occurred when she had said a prayer at Christmas. Immediately after the patient had told me this, I asked her permission to make a guess as to the words of the prayer which had initiated the attack. Surprised, she consented. Then I said, 'It was the words, "Forgive us our sins."' And so it was. When she had been fourteen years old, it had happened that her piano teacher had approached her in the most shameless manner. She had not objected to anything he did, except to sexual intercourse. She was a very religious person and she never forgave herself for this weakness."

Stekel explained to this patient the relationship between things, and advised her to confess everything. So she did, and from that moment she was cured. "The patient confessed and the puzzling attacks, for which a three-months stay at a recommended watering place had been of no effect, were gone after one hour of confessing."

This case history is very instructive. Compelled by symptoms, one being the famous lowering of consciousness, the patient comes to the psychotherapist absolutely ignorant about the nature of her problems. He sees what is wrong immediately, he does not doubt his insight, he asks permission to guess; the game can be played. Guilt, says the therapist, which must mean *the past.* The patient takes the hint and starts telling of the past. She takes out one incident and tells about it, not without reluctance, we may assume. For a woman of those days it was not at all easy to let a description of such events pass her lips. Stekel must have had some difficulty in getting it out of her. When the story has been told, Stekel explains and points out the therapy. The patient is cured.

The speed reminds one of the speed of the movies in those days. A young lady is walking through a park with quick small steps. Suddenly a man with a beard, wearing a bobtail coat, appears. The young lady's eyes look frightened, she screams, the man runs off hastily, the lady faints, and is found by a noble person who takes her in his arms. She opens her eyes, from which the fear disappears. She is grateful, and goes off with quick small steps. All this without a sound. One can be sure that this young lady will tell her psychotherapist later on that a man with a beard and a bobtail coat behaved shamelessly toward her. And if sufficient pressure is put on her, she will go into heart-rending details.

That Stekel's patient reacts to the explanation of her symptoms by becoming cured is inevitable: if the symptom is caused by repression of an incident, then the cure is effected by removing the repression. In other words, if the therapist succeeds in precipitating the patient's misery in the repression of a past incident, then the patient is obliged, by her own belief, to be cured when the repression is lifted. One is the consequence of the other. And they were cured, those patients, with a rapidity which surprises and sometimes depresses—although it should not—modern psychotherapists.

The cure does not last

For most of the patients, if not all, who were cured in this way, became ill again after some time. They had made their misery too small, and, for that matter, too untrue. The therapist then reassured the patient and invited him to make more confessions. Again he pointed at the past. And the patient went back further; he found an even earlier incident, more serious (was it not presumed he had experienced sexual attacks in his early youth?), his story contained even more emotions, the therapist was elated and offered another inspired explanation—and again the patient got well. But again he came back. And again and again. The therapist pointed further and further into the past, the patient regressed more and more. Regression became his symptom: and this was the creation of the therapist, an artificiality for which his directions had been responsible. All patients regressed further in the past. The phallic phase, the anal phase, the oral phase were only brief stops; the patients were driven back from them one by one. In closed columns they finally marched to primeval times. There they were allowed to stay, around the bones of their early ancestors.

The dangerous present

But the patients did not stay. They came back. At first they hesitated; they would really have rather not come back, it was too dangerous; but neither did they want to stay, it was too ridiculous. It was too untrue, they were ill because of other things. They were suffering from a far more dangerous disease than just the reminiscences of an unfinished past. They were suffering from the present; neurotics were and are ill because of difficulties in the present. They give evidence of a present which has become highly disagreeable—not only to them, but to us as well.

And exactly this fact—that the present is disagreeable, that it is dangerous for all of us—made the therapist search in the past. For him, too, the present was too dangerous.

Actuality and reserve

The piquant story, the surprising insight and the prompt cure, all these disappeared, or are disappearing. But the neuroses remained; they even grew more frequent. And they became tougher; treatments today are more strenuous than fifty years ago. The psychotherapists have less insight, they have become more careful and reserved. They are less inclined to explain; their opinion is that matters have become too complicated. They sail on the patient's compass. Indeed, psychotherapeutical methods have been invented in which the therapist does not explain at all, but only acts as a mirror for the patient, and merely repeats what the patient says. Of course he does not do this literally and without thought; his repetitions are meant to loosen the patient from his hopeless point of view. Nonetheless his actions are characterized by two qualities which have come to rule all of psychotherapy: reserve and actuality. The therapist is reserved because the patient has to cure himself, and every assistance makes him dependent and leads him away from being cured. He is actual because he no longer believes in the past, he believes in the present; the problems are in the present, and he must let the patient find his own way, it is his present. (The past of the patient had always been the past as known by somebody else.) The therapist also lives in this present; merely by being there, and helping to dislodge the patient from his fixations by repeating what he is saying, is enough; more should not happen, anyway, since the patient must find his own way if he really wants to get well. Reserve and actuality; it is obvious that these two qualities of modern psychotherapy are closely related.

Peace between superego and id

Patients no longer tell stories about perverted maids, sultry aunts, or lewd uncles, nor about disastrous wedding nights—unless the therapist still believes in them. Patients have also stopped talking about battles in the inner self between the two hostile camps, the superego and the id. Freud himself and his followers made this fight senseless, they brought it to an inglorious close in which neither party won, but both became weaker, more peace-loving, less inclined to fight. The superego, convinced by analytic admonitions, gave up its objections to things sexual and sent the censors home. The id changed too; it grew less violent, more humane. The changes in the relation between the superego and the id can be compared to the changes which have occurred in the relationship between bride and bridegroom. The bride of those days was just as rigorous as the superego of her time; she did not want to have anything to do with the id, of which she was not allowed to know anything. The bridegroom was more like the id, just as self-satisfied and just as lewd, even if he did behave gallantly for as long as it was necessary. His gallant behavior was the behavior of a censored id. Today the bride desires a sexual contact, of which, to her delight, she has a more or less extensive knowledge. The bridegroom meets her desire in a way that is adequate for it; he does not in the least resemble a lecher. In his wife he seeks the sexual partner, not just a sex. Bride and bridegroom are balanced, their marriage is no longer a duel. And so the war between superego and id has ended for lack of ammunition. The patients do not speak of this war anymore—unless the therapist believes in it.

The contents of a therapeutic discussion

What then do they speak of? Of the most common things, of everyday occurrences. Of things which of course illustrate the misery in which they are living, a misery with a long and depressing past, but still an actual misery, appearing in the most common everyday incidents. They talk about their work, and about their relations with other people. Especially about this last matter do they talk, about how they do not seem to be able to get along with people, and about how things are always getting into a mess. The immediate consequence of this change is that the events of the treatment are no longer communicable. How can one relate a story consisting of an almost endless series of thoroughly common incidents? It can only be done if the storyteller is exceptionally good, or if he shifts the focus from the common incidents to the extravagancies.

In the professional analytic literature, this development is evidenced by an ever-increasing scarcity of complete cases, and by the publication instead of fragments of conversations. These fragments usually contain no extraordinary facts, since they always involve ordinary things. What these fragments can show is what may be called a "derailment in relationships." Only when this derailment is clearly illustrated, is a fragment significant. And only for the same reason is the patient's whole story significant.

There is one other reason why the patient's story is significant. The derailment it shows is not unknown to the therapist; and the patient's story indicates that he shares an existence with the therapist. If I were sure I would not be misunderstood, I should say that the therapist himself is off the right track now and then. I could say this because everybody who lives consciously is aware of being on the wrong track occasionally. But perhaps it is better to put it this way: nobody knows where the right track is, and no one can say that he is on the right track. A right track cannot be discovered, either in one's own, or in the patient's, existence.

The patient suffers from a misfortune from which, in a way, everybody is suffering. The difficult conversations of which he speaks and the difficult discussions he has with the therapist, are the very discussions the therapist knows about from his own experience. The moral ambivalence of which the patient tells in his stories is the same ambivalence the therapist has in his own relations with other people. What the patient brings to his analysis is not strictly his own, it is not a strictly individual pathological difficulty, as it had been in the days of Breuer and Freud. The patient brings the effects of a "strenuous social life" as if not he, but society, were ill. The therapist does not misunderstand things; the patient *is* ill indeed. His illness, however, is a particularly bad instance of an illness from which we are all suffering, an illness which is not of an individual, but of a social, nature. Society is ill; this comes first. Only after this are there also neurotic patients. They are those who could not stand this social illness. The difference between neurotics and other people consists in this: that the neurotics break down, while other people manage to stay on their feet.

THE SUBCONSCIOUS AS EVIDENCE OF ANOTHER SOCIETY

Anomy

It is not a coincidence that the name of the disease from which society is suffering is almost as old as the theory of the neuroses. In 1897, Durkheim [40] wrote in a study on suicide that society had fallen into a state of "norm-lessness," that it was suffering from "anomy." As a result of this condition, society fails to "regulate" the individual, it does not keep him in his place; the groups to which he belongs are falling apart.

Today, much more is known about this disease, anomy. The deficiencies of our own society were defined more clearly by the study of races with a style of living greatly different from ours, some of these societies being characterized by the remarkable fact that neurotic symptoms are entirely, or almost entirely, nonexistent.

A research study instigated by UNESCO made it clear that a healthy community is characterized by four conditions: [41]

1. "First, all aspects of life are closely integrated,—work, for instance, is not something separate and distinct." This means that in a healthy community there are no gaps between work and recreation, work and play, work and religion, faith and desire, life and death, youth and adulthood. Everything is bound together in one coherent totality, with no splits anywhere. Nothing stands apart.

2. "Secondly, social belonging is automatic." Everybody belongs to the community. No one is alone; no one is given an opportunity to stand alone, not even in a certain phase of life. There is no compulsion; one belongs naturally.

3. "Change is slow and continuity is sustained by attitudes, customs and institutions." Every change is so slow that no one notices a change. So stable is life that previous generations had lived naturally, and their descendants live the same life just as naturally.

4. "And lastly, the important social groupings are small."

If these qualities are absent, what the authors call "social sickness" will appear. This sickness is characterized by the fact that the members of the community do not feel happy, and by the occurrence of circumscribed symptoms, such as psychical difficulties of different kinds, some of which are lasting: suicide, divorce, criminality, and psychosomatic diseases.[42] It is well-known, for instance, that Negroes in Africa do not suffer from high blood pressure, while Negroes in America do.[43] The morbidity of anginal complaints differs from one style of living to another, and is slight in Chinese and Negro societies.[44] Also, angina pectoris occurs more frequently in societies with a fast tempo, where the strain of life is great—*angina temporis*.[45] And so on. The connection between the nature of the community and the occurrence of neurotic and psychosomatic diseases can hardly be denied.

Considering the four conditions necessary for a healthy community, it is quite obvious that Western civilization does not fulfil even one of them. Compared to the close integration of all aspects of life in a healthy community, ours appears to be characterized by a severe disintegration. Work and play are divided in our life; the same is true for work and religion, work and sexuality, faith and sexuality, life and death, young and old. Actually, every aspect of life is separate, disconnected from the other aspects; any one aspect could be removed from the totality—if there is anything left that can be called a totality—without essentially changing it.

No community

In the second requirement, also, we differ from a healthy society. No one of us belongs automatically to the community. So little do we feel we belong to a community that anyone can be made to doubt the genuineness of his belonging simply by being asked about it. Do you feel you belong to your country? The mere question is enough to raise doubts. Do you feel you belong to a certain class? Why? Do you feel you belong to this era? Don't you feel more sympathy with earlier times? Do you feel you belong to your state, district, province? Examined closely, these abstractions have no real meaning for us. Every unity is a loose unity, perhaps still covered by a flag or a slogan, but inwardly empty and powerless. No, we do not belong to anything naturally. Even when we could still naturally belong to a unity, impediments came into existence which made every unity illusionary. In factories, where until recently community singing used to resound, the machinery now makes all the noise,[46] so much noise that it drowns out the songs and prevents even verbal communication. In other kinds of factories only a few workmen look after a whole building; sometimes there are fewer workmen than stories, so that a workman may find himself completely alone most of the time. And if there is some community feeling within a factory, then it only lasts till the end of the working day, when everybody gets into his car and the community breaks up. The workmen of the factory live in houses scattered miles apart. And where they live, there is usually no community. Some even change their residence so frequently and travel such distances that it is impossible for them to become familiar with their environment.[47] Our social contacts are for the most part fleeting. We shake hands with thousands of people, but we barely learn to know very few. Of most of our acquaintances we do not know who they are and what they do; the only thing we do know is that they are all different, that each has his own existence—and this knowledge makes our attitude toward them careful and reserved, for the least carelessness might offend another's sensitivity. An extreme reserve guarantees a certain safety; but this means only that we are all potentially derailed. We are all suffering, in Sullivan's phrase, from a "parataxic distortion"; that is, we are caught in a maze of vague contacts, which are replaceable and dangerous at the same time. Every act involves an unknown shifting of effects: at A's we encounter—in an unrecognizable and disguised form—the same deed done to B in a daring or frightened moment. Every act returns tenfold.

No stability

Thirdly: the rapidity of change in our habits of living. The rate of change is so great, and the changes frequently affect such important spheres of our lives, that inner derangement cannot be avoided.

> . . . we die to each other daily.
> What we know of other people
> Is only our memory of the moments
> During which we knew them. And they have
> changed since then
> To pretend that they and we are the same
> Is a useful and convenient social convention
> Which must sometimes be broken. We must
> also remember
> That at every meeting we are meeting a stranger.[48]

It is true: almost every one is a stranger; we should realize it. Even the few we see frequently, so frequently that from this frequency we draw the right to call them friends, even these become strangers again and again. Life changes, and they change with life, every one in his own way, every one in a different way, for life is multiform and things are multivalent. How life is going to treat us, we cannot say; where it is going to hit us is unknown. Only the effects of the change become apparent; but then it is too late, since the process of the change cannot be reversed, not with the other person nor with ourselves. He does not know what is wrong, and neither do I; what we feel is that things are different; something has changed and we adapt ourselves to this change without including what had been before. Can we blame a person for getting stuck in complexes once in a while and for visiting the psychotherapist?

The small groups

Finally, smallness of social groups. In the first place, the family. Only very recently did the family begin to recover from a grave danger, a "loss of function."

A relationship between people is never blind, never *just* a relationship, never a relationship from person to person. A relationship between people only exists when they have something in common, something in thought or something in matter. Friends are friends because of a common interest in something, because of a common hobby or a common property. Groups are only groups by the grace of a common interest, an ideal, a property, an occupation with something, with people or with matter. If a group were to lose everything it possessed, materially and ideally, it would fall apart.

Every interest and possession has been taken from the family.[49] The education of children has not rested solely with the parents for a long time. Children go to school from the time they are four or five years old. By the time they leave school forever, they are no longer able to be educated, in the original meaning of the word. The sick are not nursed at home; even the chronically sick are removed from their families more and more frequently. The old people disappear into homes for the aged more often than in the past. This disappearance is felt to be necessary by both young and old: life changes so quickly and fundamentally that one cannot expect old people to adapt themselves continuously to the ways of their children. Clothes are made at home less and less often. Food is not stored for the winter. Remedies are no longer prepared at home. Even recreation is sought elsewhere. Families who still give parties at home are becoming scarce. The custom of group singing, accompanied by the harmonica, violin, or guitar played by one of the family or a neighbor has died out—replaced by the relentless noise of a cackling or jingling contraption, recently brought to perfection by the addition of a screen, which has definitely put an end to all activity.

The backyard

Thinking of small groups, I am reminded, not without nostalgia, of the conversations on the steps in the backyard. In the front, houses might appear separate; but in the back, they used to have a common atmosphere which made differences of opinion not impossible, but which reached beyond them. And quarrels with one's neighbors were far more evidence of understanding than of difference. Today neighbors seldom quarrel; people do not know one another well enough and are afraid to learn enough of each other to start an open war. In the old days they did; the words reverberated against the walls, everybody listened attentively and with satisfaction, everyone talked about it for a few days and then it was forgotten. Or else the quarrel turned into stone and became part of the loosely-solid structure of the backyards, with their henhouses, their rabbit-crates, their cats, and their tame crows. During the summer on Saturday evenings and on Sundays, everybody was there, on the steps or leaning back on chairs, talking, telling stories, and singing. When it grew dark the stories began to predominate. The children became quiet and listened until they were sent to bed, where they could still hear the voices for hours. The group existed, it was real. When somebody fell ill, he could count on help—on soup, on eggs or some fruit. The saying that a near neighbor is better than a distant cousin originated in those days. It is no longer true. For the neighbor has become a stranger who lives next door; greetings are exchanged, but we hardly talk with him and we certainly would not sing with him. The distant cousin now has a car, and will be over in a few minutes. But he is gone in a few minutes, too, with his car; for he is busy. And for that matter, we had not kept in touch with him; actually, we had not seen him for years. If we should fall ill now, it would be wiser to go to a hospital.

The street group

The fronts of the houses, the street, made another group. A different group; even with a member of the backyard group, conversation was different at the front. People wore a different expression and behaved differently. The street belonged to the village or to the town; it was a public place in which one was observed critically. The windows with their blue window screens were perfect one-way screens; the spy-mirrors were so many eyes. No one could object, for everybody took part in the game. People just accepted the idea of behaving in a different way at the front; there they belonged to another group.

Other small groups

One did not belong to many groups: perhaps to the one at the smithy or the carpenter's workshop, and perhaps to the group of the church. All groups were severely codified; no one had doubts about these codes, and no one had any difficulties. And besides, all the groups were strongly related, since they were all rooted in the same life-pattern. If there were a fire during the night, the siren or the bell alerted everyone alike. Everybody got up, big and small; everyone got dressed and went out into the dark, and went to the fire, directed by the sound of the siren. The streets, the districts, the whole town formed one homogeneity. All groups, from the smallest to the largest—which was still a small group in comparison to those of today—reflected the same interests.

All this has gone. All small groups vanished except the family; and it is well-known how hard it has been for even this group to maintain itself.[50] Recently there has been a recovery of the family group, partly because of the disappearance of natural groups outside, and partly because there has recently been an effort to restore community life.

Larger groups

Larger groups, on the other hand, have increased in number. Almost everybody subscribes to a periodical, for instance, usually one with a certain political or religious point of view. A subscriber is thus a member of a vast, vague group of subscribers. People are also members of unions and members of clubs. Characteristic of all these groups is the fact that any one member knows the other members only vaguely, if at all. Therefore, though the group has its own existence, a member discerns little of its activities; he notices a change only because he is told of its effects in his mail. The causes of any such change are usually beyond him; they may have originated partly with himself or with a few people around him whom he knows, or they may have originated with members whom he has never seen or heard of. Nobody, except perhaps a few people at the top, sees all that happens, no one knows the exact situation. Instead of a free and certain determination of group activity, made under the eyes of anyone who might wish to see—as was true with the conversations on the steps in the back-yard—the individual is determined by the group; the group is characterized by anonymous intrinsic power, it meets the individual as an "impersonal person," it makes him a captive, and it confronts him with the codes of the moment. Tomorrow there will be new codes; they will also probably be right, for who knows after all what they contain? Each group requires a certain adjustment, an adjustment only valid for this group. Every group makes of the individual an individual of a circumscribed nature—and yet different every time. Considering that most of us are members of not one group, but of many groups, it must be clear that this may give rise to difficulties. If the relation between the group and the individual is such that the individual does not determine the group but that the group determines the individual, however vaguely, then the individual is divided within himself; he consists of as many individualities as there are groups to which he belongs. Not that he notices; an influence emanating from a group is, as a rule, vague and hard to define. Besides, the individual is not often concerned with two groups at the same time. His life is more like a kaleidoscope; with every contact his own structure changes, but the change is so slight that he does not notice it himself.

He does notice what is happening to him when he is in two groups at the same time. For he does not meet other people only in the codified connection of a group, he meets them outside the group as well: in the street, at the movies, on vacation trips, or when visiting a third person; and it is then that the difficulties arise. If a person is spending the summer vacation at the sea shore, he may think that while he is there he is exactly the same person he was before. But he is wrong; how little he is the same person, how much he has become "the seashore," which he was not before, becomes clear to him when he suddenly meets somebody who belongs to one of the large, vague, yet strictly codified groups at home. He smiles painfully, he cannot find the right attitude, and he does not feel very happy about it all. Such a meeting is "impossible"; that he should meet the other person there should not happen; yet he is there.

This is a comparatively simple and not dangerous incident. The same thing—only much more complicated and indeed dangerous—happens when a university student, who comes from a lower social level, suddenly, in the company of his friends, comes face to face with his uncle who is a farm laborer. That should not happen either, but it does; it did not happen very often in the past. Or this university student meets his father, who is a butcher, back home. It is not impossible, in these cases, that dangers are present. The two conflicting selves of the university student are not, either of them, allowed to vanish. The father (or the uncle) represents the past; what is more, he represents a past in which the student feels at home. No one can live without a past, without a past in which he feels at home, a place where his roots are. If the student eliminates his father, he eliminates a number of years from his own life, and with it the self which rests on this foundation. If he eliminates his university, and everything that is connected with it, he eliminates his future. He can go home to his father, then, but he will not feel very happy doing the things he must do there. Either way he will live a mutilated life—if he manages to live at all. If he remains true to both selves—which is by far the best thing to do—he will have to combine them, he will have to find a mode of life in which both selves are allowed to remain. Whether the civil war between the two is ever brought to an end will remain to be seen.

Plural lives

We are not ourselves; actually there is nothing we can call a "self" anymore; we are manyfold, we have as many selves as there are groups to which we belong.[51] "A neurosis is the conflict between the different social egos." The neurotic has overtly a disease from which everybody is suffering, but which makes only him manifestly ill: the disease not to be able to be one's self, which means not to be able to be identical with one's self in different contacts and in different situations.

The normal person, and even more so the neurotic, is present in every contact and in every situation in two different ways: he is manifest and he is hidden. He is leading a double life, as it

were; he is Dr. Jekyll and Mr. Hyde.[52] And it has to be remembered that there are as many Mr. Hydes as there are groups to
which he belongs. That is, minus one: for he is present in any particular group at any one moment as Dr. Jekyll, and consequently
is allowed to show the self which fits in that group; the other
shapes of his existence are put aside, they are silent, but they
whisper, their influence is not in the least abolished. Dr. Jekyll is
present; Mr. Hyde is absent in plural, and his absence haunts the
room in which Dr. Jekyll seems to move so freely.

Even if we did not know that Stevenson wrote his famous
thriller in exactly the years that Breuer and Freud were observing
the odd behavior of their patients, and extracting from their observations the foundations of the theory of the subconscious, even
then the title and theme of the book [53] would invite comparison
with Freud's theory. For what else was Freud doing than describing at first only the neurotic, but later the normal person as well,
as a split personality, split primarily in two parts; one part conscious, visible to anyone; the other part subconscious, invisible.
Stevenson, Laura Marholm, Hunt—are they not all showing, each
in his own way, what Freud explains in a psychiatric context?
Freud's discovery was a discovery made by many; but the discovery
needs to be interpreted in a different way.

At the end of the last century society had arrived in a state of
anomy. As time passed society presented the individual with fewer
and fewer strong stable connections. The individual began to
leave small groups; and related to this defection, large vague
groups, which are more autonomous and therefore more compelling, came into existence. The small, mutually related groups guaranteed the individual a solidarity with himself, but the large group
forced a self onto the individual which only functions in that
group. Consequently, although a part of the personality always
communicates, it is a different part each time; and a number of
selves always remain out of communication. What Breuer and
Freud saw was the first manifestation of an exceptionally extensive
occurrence: the manifestation of the effect of a disintegration of
society on the individual. They observed this manifestation in

the sphere in which the mutual exclusiveness of two group codes was most apparent: in the sphere of sexuality. In the large group, or rather, the conglomeration of groups belonging to public social life, sexuality was absolutely absent; in the lives of married people this sexuality was present, and what is more, present in a form radically opposed to its absence everywhere else.

Breuer's and Freud's discovery

This was what Breuer and Freud saw: the loss of a form of life, embodied in the disconnection of the individual. The individual was adrift, now in this group, now in another; the different groups could be so unrelated that at times the individual did not recognize himself. So much could he become adrift, that he lost himself. He—in this connection *she* is more appropriate—she drifted too far from home, she did not live a life that she knew, to which she belonged; instead she lived the life of another person, a person who was at home in another group. Actually she lost her own life; and when that happened, she fainted. When the woman of the last century fainted, she fell right through a group which was too dislocated into nothingness. She would have liked to stay with the group, that was not the reason why she fell; but she simply could not stay, the atmosphere of the group was too rarefied, the group was not able to bind her—so she fell.

But did she not have other selves to hold on to, selves belonging to less rarefied groups? for instance, the self from the group "home," or the self from the group "theater," or from the group "church"? She did not. Just as the student of the lower social level does not think of home when he is at the university, for the simple reason that he cannot think of it as long as he remains in this atmosphere with his fellow students, so the young lady of the nineteenth century in her dizzy moment did not think of home, of the theater, or of the church, simply because it was exactly those things she could not think of. The student still has a way out; he can think of his parents to the degree that he is able to assimilate them in the university atmosphere. He can imagine that his father does fit in with the people around him, and that his mother could be in his room when he is giving a party for his fellow students;

in his imagination he can falsify them—if they suddenly appeared before him his imaginary world would collapse—but the young lady of the last century did not have this kind of retreat: her parents were foreign, absolutely and without remedy, to anything sexual. It was *their* fault, their attitude toward sex was precisely the cause for this dizzy awkward moment. Her girl friends from the theater were just as pre-Raphaelite as she was; and the church could help her even less. So she stood there swaying, without help from anywhere, with nothing to hold on to. All the groups she once might have belonged to were absent; consequently all her selves which might have belonged to those groups were absent. There was nothing but the extremely rarefied group, personified by the man who suddenly—and in what a way! began to make love to her. She found herself in a bare room, without even wallpaper; and worse, there was no air. She gasped for breath in this atmosphere, she became like it, rarefied, inanimate, absent. She fell.

Unconsciousness

During the moment in which she is falling—that is, the few seconds between his ambiguous words, his daring gesture, or his dubious look and her falling on the soft carpet—she (for example Hunt's young lady) is nothing but the spark of sexuality that makes her fall, nothing but a few atoms of sexual breath. There is nothing more. Her parents are absent; perhaps her eyes search desperately for something that invokes her parents, to which she cannot give a name anymore. That is why she looks around so bewilderedly when she falls; there is nothing on which to focus her stare. Her girl friends are not there; when she sways, they sway with her, and when she falls, she pulls every girl of her acquaintance with her. And the church is so entirely dismissed by the man's gesture that she must search in vain for words which gave her security perhaps only an hour ago. Parents, friends, and church: they are not there during those few seconds, they are absent, they are pushed into her subconscious.

By the time she comes to, things have changed. She says she does not remember what has happened, maybe she does not even remember the man who had caused her fall, the stranger who is going to so much trouble to bring her to with *eau de la reine*. At that moment, sexuality (the spark, the glimmer, the atom of sexuality) is her subconscious, and all that the stranger had pushed beyond the horizon with one gesture is conscious again—her parents, her friends, the church. If one wants to speak of repressions, her parents were repressed when he drew her toward him—and her sexuality was repressed when he brought her to with *eau de la reine*.

Repression

Yet it is clear that the word *repression* does not cover the incidents completely; it suggests an unabridged and persisting presence of all life's attributes within the individual, in this case within the falling lady. According to the theory of repression, everything is within her all the time—sexuality, parents, friends, the church; of these attributes, however, sexuality is present in an occult way, "repressed"; and what the man does when he draws her toward him is to fight the repression, to attack the repressor, the censor who will not budge because it obeys the despotic superego. The censor—according to the theory of the repression—defends itself; that which had been repressed, however, that which has been waiting so long to escape, is going to revolt, encouraged by the man's gesture and by the consequent preoccupation of the censor. In the inner self of this frightened lady a war is raging between the id and the superego. So heavy is the fighting that she cannot stand it and she loses consciousness. And while she is unconscious her superego recovers, it sends out new censors to the threatened area with new instructions. To be on the safe side, the recent experience is also pushed into her subconscious with a new, particularly alert censor to watch it. When she awakens the young lady says: "What has happened? Why do you look like that? And who is he?", pointing at the man with the flask in his hand—the very man who had caused her this distress a few moments ago. It is the new censor's task to see that her memory of him, and certainly her memory of what he had been doing, remains out of reach.

All this is according to the theory of the repression. The first difficulty with this scheme is that if the subconscious is within her, as the theory assumes, it must be possible to find it, if necessary over the censor's dead body. But is this so? If the censor is beaten to a jelly by a long treatment, and the superego is torn to pieces, then the subconscious indeed appears to be within her. "I remember now," says the patient, and then comes the story. The censor is gone and the subconscious is giving up its secrets. Nonetheless, it is strange such extremely important knowledge can rest within a person although it seems impossible to find it. But there is another and far more serious objection to the theory of repression.

Repression of accessible matters

What the theory cannot explain is why the parents, the friends —in short, all the persons and contents of daily life which are not suspect at all, and which are in every way accessible—are absent during the short time between the man's gesture and her fall. If the theory of repression is maintained, then it has to be accepted that there are also censors at the other side of the fence, in the subconscious, watchmen of the daily world. It is not clear why the subconscious suspects secrets in the daily world; and the objection comes down to this. The theory of repression makes it clear why a certain sector of inner life does not participate. The sector is suspect, it is not allowed to participate, because, if it did, the whole person would face a dangerous situation, the situation in which a civil war would rage within the inner self. It appears, however, that not only suspect sectors are repressed—nonsuspect sectors are repressed even more frequently. Every repression requires a repressor, a repressing agent. It is not clear which agent in the individual could object to nonsuspect sectors.

The theory of repression does not make clear either, why the patient loses consciousness. Certainly, one could point to inner struggles caused by the duel between superego and id. But why should the conscious always have to beat the retreat? Why doesn't she remain upright, this lady, why doesn't she say, still standing, "I am boiling inside. I feel torn apart. The limits of my inner self are being exceeded"? If she could say anything at all, she would stammer, "I am so empty inside. There is no air. There is nothing around me, and there is nothing in me." And because there is nothing, she is quiet, she does not say anything; for there is nothing to say. And because there is nothing at all—except for the spark of sexuality—so absolutely nothing, she falls.

The variable subconscious

What the theory of repression does not really explain is why the extent of the subconscious depends on the person with whom the patient is speaking. The secret of a great therapist is that by his manner, by his particular behavior, by the intonation of his voice, by the particular kind of contact he establishes, he acts as a bridge to areas which have sunk into oblivion, or which have never been entered before, so that the patient tells him about incidents which she would not be able to remember with somebody else, and she touches on subjects she has never discussed. How can this be explained if it is assumed that the patient is the victim of a diseased inner structure? Is the gifted psychotherapist so aware of the border, that he is able to smuggle the id's goods to the other side? Or is he admitted to the superego, where, as a rule, no one even faintly related to the id is ever admitted? Considering that, according to the theory, the superego is able to see through the most clever camouflages of the id, this does not seem very likely. The gifted therapist, however, is not trying to be clever at all. On the contrary, he is a man who means what he says. The conversation between him and the patient makes it clear that the subconscious is not so much an affair of the individual (in this case, of the patient) but of two people. The subconscious is a communicative phenomenon. I will explain this in detail, but before I do so, I would like to linger a moment over a thought mentioned above.

It is this: that the patient in his contact with the psychotherapist very often explores new areas which he had never entered before. The theory of repression only recognizes old areas, present in the patient for years, but so covered with the dust of those years that they have been made unrecognizable. Yet, despite this dust of the years, new things can be treated as if they were just as old. It seems highly probable that this dust is just what makes new things seem old. The theory of repression—and it is well to remember this—is closely related to the thesis that there is sense in everything, which in turn implies that everything is past and there is nothing new. The idea that quite often the subconscious is *new* could not be fitted into this theory.

And yet this idea is true to what actually happens in every psychotherapy. Every patient who submits himself to psychotherapy is entering areas which until then had been inaccessible; these areas, however, did not exist in the patient before the treatment, and can therefore justly be called new.

The subconscious: index of communication

Hunt's young man, who had suddenly begun to make love to the girl, *knew*. This is seen by his way of looking, by his gesture. His way of looking at her and his gesture, however, bring the girl into a state of barely knowing, and shortly afterward into an emptiness, into a not-knowing. She did not know what he knew. That is why she was able to say, if she were asked afterward, "I do not know." And why, after a while, when the therapist had provided the atmosphere with greater density, she could say, "I remember." She was speaking the truth, the whole truth, on both occasions. She was even speaking the truth when, at the end of the treatment, she said what according to Freud must be considered as an indication of the success of the treatment: "I have always known." [54] For indeed she had known. This knowledge, however, had not been part of her, but of the man, of the man who had made love to her. A lover had always been very far away from her; her parents, uncles, aunts, the church, everybody saw to that. Consequently, her knowing had been far away, infinitely far away. But when another person (the psychiatrist) came nearer, her knowing came nearer with him: she began to know. After the therapist, however, came the young man who made love. But was it not sexuality that the therapist brought nearer to her, or, even better, maturity? He guided the patient into a new group, the group of lovers. If the therapist was able to approach her so closely that he was with her, then it meant that the lovers were also with her—including the man who had drawn her to him. And then what had happened was clear to her too. "I have always known," is what she says at this moment. Undoubtedly; at first this knowing had been infinitely far away; at the end of the treatment it was there beside her, on the couch.

There was even more beside her. With her knowledge of what had happened, a knowledge of the man who had been the cause of it also came nearer. And of this knowledge, too, she said, "I have always known." And she was not lying.

The subconscious is thus the index of nearness or remoteness in one's relationship with other people. I would like to give a few illustrations of this definition, which, it seems to me, has extreme significance for the understanding of neurotic symptoms, and also for an understanding of human existence in general.

Let us say that a few harsh words have been spoken between a married couple. Let us presume that in the morning when the man is putting on his trousers he discovers that a button, which he had pointed out as missing the night before, is still conspicuous by its absence. He grumbles; and his wife, who as it is has enough worries of which the man has no idea anyway, makes a few biting remarks in return. He thinks, "What a bad temper she has. And she yells, too, just like her sister." With this thought in mind he eats his breakfast and catches the train which takes him to his work. Purely by accident (as it is called) he finds himself sitting opposite a charming young woman, who shows, by her haughty nonchalance, that she is highly susceptible to male interest, of which the husband gives evidence by the way he looks at her. He has to leave the train before she does. Added to the thought "just like her sister" there is now another: "and just think —a girl like that one." He feels rather gloomy. But things get better while he works, and when he goes home at five o'clock there is nothing to remind him of what happened in the morning. He thinks he will take something to his wife, and when he sees a flowershop with her favorite flowers in the window, he buys them. When he gets home, he says to his wife: "I saw these flowers in the florist's window, and I thought I would buy them for you."

His wife happens to be a very sensible woman. She thinks, "He has been worrying about this morning. It must have bothered him, for he hasn't bought me flowers for at least three years." She is right, this woman, that is, in our eyes (the audience). She is not only sensible, she has courage, too. She looks at him and she says, "Were you annoyed this morning?"

What happens now depends entirely on the nature of their marriage. If they are getting along well, there is a good chance that he will grin and say, "I have been looking at women to find out whether they are all as bad-tempered as you are." "Did you find out?" says she, for there is no harm in this question. "No," he answers. "I did see a very charming woman, but I couldn't imagine her enjoying the job of sewing on buttons." Then both of them laugh and tease each other a bit, and that will be the end of it.

But if their relationship is not very good, things will turn out differently. Then her question is not courageous at all, it is stupid. Which is obvious. He says: "No." But just because he leaves it at that he creates more suspicion than all the flowers put together. She is aware of this; and so she says, "Then why did you bring the flowers?" With this remark she destroys his move to re-establish their married relation, embodied in the flowers. "Well," says he, "can't I go and buy you flowers when I want to?" We (the audience) know that he is evading the issue, for he knows pretty well that she is right. She knows, anyway. For her next remark is, "You must have something on your conscience. Have you been looking at girls again?" Of course this is a nasty remark, but not entirely irrelevant (in our eyes). But the man says, "That's a lie." And he adds, "If you don't like them, you don't have to have them," and he takes the flowers out of the vase and throws them out the window.

Who has been lying? We are inclined to say the man. That is what the woman says. But he says, "She's lying; I only brought her the flowers because I want some affection."

And if we should say, "But what about this morning, and what about the train?" he would probably answer, "What nonsense. It was nothing important this morning. And in the train I was only looking at a pretty woman's face, as every man does. That has nothing to do with my marriage." Every psychiatrist knows that it is impossible to make this man see that there is a connection. There is no connection for him. For this reason: the distance which divides him from his wife makes it impossible for his views to be her views. That is the fundamental cause of their difficulties. If they manage to get together again, then, yes, her views can be his. And that is what does happen when they do get together. It is not impossible that the woman—who, we will assume, was sensible enough not to proceed with this conversation—will, much later, when relations are restored and at the right moment, say, "Remember those flowers?" and that his answer will be, "Do I! I was pretty near a divorce that day."

Let us take another example: A milkman saved scores of lives during the war. With great danger to his own life, he transported Jews from one corner of Holland to another. He helped political prisoners escape, and he hid quite a few Allied pilots in his house. He did not think of the milk. Primarily because there was no milk; and secondly—and this is more essential—because he thought of other things. Then the war was over. There was milk again—and since he had to earn money, he resumed his business. But he was not happy. For his mind still turned to another life, one that had been important and full of risks, that had brought him into contact with important people, even with members of the government. Back in his old life, he felt devalued. This was brought home to him again and again when he met people from those days. They did not know him anymore.

No, that was not quite true. The important people from those days did know him, still; they even made a point of saying hello to him when they happened to meet. But the milkman observed that the feeling of equality was gone. He was just a milkman, that was obvious to him. And moreover, he noticed that the people to whom he had given his last slice of bread had become very rich, and drove off to expensive summer resorts in overgrown cars. Life became miserable for him. He could not digest what he saw. And since undigested matter is apt to pass through the body badly, or not at all, or far too quickly, a severe indigestion developed, so severe that his intestines were full of ulcers. He suffered from a *colitis ulcerosa*. He lost a fair amount of blood and looked like a ghost. And so he went to his doctor, who referred him to a specialist for internal diseases, who in turn referred him to the radiologist, who finally returned him to the specialist. The latter gave him medicines, which had no effect. This was only logical; for the intestines the specialist was treating were not ill; the intestines which were ill are not mentioned in the books of internal medicine.[55] It is a fact that the diseased intestines had caused a disturbance in the internal intestines, and thus the doctor was right to keep the patient under observation. But the diseased internal intestines are only an effect, a sign, a warning; and it is not in this relation that a specialist ever sees a patient. He sees the patient's disease as the stoker sees the furnace: he sees the ashes, the results of the fire—not the fire itself, not the heat, not the heated rooms; nothing of that.

Finally the specialist got tired of the case and recommended a psychiatrist. With the classic feeling of discomfort, the milkman followed his advice. After three or four talks it became obvious to the psychiatrist where the shoe pinched. He did not say, however, what the actual difficulties were from which the patient was suffering; for the patient would not have accepted his correct version.

Why not? Because of the censors? It is not clear why censors should have to take action against bringing to consciousness such easily understandable, innocent, even partly noble matters, nor is it clear on whose authority. I may mention that there is not much sex in it, either. Did this milkman have an overethical agent in him telling him that it is not permissible, once and for all, to view the return to his former life as a devaluation, and to blame those rich people for being rich? If this were true, then there would be censors. And yet the patient himself told how difficult it was to start his old work again: "It was tough, doctor, to go back to the milk wagon." He said that it had hurt him to be treated so distantly by those rich people. And the ladies! "They weren't going to sit down in their minks on the same chair as the one they sat on, eating my porridge during the war." No trace of a censor in these remarks.

Yet the patient related these facts differently from the way the psychiatrist would like to have them told. He treated them *en bagatelle*; while the psychiatrist considered them of primary importance. Moreover, he acted as if his annoyance were all over. "Then," he said, "I had a tough time. But it doesn't worry me any more." This shift to the past tense was too clear to the psychiatrist, who understood he was in the midst of his worries. But it was impossible to tell him; the patient would only have emphatically denied it. Why?

This question became even more urgent when things began not going too well with the patient, when his condition became more serious, when ultimately his life was in danger. Nothing—to the eyes of the psychiatrist—was clearer than the cause of this illness; and yet, the patient chose this illness above the simple realization, the seemingly simple condition for his recovery. And then he died, without ever seeing the connection which had been so obvious to everybody. He died because he did not know; did not know what to everybody else had been extremely accessible knowledge, an easily attainable insight.

How can this happen? It happened because when the war was over the patient remained floating in the air. He had not been a milkman for a long time; not for two years, to be exact. Two long years, though; long enough and intense enough to prevent him from becoming a milkman again. But he did not belong to those people he had served during the war; this became clear to him in a thousand ways. He had been devaluated; he did not belong anywhere, not to any group, and therefore he had no contact with anybody. That is why he did not understand the psychiatrist's point of view, and why he could not see what everybody else saw. His wife, his children, his brothers and sisters, his friends and acquaintances, the customers in his dairy, everybody tried to tell him; but he did not hear, because he was not there. What the others knew he could not know. He was no part of them; consequently he could not take part in their knowledge. He could not see obvious connections, because he was outside any connection. Other people's knowledge was, inevitably, his nonknowledge, his nonawareness, his subconscious. His subconscious was evidence of his dislocation.

First contact, then realization

That is the reason a psychotherapist does not try to force his views upon a patient. He does try to find out to what extent the patient is capable of a certain insight into his problems. But if it appears that the patient is blind about obvious relationships, he will quickly withdraw. If other aspects are favorable he may recommend extensive treatment—analysis, for instance. Then the patient begins to talk, and everything he says is right. The therapist does not intervene, he forces no other points of view upon him. For if the patient is outside everything and everybody, it is impossible for him to see the things other people see. Therefore the therapist lets his own views rest; in other words, he respects the patient's subconscious, or, rather, *he respects his isolation.* Only after a while will the patient be able to re-establish contact; if he does, the treatment is successful. The patient's insight into his own problems is only a byproduct, it is not necessary. The cause of the symptoms is isolation; the remedy is found in a way to end this isolation. Quite often patients recover, although without seeing the connections everybody else can see. Their recovery is a return; their insight is not essential. Most patients do give evidence of a greater insight and usually it comes spontaneously. With the re-establishment of contact, their insight into the relatedness of incidents grows. But insight remains of secondary importance.

Bovaryism

So obvious was the unmasking effect of *Madame Bovary*, that this book has been compared with *Don Quixote*. The book is still interesting; at almost every page it is evident that the author is a natural psychologist and an erudite writer. And yet it is strange that this book caused such a furore. What is it that Flaubert had unmasked? What quality of Emma Bovary's did he show so clearly that everybody felt personally involved?

No doubt it was the quality which, by Gaultier's reference to it as "Bovaryism," grew into an abstraction: "The inclination to live two lives and to be so absorbed in the fantasy life that the normal life threatens to atrophy." This is Andre Gide's definition of Bovaryism, made in one of his critical literary essays.[56] What Flaubert exposed was a fantasy life that had usurped the rights of normal existence. Emma Bovary preferred a spongy fantasy to a disappointing reality—which, however, insisted on remaining reality—and was wrecked by her preference. *Madame Bovary* was the most important novel of the last century, because Emma's disease was almost everybody's disease. It was this disease that Breuer and Freud met when they examined their first patients.

A *necessary pluralism*

This book was published in 1857; the disease discovered by Breuer and Freud must have been very widespread by then. When did it come into existence? A difficult question. At the end of Romanticism? It is not impossible. Did the French revolution disturb the order of society so greatly that everybody has suffered from a lack of unity since? Freedom, however attractive it may sound—and however necessary as a slogan it may have been at the end of the eighteenth century—is capable, more than anything else, of blowing up the structures of existence. If society has no definite structure, then everybody is allowed to choose his own direction, any direction that appeals to him, a direction which may lead to a partial dislocation. Did Emma Bovary, did the first neurotic, evolve in this way? Here is a subject for important historical psychological research. It seems obvious to me that the dualism of the inner self is peculiar to the nineteenth century; and this dualism is present in the same way in Madame Bovary, in the lady in Hunt's painting, in Laura Marholm, in van Eckeren's Eve, and in Freud's patients.

In the twentieth century this dualism has become what it had always been in principle: a pluralism. The individual has as many selves as there are groups to which he belongs. This pluralism has no need to prove its right to exist; the groups are there, they did not appear without a reason. And they exist for all of us, either in reality or potentially. We have to function in different groups, which are not alike, and each one of which is autonomous; consequently, we have to be divided within. Inner pluralism is necessary—I almost said is a necessary evil. But it is not an evil. It was an evil, no doubt, in its preliminary dualistic form; this can be seen in both Flaubert's and Breuer's work. Emma Bovary had to commit suicide, there was no other way out; Anna O, Breuer's patient, was paralyzed, half-blind, and unconscious. Of course Freud wanted to abolish this dualism from which his patients suffered. "What had been id must become 'I' " [57] was his famous comment. The complete separation of sexuality and asexuality led to an untenable state of affairs.

But if this ideal is applied to the pluralism which evolved from dualism, it may have dangerous consequences. When society offers the individual several different forms of existence all at once, then it would contradict reality to give only one advice and to accept only one pattern. The psychotherapist who removes his patient from every group except one, and who firmly establishes him in that group, is not doing the patient a service—even if he makes all symptoms disappear. He makes it too easy for himself. He is doing what the eye-specialist would do if he prescribed one pair of glasses which would allow the patient to see distinctly from a short distance, and then gave him the advice never to go outdoors, instead of giving him two pairs of glasses, one for close and one for distance vision. Of course, his advice would be effective; but at tremendous cost to the patient. In the same way the psychotherapist's advice can be effective when he says the equivalent of "Stay indoors with those glasses." The patient will be rid of his complaints; but he will have ceased to live.

Rilke and pluralism

Rilke was another author acutely aware of all this. He consulted a psychotherapist; and when it became clear to him what the treatment involved and to what goal it aspired, he withdrew from the treatment with the memorable statement that if his devils were to leave him, he was afraid that his angels also would take flight.[58] No devils, no angels, is what he says. Do not make me uniform; for uniformity does not safeguard the area it covers, it destroys it. In the night of November 3, 1899 a short time before Freud's explanation of dreams was published, Rilke wrote in his diary that the only things he was afraid of were the inner contrasts which are inclined to reconciliation; for how narrow must life be, when contrasts can even think of coming nearer toward each other.[59]

This modern conception leads to just as modern pedagogic advice. The educator, writes Rilke, should try to make many and different people out of the crowd entrusted to him; it is better to accidentally educate one child into two mutually combative personalities than by imposition of routine produce one personality out of all.[60] Rather two or many adults out of one child, than one; maturity will not be easily attained otherwise. For today maturity means living pluralistically. It is simply not permissible to deny the child its inner contrasts.

Twentieth-century man has many more difficulties than did, let us say, man in the eighteenth century; but he does live more intensely, more "consciously," and more completely. He has an insight which in the early days was had only by few.

Why 1882?

The question of why the subconscious was discovered at the end of the nineteenth century and not before has been answered. In the nineteenth century there was a loss of uniformity of life. The individual went adrift, he drifted in several directions, he pluralized. The subconscious is the evidence of his plurality.

At the same time, it is clear why nobody ever described or treated neurotics before Janet, Breuer, and Freud: there were no neurotics; they also appeared in the nineteenth century.

Hysteria

Yet hysteria has been known since antiquity. There has always been hysteria, but it remains doubtful whether hysteria has always been a disease. And particularly whether it may always be interpreted as a neurotic symptom. That hysteria occurred before means only that even in earlier times people could be dislocated. The modern dislocation is the neurosis. But in the past? It is well-known that frequently extremely religious people were the ones who showed hysterical symptoms. The extremely religious person, however, is defined by an extraordinary contact, his association with God. In the first place, and perhaps to the exclusion of all other groups, he belongs to this particular "group"; and consequently he is excluded from the groups to which his contemporaries belong. That is why a religious person sometimes bore the signs which in the nineteenth century were almost entirely reserved for neurotics. What today is a symptom of the hysterical neurotic, and considered evidence of a pathological dislocation, has always been a sign of extreme religiousness in the religious person; and it was not considered pathological. The symptoms of Teresa of Avila do not give us a right to call her a neurotic or a hysteric. Francis of Assissi's stigmata are not evidence of a pathology.

Apart from these cases, occasionally (how often is unknown as yet) there must have been people who were not able to manage the particular problems of their time—for instance, the second half of the eighteenth century. The symptoms of neurotics of that era, of Mesmer's patients for example, were not identical with those shown by neurotics today, however. There was no evidence of a pluralism.

And finally, there have always been people different from everyone else because of their originality. These are also outside the totality, and show their dislocation by symptoms; but their symptoms are not defects. This is still true; neurotic symptoms are not *always* evidences of neurosis.

Neurotic symptoms only show an extraordinary relation, a being different, a dislocation. Mostly the dislocated are people who have stayed behind, or who were pushed aside; but sometimes they are the exceptional, the gifted, the talented; pioneers, spies of the future.

Was Augustine a neurotic? Pascal? Kierkegaard, Rilke, Kafka? Or were they, above all, exceptional, exceptionally sane? Was their sanity so exceptional that it almost wrecked their lives?

Factors liable to provoke neurotic symptoms

The neurotic is defined as one whose manifestations and achievements are constantly below the optimal level, although he is not suffering from a physical disease or a psychosis. This is a definition by exclusion. There should be a more positive definition.

No one is neurotic unless made neurotic by society. A neurosis is an individual's reaction to the conflicting and complicating demands made by society. A neurosis is the pathological effect of factors which are liable to provoke neurotic symptoms and which are inherent to society.

⌐he first psychotherapist who seriously tried to realize to what extent society was causing neurotic symptoms was Karen Horney. In her book, *The Neurotic Personality of Our Time*, she discusses three important factors:

1. Modern society is characterized by a continuous competition which makes an enemy of everybody. At the same time, society requires a person to be amiable and obliging.

2. Modern society is characterized by the stirring of every need and the creation of ever more needs. But the possibility of satisfying these needs is at the same time restricted.

3. Modern society is characterized by a constant and emphatic stressing of individual freedom and by a lack of freedom for everyone. Society keeps us prisoners, while it cries out to us that we can do what we like.

No doubt there are many other factors—for instance mentally drained work,[61] physically drained work, estrangement of one's own body, and psychical conformity. But I will not go into these factors here. The most important factor (first mentioned by Sorokin) is the plurality of large groups. Most neurotics consult a psychiatrist because they have become a victim of this factor. They become mixed up with the strategies of different groups; they are not able to maintain mastery over the plurality of their own self and they run aground on the basic existence that is left. It was an exceptional and temporary form of this which brought Breuer his first patient.[62]

Neuroses are socioses

Every factor which provokes a neurotic reaction has a communicative, or rather a sociological, nature. No factor is concerned with the individual himself; the individual becomes neurotic only because of an appeal aimed at him by a complex society.

Therefore the name *neurosis* is no longer correct. This word is derived from the Greek *neuron*, meaning "nerve." Older medical science, which was inclined to be individualistic and was therefore chained to anatomy, had no room for anything but an anatomical and physiological explanation for symptoms; and since neurotic symptoms appeared to be of a nervous nature, it was assumed that these symptoms were caused by a peculiarity of the nervous substance. Neurotic symptoms were exceptional in that they progressed without the signs of an anatomical disease; therefore, it was necessary to assume that the symptoms were not caused by an abnormality in the matter, but in the function of the nervous tissue. This thought is expressed by the ending *-osis*. A neurosis was no *-itis*, no inflammation or anything of the sort, but an *-osis*, a nonanatomical, even physiologically incomprehensible, functional disturbance.

Freud and his followers proved that this conception is untenable. They showed that the neurotic symptom was a psychological symptom, although they did maintain its ultimate connection with the anatomy.

The neurotic is not ill because of causative agents within himself—agents incorporated in his own subjectivity—but because of agents from outside. It is true that he takes measures against these agents, and it is also true that as a result of these measures he may get more severely ill; if this happens, of course, he is then ill because of agents within himself. Yet the primary causative factors are outside himself. It is society which is the cause of his illness.[63]

It would be more appropriate then, instead of speaking of neuroses, to speak of *communicoses*, or rather of *socioses*; nonanatomical nonphysiological symptoms of a sociological nature. The word *neurosis*, however, has withstood the change from an anatomical and physiological orientation to a psychological one; and we may presume that it will also be able to withstand the change from a psychological to a sociological point of view.

CHAPTER 4

The miracle

The absence of miracles

In Chapter I, I discussed the behaviour of Spencer's father, and promised to return to the miracle which he removed so completely. What has happened to the miracle?

As soon as I formulated this question I am in difficulty. For I cannot get an answer; the question fades away, it meets no obstacle, there is not even an echo. My words create an emptiness.

I am not even stating the question I really mean to ask: What sort of a thing is a miracle? First I have to realize that my wanting to know where the miracle has gone—which actually means where has God gone—has become an impossible question. Where is God? What a question!

God's absence

Descartes seemed to have found an answer, though, when he put God at the beginning of things and said: This is where He should be. His argument must have been very powerful; for he proved to everybody that this was God's right place, at the beginning of things. God has stayed there.

Has He? Maybe He didn't even go there at all. When Descartes removed God from the line which connects the past with the present, and when he made Him go to the point where the line starts, it was not God who was put there, but a question mark. Descartes did not notice the difference. And now the difference has disappeared. What is God? A question mark. Question and answer seem to fit each other perfectly.

Would it be better to ask, "Where is the question mark?" I hear an answer immediately: "The question mark is at the beginning." But I also hear other answers, a storm of answers. The question mark seems to be everywhere. Is God everywhere then? Immediately the storm subsides.

I do not feel very happy about all this. My questions apparently touch on a dangerous subject. I may not be able to foresee the effects of my questions. Perhaps I will not be able to keep them under control.

Change

It must be clear to the reader that in this book I want to point out changes. Good changes, of which there are quite a few; but bad and sad changes as well. I am trying to see through these changes and to find the old shapes which have become hidden. I want to say, "See, this is how it was, and this is what we made of it; was it really necessary?" Quite often it was necessary; and it is no use being sad about it. But quite often it was not; the reader will see that in these cases I have invited him to remove the bad or sad character of the change. Sometimes the change is difficult to describe. It is easy to discuss the change in the relation between old and young; it is not difficult to show that in this matter we have made some good changes, but infinitely more bad ones. But as to God—I don't know what to do with Him. He is the fundamental problem.

If we look at them closely, we can see that all the bad and the sad changes come down, primarily, to a matter of increased distance. Future and past have become invisible; the present is in a tremendous hurry to pass us. The child today is far away from adults; adults have less real mutual contact. But all these increased distances are reflections of but one single one: the increased distance of God. It need not surprise us that today He is covered with a layer of dust so thick that anyone who wants to find Him suffocates before he even tries. Are there not many God-seekers who, after an honest start, get into so many difficulties that they lose their aim and become nothing but long-lasting agonies?

I cannot say that I am attracted to this fate. I therefore ask the reader's permission to behave like a modern man, who does not know of God, but who nevertheless is surprised at miracles and who seeks enlightenment. I hope I have enough sense not to cry out too quickly about oldfashioned prejudices, fables, metaphors, and the like; and I hope I am psychologist enough not to get entangled in the tentacles of projection. I wish to talk about miracles and to look at them from different angles. I will not dare a frontal attack; it would only land me in trouble.

The willing things

The shape in which things appear to us is remarkably variable. Not only do things have a tendency to meet us half way as far as our changing moods are concerned, but we can influence them, too; we are able, to a certain extent, to change things just by observing them differently. I can sit in my room and look at the furniture, at the curtains, at the assembled things of my existence, so unfavorably that they become hostile. They become my enemies, and after a while I wonder how in the world it has ever been possible for me to feel happy in this room with these things. If I change the intention of my observation, though; if, for instance, I resolve to draw from the things their favorable qualities, then, as a rule, it soon appears that the things which just a minute ago glared at me, start to smile and perhaps even entrust me with the sunniest aspect of their existence.[1]

This ability to change the appearance of things is certainly not possible under all conditions. There is a mood which soaks everything in a somber gloom, when the flowers have less color, and the light from the sun is nothing more than an unnecessary extrapolation of a lightbulb. I cannot succeed in changing this state of affairs very much. This is a bad day; the evil of it is primarily embodied in the unchanging unfriendly aspect of things. But there are also days when everything appears to be possessed of a new persisting light. The sun is brilliant, the colors of the flowers are unexpectedly deep, and even the smallest thing gives me its own bit of happiness without becoming in the least poorer in consequence. I cannot change this state of affairs, either.

But as a rule, things wait for our intention; they are willing. We have the freedom to make them what we wish, even if we do not often use this freedom. Before me there is a small piece of pencil which my son left on my desk. At one end it has been clumsily sharpened; the other end has been gnawed. The choice of what to make of this piece of pencil is mine. I can see it as evidence of his carelessness: why does he leave everything where it falls, why did he drop the pencil on my book so that the wet part smudged the page? It is equally possible to see this stub as an attribute of youth, which will pass too quickly, anyway; I imagine him sharpening it, his tongue between his teeth, and I can see him gnawing it. In that case I am not concerned about the smudge on the page; I hardly see it, and if I did see it, it is not inconceivable that I might draw a circle around it and write, "Here lay a gnawed, moist, and dirty piece of pencil belonging to my son," and add the date so as to afford myself a nice memory when I re-open the book in perhaps many years from now and read this memorandum, which will have been long forgotten.

But perhaps I will see entirely different things. The row of small dents shows me that my child still has his milk teeth, which I knew, of course; only I see this more clearly now, and I can examine the regularity of the impression. I wonder when his first tooth will come out, and end up reflecting about dentists. Or the color of the wood can attract my attention. I examine the pencil more closely, and when I bring the stub up to my eyes, the typical smell of pencil-wood reaches me. Immediately I am back in my own youth: I have a vague but intense memory of a stifling hot classroom with open windows, through which drifts tiredly the sound of another class singing a few rooms away from us. None of this is necessary. I can refuse the memory of my youth just as easily as I can send back the dentist who had been hiding in the stub, or I can refuse the affectionate emotion of a clumsily sharpened and gnawed piece of wood. I might want to be angry; instantly the pencil will then appear as a corpus delicti, and I do not see an image, but a compact reality. The stub is a dirty piece of wood; it smudged my clean book and it has a bad smell.

The first try

The variability of the things we observe is typical of our existence. This is what the tree of the knowledge of good and evil embodied: after man ate of it, he could see thousands of things in every object or incident. The apple tree was not just an apple tree, not just one diffuse fact which deserves but one ultimately undefined meaning. It was an infinite amount of facts; among many other things, it was a tree that gives understanding. The leap from the diffuse undefined observation to the observation of thousands of hard realities is full of dangers. For by seeing things in this manner, one can make this world a hell or a heaven; or rather, the leap from the diffuse to the multiple concrete makes the world a possible hell and a possible heaven. The leap toward the differentiated observation is the leap toward light and darkness, toward happiness and unhappiness, toward belief and disbelief; a promotion and a denigration, a becoming like God and a being infinitely far away from him. Both. God has said so Himself: "Behold, the man is become as one of us, to know good and evil." And immediately afterward, He "sent him forth from the garden of Eden." Instantly.

It has never been told of Adam and Eve before they left the garden of Eden whether they had faith or not; they had not yet arrived at that stage. But barely has man—this creature promoted to God—been expelled from Eden than he lights the first fire in sacrifice. Faith presumes a breach with God; one can only hope for His nearness, and arrange one's life in accordance with His nearness, if His distance is taken for granted.

By now I am rather getting into the dust. I think it is too dangerous to continue. Let us go in another direction.

The second try

When a person spends his vacation out of town and one day decides to go and find mushrooms, he will, without necessarily being explicitly aware of it, focus his observation on mushrooms; this means that he begs nature to show him mushrooms above all other things. Even if he is also an enthusiastic entomologist, he will still not see many insects on this particular day; many fewer, certainly, than if he had gone out to catch insects. If he is out to get dead wood for the stove, he will have no eyes for either insects or mushrooms, but he discovers dead branches which he had never noticed before. And if it should happen that his son has just fallen from a tree and broken his leg, then he will, on the way to the doctor, make the dead branches, insects, and mushrooms disappear, and will only see the bumps in the road. Never do we live in a complete world, the world pictured in a snapshot, for instance; we always live with a sort of thin net [2] over it, and most things disappear through the holes. Each time this net is thrown over reality in a different way; each time reality shows itself in a different shape.

Even when we concern ourselves with only one net, even then there are infinite series of different possibilities. The botanist, the lumberman, the pursued thief, and the tree-climbing boy, they all have, so it seems, thrown the same net over the woods, the net called "trees" (and not mushrooms, insects, deadwood, flowers, colors, gnomes, mysteries, fears, and so on); but actually they throw very different nets.[3] A certain tree seen by all four may seem the same tree photographically; but for each of the four it will be a different tree, a tree with different qualities. It may be that one of them will pass the tree without showing any interest in it at all; and that another will never tire looking at it.

It is not surprising that the transformation from simple but undefined apple [4] to desirable understanding was followed by the Babylonian confusion of tongues. No one has the same understanding: that is what the transformation means. And since words are voiced understanding, the misunderstanding is right at the door; to be exact, at the door which divides Paradise from our world. The hydraulic engineer and the girl in love may both gaze at water with undivided attention, but they should not start a discussion about what they are seeing. Unless, of course, the hydraulic engineer changes into a man in love, which means that he exchanges his net, knitted at his university, for another about which it is not so easy to decide where it was made.

To be with somebody else one has to see and hear with him. The religious person wants to be with God. He searches for God's views and he listens to God's words. Using the same figure of speech, this means that he tries to find the net that God has thrown, and is throwing, over the world. A very special net. Maybe it is no net at all, but just that over which all nets are thrown. Who can say? A net, perhaps, by the grace of which reality exists. Or maybe it is reality itself, nothing but grace; the reality which prevents all the other realities from falling to pieces?

The dust is all around me now; I will have to get away quickly. Just one question, I can just manage that. If the religious person becomes aware of God's net, will he see the miracle? Is this the miracle: God's net? It is high time to go and find some fresh air; for there is no sense in these questions. Let us try another direction.

A *third try*

"Aunt," cried out the child in the bedroom, "aunt, please say something. I am scared; it is so dark." Aunt says, "Why do you want me to say something, darling; you can't see me, can you?" But the child says, "It doesn't matter; if you talk it gets light." [5]

The child is afraid in the dark, it wants light. It is given light— light without fire, light by a word. But that is a miracle.

This is encouraging. Without our going in God's direction— and consequently being suffocated by the dust—the miracle falls right into our lap. Maybe we will find more in this direction.

And here I shall cite an autobiographical note of André Gide's. [6] It is an exceptional anecdote, indeed.

When Gide was a child, he went out with his nurse one day to pick flowers; noticing he was alone, he called out to her. She came out of the shadow of a tree into the full sunlight. He had never seen her so light and so like the summer, and it seemed to him that she was smiling at him. He asked her why she was so happy. She said, "For no reason at all; but isn't the weather gorgeous?" At that moment, writes Gide, *the whole valley became filled with love and happiness.*

It is obvious that Gide liked the nurse very much. The change in the valley proved it. I mean this literally: the valley *did* change. It visibly became filled with delight. The flowers became more colorful, the shadows grew deeper, the light was lighter, and the summer even more summery. And all this because of a few words.

This again is a miracle. Not so much because things changed without a cause—I will not say without a reason—the changes Gide saw instituted a miracle above all because in the changes he realized the nearness of another person.

I expect that many people will not accept this reasoning. Gide's observation is so entirely human, so of this world, that it can hardly be called a miracle. Is the miracle not supposed to be super-human; is it not the sudden appearance of the nonhuman, or even inhuman, in a human world? Is it not from out of this world? In the miracle God pushes aside the human world; he destroys the human world locally.[7] According to David Hume, "a miracle is a violation of the law of nature." Our world is ruled by laws essentially different from those of His sacred, supernatural, divine world.

This point of view may have had its origin in the fact that, explained in this way, the miracle ceases to be a cause for anxiety; it is located somewhere else, somewhere in the dust, or (what is actually the same thing) in supernature. When it is thus outside our existence, we need no longer reckon with it. And it is a fact that miracles are not observed anymore, they do not happen anymore; they belong, as we say, to an infantile, naive, credulous time, when the craftiness and artfulness of nature was less well understood and the gaps of human knowledge needed filling. Modern man does not have so many gaps in his knowledge, consequently there are fewer gaps to fill. He does not need miracles; the completeness of his idea of nature could not tolerate the belief in nonnatural or unnatural incidents. "It is impossible," says Bultmann,[8] "to have electric light, to have a radio set, to call in the help of modern medical drugs in case of illness, and at the same time to believe in the miracles of the New Testament." It is a modern theologist who says this, and without a doubt he is the voice of all those who consider it right—if not safe—that the miracle, this stone of offence, has been removed from our existence. We are living in a sensible world. At a turn of a button there is sound, the mechanism of which is explained in the encyclopedia only an arm's length away from our favorite armchair. There is an explanation for everything. Things that cannot be explained do not exist. The change from water into wine at the wedding at Cana need not cause us anxiety anymore; it is not necessary for this story to keep us enchanted, for the story dates from primitive times. Nothing of the miracle would have been left if the wedding at Cana had been filmed.

But neither is there anything left of the light seen by Gide. One can be absolutely certain of the fact that photographs taken before and after the nurse spoke would produce exactly the same picture. And yet Gide observed a change the memory of which remained with him through life. The statement that miracles never show up on a photograph needs the immediate amendment that a photograph never shows what we see at the most important moments of our lives, anyway. Our mental picture of our first classroom in school—a photograph has nothing to do with it. As a child, we look at the sea for the first time—no photograph can ever truly portray this moment. One day we experience the burning heat of the South of France for the first time—never can a photograph capture the vibrating landscape, which tasted like wine.

The miracle: a human occurrence

Anyone who believes that the miracle is a nonhuman, extra-human, sacred affair has placed it at such a distance that he need not worry about its untimely return—a return, moreover, which he would think highly unlawful. He has made the miracle an attribute of God—although it is obviously an attribute of man. God does not believe. To believe is our affair; we believe, and it is by our belief that the world becomes a creation, it is by our belief that God becomes present, present in the only place where we can rightly speak of His presence or His absence: in the world of substantial things, in our world. When these things give evidence of His presence, then a miracle is taking place.

It will not happen at random. One can hardly expect God, in a playful mood, to step on earth occasionally, to do a few things against the laws of nature, and then, just as unpredictably, return to his own domain (which cannot be anything but an as yet unexplored corner of the Universe). God's absence or presence cannot be compared with the absence or presence of a meteor, which comes from an undefined infinity, becomes visible for a few moments, and disappears again into infinity. There must be sense in God's becoming visible. His visibility is the nearness between man and man. There is no other nearness. When God is with us, He does not appear as a transparent ghost in the realm of the dead. He stands face to face with us as an acquaintance, a friend, a wife, a husband, or a child. Or as young Gide's nursemaid.

There are bad nursemaids too, unfriendly, heartless, selfish females. Had Gide been walking with one of them he would have experienced a different change under the same circumstances; for her words would have visibly filled the valley with childish grief and loneliness. Things would have shown God's absence. A negative miracle, the negation of a miracle, but nonetheless not less miraculous. Has it not been known since antiquity that false miracles occur? The true miracles, God's miracles, are known to reveal the nearness between man and man. Bread and wine are multiplied: this means that Jesus Christ is present and that His presence brings nearness to everyone else present. In their abundant nearness, everything becomes abundant, they cannot even finish it.

Extramundane facts

This direction has apparently led us to the goal. Without getting into too many difficulties, we have arrived with God. It is still not very clear around us—those last sentences were rather foggy. We had better be very careful as we go on. Let us now examine the miracle directly.

In most cases, the miracle is considered to be a fact or occurrence unconnected with the observer. A fact to be observed like any other fact. Cardinal Lepicier said, "The miracle is a fact, and as such it is an object of experience." [9] A fact, however, which in one respect is essentially different from other facts, in that it does not belong to the realm of daily facts (which we usually call natural facts), but instead belongs to the essentially different realm of the supernatural. God is supposed to intervene in the daily facts and insert a fact of another nature. The miracle is "a supernatural fact and under that aspect it belongs to the invisible world; it presupposes a divine intervention." [10] Such a definition is apt to provoke unchecked daydreaming. For instance:

One morning I open the door of my study, and as I enter the room I see nothing out of the ordinary. But when I proceed to my desk, I find myself looking at Job, Job from the Old Testament, sitting behind my desk in the most deplorable rags imaginable, and with a body that would attract my medical attention if I were not transfixed and incapable of anything except boundless amazement. I try to fight this amazement by assuming that somebody must be making a fool of me, for I can see no other comprehensible reason. But then, just as I have restored the natural order of things with this thought, and as I am about to take the necessary steps, there goes Job—into the air, chair and all, to remain floating, halfway to the ceiling. The steps I intended to take fade away. I am witnessing a miracle. My last doubt is removed when Job blows out through the closed window, and with a benevolent gesture sails through the expanse of heaven to disappear through a hastily opened doorway of clouds—while my chair, with a thundering crash, falls back in its customary place.

This is a slightly blasphemous daydream. And yet, is it not equally blasphemous to assume that a statue would deign to twist its stone lips into a smile for the benefit of a few devout souls? Every miracle, as defined by Cardinal Lepicier, is necessarily blasphemous, because it irresponsibly, arbitrarily, willfully, and therefore insultingly interrupts God's creation, which in itself, as a human abode, is the expression of a great magisterial miracle.

Invaded nature

This aspect of the miracle was illuminated by C. S. Lewis simply and clearly in his book, *Miracles*. He writes:

> If we open such books as Grimms' *Fairy Tales* or Ovid's *Metamorphoses* or the Italian epics, we find ourselves in a world of miracles so diverse that they can hardly be classified. Beasts turn into men and men into beasts or trees, trees talk, ships become goddesses and a magic ring can cause tables richly spread with food to appear in solitary places. Some people cannot stand this kind of story, others find it fun. But the least suspicion that it was true would turn the fun into nightmare. If such things really happened they would, I suppose, show that Nature was being invaded. But they would show that she was invaded by an alien power.[11]

As long as nature remains what she is, such things do not happen. Miracles are against nature, they are facts *contra naturam*, as the time-honored definition has it.

Contra naturam

But whether the miracle is a fact *contra naturam* depends ultimately on our conception of nature. If nature is understood to be the reality of science—in other words, a reality distilled from the other, total, general, daily reality by a narrowly circumscribed, uncommon, acquired, and in every way artificial, point of view—then, indeed, miracles involve things so far removed from their common nature that they can no longer show the presence of God. If Gide's valley is seen as a geological cleft in a geographical landscape with atmospheric influences and a classified vegetation, no change caused by words will ever be observed. God has been removed from reality so thoroughly that it is impossible for Him to appear. If within this conception of nature God is still expected to appear, it will have to be assumed that He can appear as a physical fact among other physical facts, as a child for instance: as the child Jesus, who plays between the oak tree and the maple tree, and who can be approached in the same biological way as the trees can be approached. Believing in the miracle in this way is actually not believing in it. For in the first place, reality—which is, above all, a realization of our understanding with God—has been reduced to a system of scientific facts; this means that God has been removed from this reality. And in the second place, if He is then, after all, requested to reappear in this reality, which has become foreign to Him, in the shape of an "objective" fact among other "objective" facts, then this means that God dies. The conception that the miracle is *contra naturam* does not only mean that, as a miracle, it disrupts nature; it also implies that the miracle which appears in the resulting cleft shows itself as a (pseudo) natural, (pseudo) physical, and (pseudo) chemical fact. Belief in the miracle, as defined by Cardinal Lepicier, is belief in (pseudo) science.

Spoiled facts

Lepicier mentions the miracle in which the Messiah walked on the surface of the water as if it had been solid earth. He then states that this miracle can be interpreted in two ways. Either Jesus Christ had ordered the water to assume its solid state, so that as ice it could support His body; or else he achieved another state of His own body, a state without weight, so that it would not sink in the water.[12] There is no other possibility. But these words show that the miracle has been made adequate to nature. The miracle has been made a fact like any other fact, with only this difference, that it is an abnormal fact. It is a spoiled fact. For how else can we consider ice that is not ice, or a body without weight?

Credibility of the miracle

The person who believes in the walk on the water in this way, does not actually believe in a miracle; *he believes in a spoiled nature.*

The belief that Christ walked over the surface of the water originates in the belief in which this walk occurred. Matthew comments on it sufficiently. The disciples were in danger, their ship was in a dangerous storm, it seemed that they would be wrecked. They could not reach the coast because of a land breeze. And this was not a neutral coast, it was their own land, the country where their master resided. In their difficulties they were with Him. That was their faith; that they were with Him. In this belief the miracle happened. So much were they with Him, so strong was their belief in Him, that Christ came to them. There is nothing supernatural in this. Everyone has experienced what happened. If I should be with you in this way, dear reader, you will have come here. That is the secret of all thinking, and of all longing: bringing the other person or other thing near. Of course you can remain in your chair, I don't care; I am thinking of you, and you will come. When Christ came to them, and as they saw Him more clearly, they went to Him with new hope. Peter even left the boat.

What? we will ask. Did he just step over the side? And then we are caught in Lepicier's argument. The question is not really fair. It does not matter whether Peter stepped over the side or not. It does not matter whether he left the ship or not. Because he did. There is nothing supernatural in it. When I am with you, dear reader, I said a moment ago that you will come to me; but it is entirely impossible to say where we are going to meet. At your or at my home? Either is equally true—and equally untrue. If I am thinking of you, I am thinking of you where you are, even if I do not know you; at the moment I am thinking of you I am still to be found at the place (unknown to me) where you (stranger) might happen to be. But I am still at my place, and I have not even stopped writing.

It is quite clear that geography does not play a role in the world of a person who says: "I shall be with you tomorrow evening," and the person to whom he says this happens to be in a train which will depart for Switzerland in a few minutes. And yet he is not lying. This is realized by the one who hears these words, who is probably eagerly listening. It is realized even more strongly by this person the next day, in the evening, at the hour she knows the other person is thinking of her; she even becomes quiet because of it. One would not expect her to sit down and write, "You said you would be here tonight, but I don't see you. I should have known you couldn't be here, for I knew that you couldn't get on the train." Of course not. Such a letter would be a no-confidence motion in respect to the affection expressed in the honest promise, "I shall be with you tomorrow evening." It is just as much a no-confidence motion in Peter's faith to ask whether he stepped over the side. Peter was with Christ. When Christ came to him in the turbulence of the sea, he went to meet Him. But no sooner does he believe in the storm around him more strongly than he does in Christ, than he almost drowns. Christ saves him by an even greater nearness. He reaches out His hand and says: Why do you doubt me? "Tomorrow evening," says the man on the platform to his beloved, "tomorrow evening I shall hold your hand." It is so believable, this belief.

Contra miraculum

But I must admit that the combination of belief and credulity has a bad reputation. We are so used to combining belief with nonhuman or antihuman affairs, that connecting the miracle with our daily existence, as was usual in the middle ages, does not sound very convincing. It is said that the miracle belongs to a super-natural, and not to our natural, daily existence. But what is the nature of our existence if it does not contain the (so-called) super-natural as well? What would our life be like if it had no part in that other life, which the word supernatural threatens to estrange from us? Maybe our life is even mainly this other life, just as nature, which we see around us, is mainly the "other" nature, nature in its original meaning of "that which was born," a fact of creation, a fact of a world which exists only with God's attention. In our belief this attention becomes apparent; the world gets its shapes so essentially belonging to it, things are shaped, created; it is in this world that the miracle takes place. First comes faith in the world as a creation; then comes the observation of the miracle. The miracle is not *contra naturam*; it is the nature of the *contra naturam* world which is *contra miraculum*.

The miracle as the habitual nature of things

One cannot think too "naturally" about miracles. When the Jews arrived at the barrier of the Red Sea shortly after their exodus from Egypt, "Jehovah caused the sea to go back by a strong east wind all the night and made the sea dry land and the waters were divided." [13] This was a completely natural occurrence, which derived its miraculousness from the faith of Moses and his followers. It is this faith that says, "And the children of Israel went into the midst of the sea upon dry ground, and the waters were a wall unto them on their right hand and on their left" [14]—but a photograph would have made nothing of it.

And one cannot think too humanly about it either. When Jesus Christ came to Nazareth, He "could there do no mighty work." [15] Jesus was not surprised about His lack of power, nor about nature in Nazareth, which, like a modern landscape, left Him no opening for His supernatural interference; but "He marvelled because of their unbelief." [16] Our belief is the condition of the miracle. Without our belief, apparently, no miracle can happen; the miracle is present in our belief, it is the habitual state of things.

One need not change the usual aspect of things to experience miracles constantly. If, however, our disbelief has chased away this aspect, if it has denaturalized things to "natural" facts, then nothing like a miracle will ever be seen. "The miracle occurs to the extent to which our belief is concerned with it." [17] If we believe in God's nearness—that is, if we believe in the nearness of man—the miracle is there; but if we consider the miracle apart from anything else, if we take it out of its environment, if we disconnect it from the belief of which it is a condition, if we put it in front of us as a fact with the intention of finding an answer to the question of questions in this way, the question "Where is God?", then we have driven out His presence, we will have made the glory of things evaporate; and in our hands is left unshaped matter, matter dating from before the creation. God is near for those who believe; disbelief results in His absence.

I could finish this chapter now. The miracle has been saved; it need not disappear, it only had to get rid of a perturbing shape. Perhaps the reader is of a different opinion; but I am well satisfied. I was even able to end this discussion with a rather dusty observation, without disturbing the dust too much. It was not even necessary to drag eschatology (this Cartesianism with a negative prefix) [18] into the argument. It gives me satisfaction that a few passages from the Bible even found their way in without too much difficulty, and that Mark's communication provided a satisfactory ending to the argument.

And yet—are all the considerations that have been discussed in this chapter wrong?

Actually it is strange that the Evangelist was so honest. He says that Jesus, who is God, could do there no mighty work, although he is omnipotent. Does this mean his power can be compared with the power of the hypnotist, who makes a whole audience shudder with cold while actually it is rather warm? The hypnotist can only do this because the audience believes in him. Why does Mark make this comparison so easy? He might have known that disbelief would jump at it. The more I think of it, the more it amazes me that the Evangelist did not use other words. He could just as easily have written: Jesus did not mind performing miracles, but the people who lived there were not worth it. Or, more theological: In Nazareth Jesus' second nature showed itself; there He was a man, and not God. Or, without any comment: He did not perform miracles in Nazareth. What on earth could have moved Mark to write: "He could not do it, because they did not believe in him"?

Innocent honesty

It could only have been his honesty that made him write this. Mark was an honest man. An exceptionally honest man; he did not even want to use a *pia fraus*, which really was not hard to find. He was honest, and because of his honesty he stayed out of trouble; while we stare at one of the most amazing texts in the Bible, he writes on as if there were nothing wrong with what he said.

And there was nothing wrong; that is the only explanation for the serenity of Mark's words. The words which harden our disbelief, which even lead to disbelief, must have been entirely without danger for him. Nobody saw anything extraordinary in this text; I do not think another explanation is possible. The reality of the miracle was so beyond all question—for those who believed, as well as for those who did not—that this text could not be mis-understood.

It is as if today someone says, "Last year I was in Spain and I was very thirsty; I asked everybody I met for water, but nobody understood, I couldn't make them understand." No one would, as a result of this story, doubt the reality of words as a mean to convey understanding. For the thirsty man the means was unsound because he did not speak Spanish, and the Spaniards did not speak any other language. He used a lot of words, he did express his need clearly enough, and yet nothing happened. The Spaniards must have looked at him with bewildered expressions. So, more or less, must the people of Nazareth have looked. They did not understand Jesus; that was their disbelief, and that is why nothing happened. The reality of the miracle is not affected by it.

What reality? What is the reality of the miracle? Just now I thought I knew, and now it seems more obscure than ever. The reality of the light in the spare bedroom? The reality of the sun and the colors in the valley for the two who were gathering flowers? If it had been this reality Mark would have written in a different way, for then what he did write would have been too dangerous. Actually, if he had meant this reality, his story would have been wrong altogether. Then he would have written: Jesus did perform miracles, and we saw the miracles, but *they* could not see them because they did not have faith. But instead he wrote: He could not perform miracles, nothing happened. But then have I been wrong? Are miracles "natural facts," after all? Facts among facts? Miraculous facts? *That* is the way they are related in the Gospel.

When the wedding party in Cana ran out of wine, Jesus had the jugs filled with water. The organizer of the party did not know of the experiment, which was Jesus' first miracle. (I am not quite ready for it, He said to Mary.) Then, when the party-giver tasted it, he said, "We should not have left this wine to the last, for it is the best we have had." This story is either founded on physical facts, or it is made up. It does not seem necessary to cite more examples. Metaphors violate the Bible. Another spirit is coming toward us.

The changing character of the miracle

It is such a different spirit that I could not take back anything I said in the first part of this chapter, however much I should want to. The miracles of our time are subtle miracles. Apparently God is not allowed to show Himself in any way except the way that things appear to us; not in the things themselves. And it is quite clear why. The things have suffered so much from the treatment of many ages, that the damage cannot be undone, not even by God. Especially not by God, because the damage is His absence. The only thing God can still do is to put Himself "against" the substratum of things; He can pretend, and pretending, He can bring back to our minds a past that was more glorious, more real. A past of a fair reality, which tolerated God, and in which He walked in and out. One said "Good morning" to Him, and if there was not enough bread, He made some. Nobody said He could not; for the laws of this inability had not yet been invented. Do you believe in this, dear reader? I do not; but I wish I did. You do not either; but you wish you did. Our belief is of another sort. We believe in each other—and we say that there is no other belief. We believe in what we see—and we say there is nothing beyond it. And if we are honest, we really cannot do anything else.

It is difficult to see it any other way. If we should believe in miracles now, miracles in the spirit of the Gospel, if we should see them as "facts," "facts of reality," we would not sleep at night because of the injustice. An innocent man has been brought to a concentration camp. A slight offence enrages one of the guards, who hangs the prisoner from a tree by his hands, and then slices his skin in strips. It gets warmer; flies come down on his bloody body, and his wounds become infected. After a few days the man is nothing but purulent pain; but he is still alive. Nothing happens. The man is religious; he prays for deliverance. Nothing happens. Not a trace of a miracle. Set this against the wedding party in Cana which by a miracle got more wine.

I know that every theologist will point out that the miracle is supposed to have had the character of a token; the miracle meant fulfillment, it referred to ultimate victory. But who can leave it at that if he sees this dying man? Could not there have been one miracle less in the Bible, and one more here, there where the man is hanging? And besides, would it not be a wonderful token if the man who hangs there writhing in extreme wretchedness stands a moment later completely cured. What a token!

But to believe in a miracle, now, is blasphemy. Because God cannot do it anymore. He cannot help the poor devil. Or should we think that He could, but does not want to? That is what I meant by blasphemy. He cannot do it. We have made it impossible for Him. He has said goodbye to us, as it were. He has said: "If I do not belong to it anymore, you will have to do it yourselves; I shall stay out of it." That is why our "doing" is so successful. That is why miracles do not happen anymore. But they once did.

CHAPTER 5

The subject and his landscape

Projection

I began the previous chapter with the assurance I would not make use of projection. By doing that, I made it difficult for myself. The theory of projection solves the problem of the miracle with these few words:

The person who sees a miracle thinks he is seeing it; in reality, he does not see anything. He only sees an inner occurrence, something taking place in his soul; an occurrence, however, which he imagines, which he throws out of his inner self, which he "projects," which he apparently manages to move from his inner world into the outer world so successfully that he is no longer able to identify it. He is the victim of a delusion. The reason behind the delusion is not hard to find. The person who sees a miracle lacks something, he needs something; and he tries to fulfill this need, by making up a fulfillment and then forcefully throwing his fantasy into the outside world. For what is outside is real, is convincing. Inside there are only fantasies, glimmering unreality.

What is inside is not convincing. The party in Cana were not satisfied with the quantity of the wine; they imagined another few jugs, threw out this fantasy, and drank more wine—although in "reality" they did not have a drop more than before.

The person who prays does the same thing. The man who prays does so because his subjectivity longs for compassion, and no one gives him any; so he imagines someone who consoles him, and then throws out this fantasy. Or it is courage that he lacks, and nobody gives him any words of courage; so he finds the words himself and puts them in an Almighty's mouth. He makes Him almighty, and he makes Him speak.

And the same is true for the person in love. The beloved's qualities are actually only frustrated wishes and their compensations, inconveniences of the lover's inner self, dust traps in his superego; he throws these out of himself, into the air, and through the air to the other person, who almost sinks beneath the burden.

Metaphysical tricks

How does this lover do it? How does he manage to cut the subjective knots away from the network of his inner self, to separate them from it, to smuggle them through the metaphysical curtain which envelops his inner self, to push them into the free air, to throw them over the other person, to fasten them so thoroughly that the other person changes, changes to such an extent that the projector accepts these changes as real, so that actually he loses sight of reality? How does he perform these metaphysical tricks? The theory of projection is never entirely clear about it. The theory suggests understanding, although understanding is never so absent as in its own procedures. No one understands these procedures—which nonetheless are used by everybody. Why? Why is it that we do not see the lack of understanding implicit in this theory, and why do we value the understanding it does not contain? What necessitated this theory? For that must be the solution: the theory of projection must have been a necessary theory, because if it were not, everybody would object to its obvious faults. In this chapter I intend to answer the question of why the theory of projection is necessary.

Remembrance

In a chapter of his diary, published in 1953, Jean Cocteau described what happened to him when he was walking down the street on which a large part of his youth had been spent. He had been in the neighborhood before; but a vague diffidence, known to us all, had restrained him from going further and looking at his old house. But this time he did enter the porch of the house, and in a few moments he was in the back yard. He saw that the trees had grown higher, and he was trying to identify other changes, when a suspicious voice asked him the reason for his presence. His honest answer could not convince the man, and after a few minutes he found himself back in the street. Cocteau, who did not want to lose the charm of his past too soon, recalled the way he used to walk through the streets and on the pavement. He remembered that he used to walk close to the houses, trailing his finger along the wall.

Who did not do that, when he was a child? The gates were a special attraction; hand and finger would leap from one spike to the next. The porches involved the delightful necessity of climbing the steps; the finger then traced the panel on the door; one was almost assimilated by the unknown behind it of which sometimes the smell reached us. No porch, no door, no gate was neglected. We would not have dared to forget even one of them, convinced as we were that the silent reproach or the dumb complaint of the one we forgot to touch with our finger would come down on us. The obligation made us bold. Sometimes the porches were very deep— they have never been so deep again—and very occasionally we even had to force ourselves bravely into long dark passages which implied unexpected and, in our eyes, dangerous incidents. But we had to; the door at the end of the walk was relentless. A child feels compassion for forgotten things. If he is to feel every tree along the road, then it is impossible for him to leave the lone tree, far to the side, devoid of his benevolent touch. We lose this compassion. We no longer believe in the aliveness of things and consequently we are deaf to their entreaties. The habit of tracing the unevennesses of the walls with one's finger gets lost. We don't do it anymore.

But Cocteau did. Thinking of the past, he trailed his hand along the wall. But he was not satisfied with the result; he felt something was missing. Suddenly it became clear to him what was wrong: he had been smaller as a child, his hand had touched surfaces which he missed as an adult simply because he was drawing a different line. He decided to repeat the experiment, but this time he bent down. (In Paris one can do such a thing.) He bent down, closed his eyes, and let his hand trace the wall at a height which had been natural in the days he went to school. And immediately appeared what he had vaguely been expecting. "Just as the needle picks up the melody from the record, I obtained the melody of the past with my hand. I found everything: my cape, the leather of my satchel, the names of my friends and of my teachers, certain expressions I had used, the sound of my grandfather's voice, the smell of his beard, the smell of my sister's dresses and of my mother's gown." [1]

The wall or the brain

Cocteau's notes oblige us to ask: where did his memories come from? This question will not be received with ease, for we have become used to the idea that we cannot localize the psychic. There were times courageous enough to do it; in the previous century, for instance, it was held that the psychic was localized in the brain—in the gray matter, in the white matter, in the liquor, in the blood vessels of the brain, depending on the particular interests of the anatomist. But no one ever found anything in the least psychical. They did find cells, fibers, blood, and brain liquor. And since then they have given up, consoled by the assurance that the psychic is spaceless and consequently need not be localized. This assurance was only a flattering unction to the wounded soul, though. For we do live in space, and there is no psychical, nor even spiritual, affair which does not enact itself in space. In which space? That is exactly the question which occupies us at the moment: where were the memories which Cocteau managed to recover? First they were not there—Cocteau searched for them in vain—and then they were. Where did they come from, and where were they at the moment of their reappearance? By all means these are justified questions!

Questions to which there seems to be but one answer: the memories recalled by Cocteau were stored in his brain, but he could not reach them. When he found them again, it was because he was admitted to them; his finger and the wall had provided him with the key, that is all. To remember means to go back to the impressions of the past which are stored within us. The actual penetrates through the doorways of our body and reaches the brain where it is stored. Memories are within us, within our inner life; what else can this mean but in our brain? The evidence is before us: if a disease, a degeneration of the brain in old age, for instance, or a lesion of the brain, damages certain parts of the brain, remembering becomes more difficult or even impossible. Whole years of memories may vanish in this way. Without brain, no memory; this conclusion is undoubtedly correct, just as correct as the famous conclusion that without phosphorus thinking is impossible. Yet phosphorus is not the thought itself, it is only a condition. A necessary condition, certainly, but just as adventitious. Without vocal chords, no speech. Yet the vocal chords are not speech itself. Speech is possible because of an understanding, a verbal understanding which utilizes lungs and vocal chords. In the same way a memory utilizes physically engraved memory traces; in the same way thoughts utilize phosphorus, and the evening walk uses the leg muscles. When we are trying to remember something, says Jean Paul, we feel "how we are urging our brain to co-operate." [2] "Please help me," cries out the person who wants to remember to his brain. "Please help me; I should like to do it by myself, I could almost do it by myself, just give me one grain of retained remembrance and I will make it a memory." The person with the damaged cerebrum calls out in vain; he can remember all right, but his brain does not co-operate, it refuses its slight but necessary assistance. And a paralysed person can walk: *he* can do it, but his legs leave him in the lurch.

And so does the dead person live; *he* can live all right, if only his body would co-operate. He waits for a new body to serve him.

Cocteau did not write, "When I traced the wall with my finger the memory awoke in my inner self," although he might have put it this way if he had wanted to express himself psychologically. Nor did he write, "When I traced the wall, I was admitted to the engrammes in my brain," which is what he would have said if he had had a preference for an obsolete neurology. What he said was, "Just as the needle picks up the melody from the record, I recovered my memory. My finger picked up the melody of my youth—*from the wall*." The question about the localization of the memory has thus been answered: the memory was in the wall, even if engrammes had to lend their assistance for Cocteau to recover them.

We must be reasonable, though. Doesn't Cocteau's observation belong to those many, unreflected, ready, more or less poetical and therefore not very scientific, observations which may be impressive because of their originality, but which cannot stand a closer examination? "The memories are within the wall"; does this mean anything, or is it just a peculiar way of saying things? For a wall, one has to admit it, contains just a few memories as—brains, for instance. A wall is made of bricks, is it not? Memories are made of another matter. What *sort* of matter remains a problem. Certainly not of brain matter; but even less of the matter handled by bricklayers. Let us make Cocteau repeat his experiment, but pay more critical attention this time to what the wall—the wall of the bricklayer—has to say.

The test

Let us assume that Cocteau, impressed by the seriousness of our words, repeats his crouched walk. We have arranged for him to be accompanied by one of us who does not share his belief in the presence of memories in the wall. It is quite certain that Cocteau will rise up after a few steps and say, slightly annoyed, that he does not discern anything like his original perception. What he feels is a wall, a windowpane and a cellar window;

bricks, wood, and iron—nothing else. No memory of any kind can he wring from the wall, only a little dust. His companion—and every one of us, with only a very few exceptions, with him—feels satisfied with this result. What happened the first time, he would lecture Cocteau, was identical with what happened just now. Then the finger did not pick up anything, either, merely a few tactile impressions of a neutral character. But these impressions were conducted to a sensitized apparatus. Hadn't Cocteau just been turned out of the domain of his youth by a suspicious janitor? He was still under the spell of his returning memories, the spell of his affected engrammes. His brain was in a certain state of excitement. He wished to continue this agreeable sensation, and in this mood he walked along the houses; he made them "pregnant." Only then were the tactile impressions able to realize what had been expected. It was by association that his finger's observations reawakened the memories which had been stored in his head.

A *private wall, or everybody's wall?*

Cocteau will have listened to all this without much comment. I dare say that he would consider the psychology present in the arguments of his companion an extraordinary science. An unfriendly science. For does not this experience make him one illusion the poorer? For that is what he would have to call his first impressions—illusion. Before the test he might instead have spoken of a reality, a hard pungent reality, for the impressions almost overpowered him. Whichever it is, no one would expect Cocteau to repeat his experiment; this test has proved *conclusively* to him that his finger does *not* pick up melodies, but soot and chalk. The wall has been spoiled.

Or rather, the wall has been saved. The wall, touched by Cocteau when he was accompanied by his critical companion, is *our* wall. We all find soot and chalk on it. Isn't this what the observations of his critical companion ultimately implied? Was he not trying to get Cocteau out of his subjectivism, to deny him his subjectivism? It is not permitted to own a wall all by yourself, is what the companion meant to say; the wall is our common property. This must be what he meant to say, nothing else; for the other things he said were not true.

Impermissible truth

I think Cocteau would have discovered it for himself after a few days. Thinking back about what had happened, he would have wondered whether he had been robbed of an illusion, or, perhaps, of a real and true reality. If it were only an illusion— so he might think—if I only picked up projections and chalk from the wall, then it must be possible to find the memories by myself just as well, or even better; and yet I cannot. "Intro- spectively" I am not able to recover this memory, which took me by surprise, and which suddenly struck me by its intense feeling of reality, there on the pavement. What I can recover introspectively has no more than a slight resemblance to what happened on the pavement. My introspectively recovered memo- ries are bare and lifeless; they are the skeleton of my memory, no more than that.

This argument is flawless. Cocteau was perfectly right when he wrote that his finger picked up the memories from the wall as the needle picks up music from a record. But it is unper- missible. What he should have done, as a modern man, was to move his memories to his inner self, hidden them with his physical shape. He should have written, "When I touched the wall—which is the same wall for everybody and which has nothing to do with anything human—tactile impressions, re- corded by the sensitive organs of my fingertips and transmitted by the nervous system connecting these organs with the brain, excited my brain's engrammes, which in their turn conveyed the memories they contained to my consciousness. Then I fooled myself and everybody else who read my diary; for instead of keeping my memories within my inner self, I removed them from my person and put them on the wall." No one would ob- ject to this confession; for Cocteau would not have robbed any- body of a wall with these words. He would have left the wall what a wall should be in our day: a wall of bricks and plaster, a series of chemical formulas, our common property. The human element is within us; it is nowhere else. The world is not contaminated with anything human; it may *seem* to be contaminated with it, but the theory of projection shows up the true nature of the contaminations: they are misplaced sentiments.

Was this theory invented to guarantee an identity of the world for everybody, or, perhaps more accurately, to put a stop to an ever-increasing subjectivity of the world? Is it its task to save things from individualism, and to make them accessible to everybody? Again we are confronted with the question which dominates this book: What has happened, then? Has a universal feeling of relatedness with things been lost? Have things become "adrift," have they been drifting away from "us all" to such an extent that intervention was necessary to keep them for "us all"?

I shall show the way to the answer to these questions by discussing a simple case history.

As a child, this patient did not share in the pleasures of other boys. He did not climb trees with them, he did not swim in the river with them, he did not jump from one cake of ice to another with them, and he did not annoy adults. This last pastime he even thought improper; and he was supported in this opinion by his parents, who taught him respect for his elders and who told him that climbing trees, swimming in the river, and jumping on ice floes were dangerous, much more dangerous than, for instance, playing the violin, which for this reason they recommended particularly. He did play very well indeed, this boy; but that was less surprising than some visitors implied, for he spent all his time playing. He had a callous on his chin from playing the violin, but his skin was soft everywhere else; the palms of his hands were smooth and rosy like the hands of a sick person, and there were no scars on his knees. When he grew up he started to notice these differences with other boys, who could use their hands, and who knew the way. It used to make him sad; but he dispelled his sadness with the sound of his violin and after a while he was no longer aware of his misery. He played and played and did not notice other people. When he had to choose his life work, his parents had known for a long time what he wanted to be and they wanted it with him. He would go to the conservatory; he had a great future as a violinist. But in order to be admitted to the conservatory, he had to play for an expert.

That is nothing to worry about, said his parents, and the boy agreed. Nonetheless he was anxious about it, and when the day had come he was sick with nervousness. He did not eat, he did not drink, and he made excessive use of the toilet. In the train he felt miserable, and when he met the expert he was so confused that he needed some time to recover himself. He played rather spasmodically at first, but gradually he felt more at ease, his courage returned, and finally he played as if he were at home, gravely and with great skill. The expert listened and looked at him; he looked at him closely, and he understood, he understood much more than the player suspected. When the boy put away his violin, the expert told him that he had played very well. "You have been studying very hard," he said, "your technique shows how hard you must have worked, but . . . it does not show real talent. Go on playing," he added, "but if you will permit me to give you advice, do not come to the conservatory."

What else the expert said, the boy could not remember. Nor did he remember how he left, and how he found his way to the station. He came home feeling dazed. His mother said, "What is wrong with you?" for he was very pale, and he fell in a chair exhausted. "What is the matter?" He felt sick. He did not even answer his mother's question whether he had been sitting in a draught in the train. When she asked him what the expert had said, he vomited. "You are ill," she said, "you had better go to bed." She made him a hot-water bottle, she gave him an extra blanket, and she took his temperature—which was normal. The next day he was no better; he was even worse; he could not eat and he could not walk. It seemed as if his legs were paralyzed. "I thought something was wrong with his legs," said a neighbor who had seen him come home. "He walked like a cripple." The doctor was called in.

"What is wrong with you?" asked the doctor. The boy told him that he felt ill. "Since when?" "Only since yesterday."

"What happened yesterday, did you eat something that didn't agree with you?" "No, nothing particular had happened." "Well," said the doctor, "take off your pyjamas and we will have a look." But the examination showed nothing. The doctor made out a prescription and told the mother he would be back the next day—for those paralyzed legs intrigued him. "Did nothing at all unusual happen to him?" he asked the mother. "No," she said, "he had to play at the conservatory, maybe he caught a cold in the train." "Any success?" asked the doctor. "No," said the mother, "actually he had been ill before he went. He had been to the toilet at least six times." "Send me some feces and urine," said the doctor.

The feces were normal and so was the urine. The doctor could not find anything wrong, but the legs remained weak and the boy still felt ill. After a week the doctor called a neurologist and told him that he had a case that had him puzzled: a boy who, on the fifteenth, had diarrhea in the morning, who came home from the train barely able to walk, and who had had paretic legs ever since. His reflexes were normal, temperature normal, sedimentation rate normal. Would the neurologist look at him? The neurologist came and listened to the story. He examined the patient carefully, but he found nothing wrong. "When did it start?" he asked again. "The fifteenth," answered the patient, "during the morning." He remembered, since his mother had talked about it a few times, that he had had diarrhea in the morning. "Where did you go?" asked the neurologist. "I had to play for an expert, for the conservatory," said the patient, "but I did not do very well, I felt sick." That was what his mother had said, and he agreed with her. By this time the patient was hardly able to stand on his legs. The neurologist could not do anything about it while the boy was home; and as the symptom seemed rather serious, he recommended hospital treatment.

In the hospital it became clear that the patient was physically sound. His legs improved a little, but he still could not walk. The nurse, however, reported that the mother treated him like a baby, and the son accepted this treatment. Considering these factors, the neurologist began to suspect another connection, and called in a psychiatrist. He reported the results of his examinations and laboratory findings, and said that in his opinion, on that day, the fifteenth, the patient must have had the disappointment of his life.

The psychiatrist approached the patient in a way which immediately set him apart from all the other doctors. The patient showed slight surprise, but he got used to it very soon and briskly answered every question. But when the psychiatrist asked him, "What did happen at the expert's?" the patient said, "Nothing," and his expression got taut. "They told me you were not admitted to the conservatory." The patient could not deny it, but said he had been ill at the time. "How did you feel when you left him?" "Terrible," answered the patient. "It was as if the houses were falling down on me. And the people were so strange. Everything was strange and horrible—I don't know how I managed to get to the train." "And how did you get home from the train?" "I don't know," said the patient. "I don't remember, everything was strange."

"But," went on the psychiatrist, "weren't you very disappointed to hear that you were not admitted to the conservatory?" "I guess I was," said the patient, "but I was sick—and I can always try again." (That is what his mother had said.) "When are you going to try again?" asked the psychiatrist. The boy didn't know; as long as he was ill he need not think of it. When the psychiatrist asked him whether he didn't long for his violin, the patient was surprised to discover that he was not interested at all in his violin; he preferred not to think of his violin, it made him sick.

A *not unusual story*

To prevent any misunderstanding I am going to interrupt myself to emphasize the fact that this is not at all an unusual story. Every psychiatrist has a few cases among his patients whose histories are, in general terms, not unlike the one related here. It might, moreover, not be inappropriate to point out that the doctor and the neurologist did their work conscientiously. The reader knows the story hidden behind the conversations; the doctor did not, he had to grope in the dark, he was even intentionally led astray—or so it seems. By far the majority of patients come in with obscure stories. If their stories were transparent, "right," they probably would not have needed to consult a psychotherapist. Their "right" story would prove that they belonged to the group to which the psychiatrist belongs, that is, that they belonged to "everybody"; the very fact that they are patients means that they stand alone. They are estranged even from themselves, from that part of their inner self which belongs to the other people: their daily self. They live in a constant self-deception.

As for the patient whose problems we have been discussing, this self-deception is so obvious that a layman would be inclined to expose it immediately. He would say, "Listen. There's nothing physically wrong with you, so it must be mental."

Nobody can escape from the logic of this conclusion, not even the patient. Even if he does feel physically ill, even if he cannot stand on his legs because of his paralyzed muscles, he must believe in the results of a conscientious examination. And as he cannot doubt the generally accepted dichotomy of the human existence either, he can only locate his disease in the "psyche"— even if he can hardly realize what it embraces. The reason the patient nonetheless secretly persists in believing that it is his body that is ill is that the conception of the human body which the doctor (and every informed layman with him) has at his disposal is not the one accepted in daily life.

"It is a neurosis. You were spoiled by your parents, and you put up with it. You are an impossible person. They talked you into playing the violin, and you put everything you have into it. It would have been much better if you had romped with your friends a bit more. Do you have friends? No? Do you have a girl friend? No? You are married to your violin. But you have no talent; that is what the expert said. When he told you you are not very good, it was the first sensible thing you heard for years. You came home without a violin, but with no illusions, either. And now you are in bed with an inferiority complex."

It is true, every word of it. But the patient replies, "No, no,

it is not true. It is not that. I do understand; but it is not that."
And then he is silent. And so is the other person, for he has
fired his last shot. He may think, "It's impossible." Maybe he will
even say, "How can you possibly fail to see it?" But the patient
very definitely cannot see it. The man says, "I shall come again."
The patient says nothing. And when his mother comes and
asks him whether he has had a nice talk, he says, "I don't like
that man, I don't want to see him again." "But what did he say?"
asks his mother. "He said I was pretending." The mother is
astonished at such a lack of understanding.

The neurotic's and the normal person's understanding

She does not know that the psychiatrist shares this lack of
understanding, for he is very careful not to give his opinion. The
patient would not accept it anyway; he would find him offensive
and he would stop seeing him. If the psychiatrist sees him in the
hospital, the patient would leave the hospital, and he would tell
everybody for years to come that nobody was able to understand
him.

What is perfectly obvious to anybody else is obscure to the
patient. I have given this discrepancy enough attention above.
The patient does not belong to "everybody," so he is unable
to share everybody's opinion. He has to say no to this opinion. He
could only say yes to it if he began to belong to everybody. The
psychiatrist realizes this; his task is to break through the isolation
in which the patient has been caught. For the time being he is
not going to bother with what has happened at the expert's;
nothing could be gained by that.

There is another side, however, to this odd and so usual misunderstanding between the neurotic and the normal person. The
patient says, "My legs are paralyzed." The normal person says,
"Your legs are all right." The patient says, "The houses seemed
to fall down on me, the city looked horrible, and the people were
strange." The normal person says, "The houses were as straight
as ever, the city was normal, and there was nothing wrong with
the people; the only thing that was wrong was your inner self,
your subjectivity, your 'psyche.' Everything else was a mistake."

Yet the patient is thoroughly convinced of the reality of the irregularities. He is not able to walk; he can hardly find a stronger proof for the correctness of his point of view. He still remembers the impression the city made on him. Of course he does admit that it is odd to have an impression which is not shared by anybody else, but he is still convinced that if he dared to go out, this same impression would almost kill him. No reasoning can diminish the force of that one moment's impression. The houses were slanting forward, the streets were horrible, and the people were really strange. The person who suffers from agoraphobia shrinks back from the overpowering aspect of public places, while the normal person never gives it a thought. To the neurotic the reality of his disturbances is irrefutable.

What is the meaning of this misunderstanding between the neurotic and the normal person?

The expert's words

The expert had said, "You have no talent." With these words a significant change took place. The patient became pale, he swayed on his legs, there was a mist before his eyes, and a rumbling emptiness within himself. He stumbled down the stairs, he looked aghast at the houses, walked through horrible streets to a horrible train, and from this horrible train walked home, feeling horribly ill. There he crept into a reasonable bed. How could the expert's words have instituted these changes? This can only become clear if we understand the significance of the expert's words. And that, in its turn, can only be understood if we realize what the violin meant for this boy. What did the violin mean to him before he went to the expert? What had made him pour all his energy into it, even though he had no talent? The answer is obvious; he had been compensating for a deficiency. He did not play the violin because he felt attracted to it, he played the violin because deficiencies pushed him into it. Especially when he had grown a little older and compared himself with other boys of his age, he realized (in whatever way) that he had to excel in something if he ever wanted to be able to stand comparison with them, that is, if he wanted ever to belong to them. His violin was his membership card. If he met a cousin at a family reunion who by comparison made his insufficiency more obvious to him, he had always had something to which he could secretly refer; his violin. He had something, too; *he belonged to them.*

The expert ended this. He said—in soothing words—you have no talent. With these words he had torn the membership card to shreds. The patient fell out of the totality to which everyone else belonged, and he found himself alone. He had fallen out of their world. And immediately another world made itself known to him, a miserable world, a very lonely world. A world of his own. He saw the houses slant, he thought that they would fall down on him. The world was falling to pieces—on him. The streets were unreal, the people were strange—estranged from him. So awful was this world of his own that he could not walk in it, his legs gave way. And when he was asked, "What is wrong with you," he answered, "My legs won't work, everything around me is so horrible." Wasn't he right? What he said was quite true.

A *necessary correction*

He did not say anything about his inner self. In this aspect the patient is like us. If we are asked how things are, we answer, Fine, I feel fine; work is all right, I have nice friends, a nice house, and so on. We mention exterior things. Nobody ever talks about his inner self. Neither does the patient. I feel bad, he says, the streets glare at me, the people are strange and my legs are paralyzed. From ourselves we accept an exterior description, but not from the patient; from him we want an interior description. If he is to indicate how bad he feels, he is supposed to speak of an inferiority complex within himself, of a struggle for power within himself, or of a battle raging between different agents *within himself*. That is what we should be satisfied to hear. If he begins to talk about his paralyzed legs, and about the streets and the houses, we feel annoyed and we leave him; what he says is not true.

For where would we be if we granted any individual a right to have a world of his own? A world in which everything looks different, a world in which things have another substantiality? Soon there would be more and more people who would demand the same right. Things must retain their stability, they are the condition of our understanding. Even more than that, they are understanding itself. Things may no longer be able to provide an understanding with God, but that cannot be helped. Actually, things barely provide an understanding between man and man; they provide only a minimal understanding, an understanding at a minimal human level, which is, however, the maximum understanding possible. They provide an understanding of the utmost factuality, and this must be retained. No one is allowed to take it away from us, not even the patient. If he were, our common existence would fall to pieces.

Minimal understanding

What must be retained is the understanding contained in the words from one bricklayer to another: "Give me that brick, will you?" One bricklayer's brick is the other one's brick. And their brick is our brick. This brick must not be lost; but a poorer understanding could hardly be imagined. A far richer understanding, for instance, is the one achieved between two travelers who look with wonder at an old church, and who start to talk about what they see, about those bricks. On the other hand, perhaps it is a good thing that this second kind of understanding is disappearing. It is too dangerous, it demonstrates a lack of understanding too easily. How readily can one imagine a third person who might hear the whole conversation without understanding a single word. We are so fragmented and classified into so many vague, large, autonomous groups that if we wished to retain these richer forms of understanding, we would all wrap ourselves in fatal confusion. We believe—for our own protection—in only one brick; we maintain the poorest, the easiest, the least dangerous sort of understanding; and everything else—again for our own protection—is called projection. We are compelled to believe in the sort of brick that will allow us to feel together. And it is our need to feel that we belong together that made us reduce it to this sort of brick.

If this is true, then it is quite clear that the patient cannot be permitted a brick—or a street, house, city, train, or nature—of his own. He must be projecting; what he sees are his own personal impurities. It is not the brick that is impure; that is only an appearance. The fact that the patient is driven to bed by the brick he sees—which means that an aspect of reality is simply pushing him aside—is not permitted to impress us. We smile reassuringly and say, "You are projecting, what you are seeing is within yourself."

"But there is nothing within myself, I do not know of anything within myself." Of course not; his knowledge is contained in the brick, in the houses, in the city, in the train which brought him home. We sweep all this knowledge together and we bring it to him. "It has to do with you," we say—for otherwise our world would stagger.

"But I am really not aware of anything within me," the patient will protest weakly. Then we become very serious and we say with irrefutable authority, "In that case, it is in your subconscious."

The body and minimal understanding

And yet, the patient is right. Like Cocteau, he can refer to the insuperable character of his observations. His doubts—the doubts we are forcing upon him—disintegrate when they are set against the reality of his experience. So great is this reality that he is driven to bed by it. In the long run, however, his doubts will grow and grow. The solemnity of the doctors and of everybody around him will make him believe gradually he is suffering from a diseased inner self—and not from the evil which actually is the cause of his suffering, the evil of living in an individual, extremely lonely world. The thing he will cling to longest is the disease of his body; apparently the character of reality of a physical disease is hardest to invalidate. That the houses did not really change is a fact which the patient may be inclined to believe, even if this belief is denied every time he goes outdoors. But to believe that his legs are not really paralyzed—no, he cannot believe that. He cannot use them, he feels for himself that they are weak—isn't that enough evidence? The body is the last refuge of the disease from which the patient is suffering, a disease which has us all in its grip, but from which we escape by rigorously impoverishing our understanding. A brick is a brick, the patient will accept that. But a leg is a leg—that is, as yet, another matter altogether.

The factualization of our understanding—the impoverishment of things to a uniform substantiality—and the disposal of everything that is not identical with this substantiality into the "inner self" are both parts of one occurrence. The inner self became necessary when contacts were devaluated.

When did this happen?

If a rather vague determination in time would do, it might be enough to point out the difference between St. Augustine's *Confessions* and Rousseau's. Gusdorf has called attention to this difference in his book, *La decouverte de soi.* Augustine, believing that the approach to himself is an aspect of his relation to God, wishes to speak of God and not of himself; Rousseau means to speak of the self of the individual, the "self" which is of significance because of itself. Augustine has no knowledge of this self, he does not know the self of this self-satisfied individualism; Rousseau points out, at the very beginning, that he will only concern himself with the description of the individual, himself, *"moi seul,"* Rousseau. "When the trumpet of the last judgment will sound, I shall come to present myself before the supreme judge with this book in my hand. I shall say in a loud voice: In this book is written what I have done, what I have thought, and what I have been. I have told the good things and the bad things with equal honesty. I have neither subtracted anything from the bad, nor added anything to the good." [3] These bold words would have been entirely alien to Augustine. But, in his turn, Rousseau had no idea of the boldness which later times would add to his. If he had lived today, Rousseau could not have left it at that. If he wished to appear before the supreme judge as an honest man, he would have had to add: "And in the folder in my other hand you will find, Oh, Lord, the result of an accurate psychological examination." Perhaps he might even have added, with a humble inflection of his voice, "After me comes the psychiatrist who analyzed me; no doubt he will be able to fill in all the gaps in my thoughts and actions." There is no essential difference between Rousseau's words and these later additions.

Luther

Is it possible to determine the birth date of the inner self with greater accuracy? I will try. I shall discuss a few historical events which occurred between 400 and 1770 A.D. and put forward suggestions about connections between them. This reconnaissance will also be based on Dilthey's book, *Auffassung und Analyse des Menschen im 15 und 16 Jahrhundert*,[4] which emphasizes Luther's part in the personification of religion and its disappearance from public life.

In his essay "About the Freedom of a Christian" (1520), Luther made a distinction which became exceptionally significant. He distinguished the "inner" man from the outward and physical man. He needed this distinction, for he intended to dissent from a wrong conception of religion in order to assume a religious life which, to his mind, was more pure. Luther preferred the inner man, for the external and physical man is concerned with extraneous and physical things and is suspect for that reason. Luther had come to recognize extrinsic things as appearances and deceptions. "It is no help for the soul whether the body is wearing holy robes, as priests and clergymen do; neither does it help the soul whether it appears in churches or in holy places, nor whether it touches holy things." All this is of no importance; an evil man can do all these things just as well as a good man; any dissembler or hypocrite can. Consequently, it does not harm man to wear unholy clothes, to enter unholy places, and to touch unholy things; all this is of no importance. What is important is the inner man, the soul; for the soul has faith, the soul hears the word, and knows it must retain it. "The soul can do without anything except God's word, and without God's word it has no use for anything. But if it has God's word, it does not need anything else; in the word it has pleasure, food, gladness, peace, light, art, justice, truth, wisdom, freedom, and an abundance of other good things."[5] Man can do without all extraneous matters; the only objective thing he needs is God's word.

Lessing and Schleiermacher

But this state of affairs did not last. Lessing, two hundred and fifty years later, doubted even this last extrinsic necessity. In his *Axiomata* he asks the question whether man can have faith without knowing God's word; he ultimately answers this in the affirmative.[6] The evidence of faith, which after all is faith itself, depends on an inner experience. This idea, cautiously put forward by Lessing, was developed fully by Schleiermacher, who, in his *Dialektik*, wrote that God is not given to us immediately, and that we have only understanding of God insofar as we are God ourselves, which means insofar as we have God within ourselves.[7]

Faith is not action had been said by Luther; action appeared to him to be contaminated with the objects involved in the action—the clothes, the candles, the relics. But Luther had clung to a faith that was knowledge, knowledge of something (there is no blind knowledge), knowledge of an extraneousness: the Word. Schleiermacher drops even this knowledge. "Faith is neither knowledge nor action; it is a trend of feeling, or a trend of the undividable self-consciousness," [8] is what he wrote in his *Theory of Faith*. The phrase, "a trend of the undividable self-consciousness" is especially significant; according to Schleiermacher, faith is a directly given quality, there is no need for an external intermediary. Faith is a matter of the inner self, an absolutely inner quality. And although these remarkable texts do not always agree with other texts of Schleiermacher's, these words do complete the transference of faith to the inner life. Anyway, the nineteenth century took the transference of faith to inner life more and more seriously; and the psychology of religion shows that by the beginning of this century, faith threatened to become a quality belonging entirely and only to the inner life.[9]

The necessary inner life

Luther was driven away from things because he had grown to suspect them. He knew how wrongly they could be used and how they were able to absorb a dangerous religiousness. The things he saw in Rome had filled him with amazement; that, apparently, was the meaning of the holy robes, the holy places, and the holy objects. His bewilderment is identical with ours when we see what the neurotic makes of things. And so is his reaction. We say: The world is a substratum, solid matter and nothing else; anything else that could be said about it is a human creation, projection. Luther said: The robes, candles, and relics are matter, nothing else; anything else that is said about it is a human creation, vanity. Luther did not know the word, projection.

Anything else that could be said about the world is projection because we will not and we cannot do without objects as means of understanding. Anxious to avoid a new Babel, we would rather reduce things to an extreme poverty. Was Luther moved toward just such a devaluation of extraneousnesses because he too feared a loss of understanding? Did Luther transfer things to a hastily constructed area called the "inner self," because his contemporaries were escaping from an all-embracing totality and were threatening to come adrift? One remembers how much against a rupture he was. "Do not leave each other," was what, after all, his aversion toward candles and robes meant. "Let the objects become poor—so long as we can stay together." But he had come too late.[10]

A smiling inner self

In the year Luther published his treatise on freedom, Da Vinci died. He left a canvas which portrays visibly the turn from outward to inward. Da Vinci's *Mona Lisa* and Luther's manuscript are essentially identical.

It is well-known how Da Vinci's contemporaries came, curious to see the smiling woman. The interest continues to our day. Why does she smile? What makes her smile so eloquent—and so secretive? What is it that she is confiding to us and keeping from us at the same time? No one who looks at this painting can escape these questions.

Her smile seals an inner self. Her contemporaries came to see her because they could behold a new way to live. They could see the face of later generations. What they saw was the inner self, although they did not know it—the secret inner self, the inner world in which everything the world has to offer is shut away. And a smile watches over this inner self. Mona Lisa holds that which is known, and she hides it. After this, that which is known will be that which is hidden, that which is unknown. And as time goes on everything will be within her, at once known and unknown. In Rilke's words, she is the first who "contains within herself all that is human."

At the same time she is the first (it is unavoidable) who is estranged from the landscape. The landscape behind her is justly famous; it is the first landscape painted as a landscape, just because it was a landscape. A pure landscape, not just a backdrop for human actions: nature, nature as the middle ages did not know it, an exterior nature closed within itself and self-sufficient, an exterior from which the human element has, in principle, been removed entirely. It is things-in-their-farewell, and therefore is as moving as a farewell of our dearest. It is the strangest landscape ever beheld by human eyes.

"This landscape," said Rilke, when he tried to put into words what is contained in the mountains, the trees, the water, and the bridges behind the smiling woman, when he wanted to express what all this lack of horizon implies, "This landscape is not the portrayal of an impression, it is not the judgment of a man on things at rest; it is nature coming into being, the world coming into existence, unknown to man as the jungle of an unknown island. It had been necessary to see the landscape in this way, far and strange, remote, without love, as something living a life within itself, if it ever had to be the means and the motive of an independent art; for it had to be far and completely unlike us—to be a redeeming likeliness of our fate. It had to be almost hostile in its exalted indifference, if, with its objects, it was to give a new meaning to our existence." [11]

A growing inner self

Today the inner self has an impressive history. Rousseau was certainly wrong when he began his confessions with the words: "I am going to attempt something that has never been done before and will never be attempted again." [12] He was right as far as the first part of the statement was concerned; in the matter of form, the description of a solitary inner self, his confessions were a novelty. But as to the second part, history has certainly proved him wrong. In comparison to the inner self which came into existence after him, his was insignificant and poor. James Joyce [13] used as much space to describe the internal adventures of less than a day than Rousseau used to relate the story of half a life. The inner self, which in Rousseau's time was a simple, soberly filled, airy space, has become ever more crowded. Permanent residents have even been admitted; at first, only the parents, who could not stand being outside any longer, required shelter, finally it was the entire ancestry. As a result the space was divided, partitions were raised, and curtains appeared where in earlier days a free view was possible. The inner self grew into a complicated apartment building. The psychologists of our century, scouts of these inner rooms, could not finish describing all the things their astonished eyes saw. It did not take them long to surpass Joyce, and their work became endless in principle. The exploration of one apartment appeared to disturb another; and if the exploration moved to the next place, the first one again required attention. Something fell down or a threat was uttered; there was always something. The inner life was like a haunted house. But what else could it be? It contained everything. Everything extraneous had been put into it. The entire history of mankind had to be the history of the individual. Everything that had previously belonged to everybody, everything that had been collective property and had existed in the world in which everyone lived, had to be contained by the individual. It could not be expected that things would be quiet in the inner self.

The landscape

Almost unnoticed—for everybody was watching the inner self—the landscape changed. It became estranged, and consequently it became visible. In April, 1335, Petrarch climbs Mont Ventoux near Avignon, and was surprised and delighted at the view; he was seeing the landscape behind Mona Lisa, the "first landscape." But he apologized, afraid of having earned God's wrath; what he saw was Luther's robes, the jewels of Savonarola.

Four hundred years later Rousseau lay the foundation for the great change. The first observations on what since then has been called a "sense of nature" are contained his *Confessions* of 1728.[14] That this is not coincidence is quite clear now. In the *Nouvelle Héloise* (1761), the emotion felt upon observing Nature was completely described. Like an epidemic the new sensation spread through Europe. Every one wished to see what Rousseau had seen, to experience the same ecstasy. Everybody visited Switzerland and climbed the Alps. This had not happened before Rousseau.[15] It was then that the Alps became a tourist attraction. Previously they had been an obstacle; a walk through the mountains had had few delights; the views were not in any way exceptional. Even in 1750, Hénault, a poet and a friend of Voltaire's, crossed the Jura and the Alps without the least enthusiasm, merely observing, "There is always a creek at my side and rocks above my head, which seem about to fall in the creek or upon me." [16] These words would nowadays disqualify him as a poet—besides compromising his claim to be a human being.

Yet the estrangement of things, which brought Romanticism to ecstasy, belongs, for the most part, to the past. Many of the people who, on their traditional trip to the Alps, ecstatically gaze at the snow on the mountain tops and at the azure of the transparent distance, do so out of a sense of duty. They are only imitating Rousseau; they are simulating an emotion which they do not actually feel. It is simply not permissible to sigh at the vision of the great views and to wonder, for everyone to hear, whether it was really worth the trouble. And yet the question would be fully justified; all one has to do is see the sweating and sunburned crowd, after it has streamed out of the train or the bus, plunge with resignation into the recommended beauty of the landscape to know that for a great many the trouble is greater than the enjoyment. To a few the landscape is still delightful. But hardly anybody feels the delight is so great, so overpowering, that he is moved to tears.

For things have moved further away from us so that today they reveal the distance far more than the emotion that goes with it.

Petrarch was delighted; his delight was caused by his seeing a reduction. (Otherwise he would have seen nothing.) Rousseau was deeply moved; his emotion was the sort felt by a mother when her child goes out alone for the first time. Rousseau and Petrarch made us believe that theirs was a discovery of something worthwhile, of a valuable matter which people for some inexplicable reason had never seen before. That their discovery was the discovery of a loss only became apparent in the twentieth century.

The complete inner self and the completely estranged exterior

Modern psychology became possible because of an interiorization of all human realities. The interiorization founded a new domain: the inner self; psychology is its science. And of this science Freud is the undisputed master.

In 1915 (the date is significant), Freud expressed the following thoughts.

"We assume," he wrote, "that the human being has a certain amount of love, called libido, which, at the beginning, while remaining within the borders of its own self, is directed at its own self. Later on in the development, actually from a very early state on, this love detaches itself from the self, it aims itself on things outside, which are therefore, in a way, incorporated within us. If the things get lost or if they are destroyed, the love or libido which we had attached to those things, will become free again. This love can then aim itself on the things that took the place of the first things, but it can equally well return to the self. It appears that the latter is painful. Why it should be painful, why the detachment of things causes suffering, we do not understand; we are, as yet, unable to infer the painfulness from anything. What we see is that the libido clings to things, and that it does not want to give up things even if good substitutes are ready for it. This is the grief, the sadness, about the perishing of things and of people." [17]

These words could not be clearer. The *fons et origo* of the human existence is the libido; energy of the inner self. Nothing would seem more natural than that this energy remain close to its original source, within the I, within the subject. However, it does not happen this way. The energy partly detaches itself from the I and conveys itself to outside objects. The objects themselves are of secondary importance in the human existence; they remain foreign to it, and ultimately they are of no significance at all. If the objects get lost, the libido attached to them can be transported to other objects; or, if this is not feasible, it can return to the source from which it originated. If this is what happens, the libido will come home, and one is inclined to expect some satisfaction from it. Against all expectations, however, there is no satisfaction at all; on the contrary, there is suffering, mourning, and sadness. Why this suffering, mourning, and sadness? It is an enigma. "Suffering and sadness is a great mystification to the psychologist."

This is a painful remark. Sadness because of things lost—it cannot have been exceptional in the Vienna of 1915. Did the psychologist understand nothing of this grief?

Ultimately the enigma of grief is the libido's inclination toward exterior things. What prompts the libido to leave the inner self? In 1914 Freud asked himself this question—the essential question of his psychology, and the essential question of the psychology of the twentieth century. His answer ended the process of interiorization. It is: the libido leaves the inner self when the inner self has become too full. In order to prevent it from being torn, the I has to aim itself on objects outside the self; ". . . ultimately man must begin to love in order not to get ill." [18] So that is what it is. Objects are of importance only in an extreme urgency. Human beings, too. The grief over their death is the sighing of a too-far distended covering, the groaning of an overfilled inner self.

"The alarming thing is," he said, "that this time it isn't only the changeable things that are changing, but the unchangeable as well. Anyhow, that's the danger—even for me. Not only dress and manners and bank balances and the social order, but the sea and the sky and—Westminster Abbey."

"Westminster Abbey?" the girl repeated.

"That and Gray's country churchyard," he answered. "The sea, the sky . . . not only the sky and the sea are in question. The song of birds, firelight and sunlight, the woods, the turn of the seasons, the earth itself and the smell of it, the whole natural magic going on behind our little journey from the cradle to the grave. Well," he said, "you have to choose. What are they? Are they still what they have always been: the perspective of our mortality and, for some of us, an emblem or at least an analogy of our immortality? Or have they become, as it were, infected by our impermanence? Are they little more than a stage-setting to our personal and social drama? It's a question of relationship and of our view of that relationship. Are we related to them at all, as mankind has always supposed? Is the earth that we touch a part of ourselves, or has it become just a thing we walk on, like a pavement? Are we becoming, in our consciousness, separated from the stars— as indifferent to them as we are to the electric chandeliers in the lounge of an hotel? Are we being driven, or driving ourselves, into exile from the unity of nature? It is a simple question." [19]

The answer to this "simple question" is less simple. What I have said about it here is not nearly enough. Not only because my historical review was hasty, and I could therefore only point out isolated incidents, but primarily because the answer from the present, the answer from the middle of the twentieth century, is lacking. The answer is important; it inaugurates the recovery of a fatal separation.

Epilogue

"Man arrives at every age of life as a novice." [1] This thought has never been popular in psychology. Starting from the postulation of unchangeability, the psychologist prefers to locate the adventures of life in a far past, so that he can describe life as a "development," as an unfolding of endowed potentialities. The continuity created in this way is the continuity of remembrance. As we look back on life, it seems to have flowed gradually, without anything new happening. But life itself deals with what is coming; it looks into the future and is curious.

The same is true for the historical past. Looking back, we see the history of a race, or of mankind, as continuous, one era gradually following another; historical personalities only acted as necessity made itself known to them. But at that moment when history is being created, everything is uncertain. Nothing is necessary. Historical persons act, they are not driven. The course of history is in the hands of a few bold men. History is the history of the great men, [2] of great deciders, and consequently of the bearers of a great responsibility.

In this book we have looked back many times; for us the past had to appear as continuous, for to look back means to make continuous. If, however, we could transfer ourselves to the past, that is, if we could make the past present, if we were to try to understand the meaning of words and actions when they were not yet changed by what happened afterward, things would appear in a different light. Then we would catch our breath, and we would discover with satisfaction or with horror that decisions were made this way and not otherwise. This is the state of mind that I wish the reader to assume when he is present with me in the room in Ulm, anxiously following what happened in that room, and finally mourning its outcome. It was not really *necessary* for Descartes to give objects the meaning of extensiveness, thereby making them equal and laying the foundation for the continuity of things.

It is in this state of mind that I wish him to go with me into Breuer's consultation room, where he follows, full of curiosity, the demasking of hypocrisy. This matter could have turned out quite differently. And in this state of mind the reader will catch his breath when he finds Freud, in the desperation of the moment, turning away from the present, where the cause of his patients' illnesses was located, to the past; and thus making them suffer from the past and making our existence akin to their suffering. It was not necessary.

I wish the reader to realize that historical psychology, as a science of changes, leaves no room for historicism. It may seem as though it does, since the historical psychologist has to look back now and then; however, the continuity, which is the result of his looking, is broken up because he puts himself in the historical situation with the emotion adequate to that particular situation. Descartes was excited when he saw the beginning of a new science, Breuer was far from dispassionate when his patient was drinking her glass of water, Freud was, according to his own words, desperate. Scientific discoveries are emotional discoveries. And it is this emotion which gives the true evaluation of the scientific judgment: reasonable emotion.

References

CHAPTER 1

1. In 1878, Wilhelm Wundt opened the first psychological laboratory. Stanley Hall founded the first psychological laboratory in the United States in 1883. From then on laboratories were added to every psychological institute.

2. *Mein Weg zum Chassidismus*, included in *Die Chassidischen Bücher*, Schocken, Berlin, 669.

CHAPTER 2

1. "Nostre enfant est bien pressé: il ne doit au pédagisme que les premiers quinze ou seize ans de sa vie; le demeurant est due à l'action. Employons un temps si court aux instructions nécessaires. Ce sont abus; ostez toutes ces subtilitez espineuses de la Dialectique, dequoy nostre vie ne se peut amender, prenez les simples discours de la philosophie, sçachez les choisir et traitter à point: ils sont plus aisez à concevoir qu'un conte de Boccace. Un enfant en est capable, au partir de la nourrisse, beaucoup mieux que d'apprendre à lire ou escrire." Montaigne, *Essais, Livre premier*, ed. by Garnier, 175–176. What was meant by *"discours de la philosophie"* before Descartes' time was explained by Montaigne himself. He wrote that a child benefits from hearing: ". . . what God has ordained you to be, who we are, and to what purpose we were born." And: ". . . what is knowledge and what is ignorance, what is aimed at by studying, what is the difference between a craving for fame and a craving for wealth, the difference between servitude and servility, and between licentiousness and freedom." And: "How to live well and to die in the right way." And so on, all this under the title *"discours de la philosophie."* As is apparent, he meant mostly subjects of ethics; without exceptions, however, these are subjects we prefer to spare our children.

2. *Some Thoughts Concerning Education* (1693).

3. "Raisonner avec les enfants était la grande maxime de Locke; c'est la plus en vogue aujourd'hui: son succès ne me paraît pourtant pas fort propre à la mettre en crédit; et pour moi je ne vois rien de plus sot que ces enfants avec qui l'on a tant raisonné . . . Le chef d'oeuvre d'une bonne éducation est de faire un homme raisonnable: et l'on prétend élever un enfant par la raison! C'est commencer par la fin." J. J. Rousseau, *Émile ou de l'éducation*, 1762, ed. by Garnier, 71.

4. "La nature veut que les enfants soient enfants avant que d'être hommes. Si nous voulons pervertir cet ordre, nous produisons des fruits précoces qui n'auront ni maturité ni saveur." *Ibid.*, 73.

5. "Employez la force avec les enfants et la raison avec les hommes; tel est l'ordre naturel: le sage n'a pas besoin de lois." *Ibid.*, 74.

6. "Qu'il sache seulement qu'il est faible et que vous êtes fort; que, par son état et le vôtre, il est nécessairement à votre merci; qu'il le sache, qu'il l'apprenne, qu'il le sente." *Loc. cit.*

7. That Rousseau wants to keep this authority emphatically implicit is connected, in my opinion, with the greater vulnerability of the child, which was beginning to appear even then.

8. ". . . ce moment de crise, bien qu'assez court, a de longues influences." *Ibid.*, 236.

9. "La psychologie de l'adolescence est un beau sujet d'étude, mais il est aussi neuf que beau. Une page fameuse d'Aristote, il y a deux mille ans, et maintenant treize cent pages de M. Stanley Hall; et dans l'entre-deux rien ou presque rien." G. Compayré, "La psychologie de l'adolescence," *Revue philos.*, LXI (1906), 349. Quoted by P. Mendousse, *L'âme de l'adolescent*, Paris, ix.

10. "Dès quatre ans accomplis, le père lui amende de Paris un précepteur, Jean Costin, homme astorge et impiteux qui luy enseigna les lettres latines, grecques et hébraïques à la fois. Cette méthode fut suivi par le père Gion, son second précepteur, si bien qu'il lisoit aux quatre langues à six ans. . . . A sept ans et demi il traduisit, avec quelque aide de ses leçons, *le Crito* de Platon." *Mémoires de Théodore Agrippa d'Aubigné*, Paris, 1854, 4–5. This autobiography is written in the third person.

11. "Il répondit que l'horreur de la messe lui ostoit celle du feu." *Ibid.*, 7.

12. Mme. Périer-Pascal, Blaise's sister, reports in her *Vie de Pascal*: "Mon père lui dit, en général, que c'étoit le moyen de faire des figures justes, et de trouver les proportions qu'elles avoient entre elles. . . . Mon frère se mit à rêver sur cela à ses heures de récréation, et étant seul dans une salle où il avait coutume de se divertir, il prenoit du charbon et faisoit des figures. . . ." *Oeuvres Completes de Blaise Pascal*, Hachette, Paris, 1887, I, 2. This note seems so unbelievable that later critics doubted its authenticity. See, however, F. Strowski, *Les pensées de Pascal*, Paris, 1930, 12.

13. *Johann Heinrich Jung's (genannt Stilling) Lebensgeschichte, Eine wahrhafte Geschichte von ihm selbst erzählt*, Deutsche Bibliothek, Berlin, I, 57.

14. J. H. Campe, *Allgemeine Revision des genannten Schul- und Erziehungswesens*, Wolfenbüttel, 1786, V, 94–95.

15. Campe does say that he is speaking of the children "*unserer verfeinerten*

Stände," but he does not differentiate them into one group able to cope with the adult material, and another group unable to do so.

16. As far as the arts are concerned, child prodigies are an exception to this rule. I will not go into the reasons for this in this book.

17. N. Elias, *Ueber den Prozess der Zivilisation*, 1937, I, 244. The anecdote is taken from the very readable *Memoirs* of Hortense de Mazarin, published in Cologne in 1675 (in this edition, 11).

18. H. Bergson, *Essai sur les données immédiates de la conscience*, Alcan, Paris, 1888, 124.

19. François Villon (born 1431), *Ballade des dames du temps jadis.*

20. Edmond and Jules de Goncourt, *Journal*, 19-I-1865: "Comme le passé s'évapore! Il arrive un moment dans la vie où, comme dans les exhumations, on pourrait ramasser les restes de ses souvenirs et de ses amis dans une toute petite bière, dans un bien petit coin de mémoire." Cited in G. Gusdorf, *Mémoire et personne*, 1951, I, 281.

21. According to Freud, the disappearance of most of our youth memories is caused by censoring of our passions, which could be freely expressed in our first years of life. ("Starke Mächte als der späteren Lebenszeit haben die Erinnerungsfähigkeit der Kindheitserlebnisse gemodelt, dieselben Mächte warscheinlich, an denen es liegt, dass wir uns algemein dem Verständnis unserer Kindheitsjahre so weit entfremdet haben." *Zur Psychopathologie des Alttaglebens*, Chapter IV.) In Halbwach's opinion, youth memories are inaccessible to adults because the adult way of thinking is socialized. The child exists outside the adult community; it has experiences and thoughts which could not possibly penetrate into the social state of adulthood. M. Halbwachs, *Les cadres sociaux de la memoire*, 1925.

22. M. Proust, *A la recherche du temps perdu*. The first book, *Du côté de chez Swann*, appeared in 1913.

23. *La vie quotidienne*, Hachette, Paris.

24. Eileen Power, *Medieval People: History as Shown Through the Daily Lives of Ordinary People, Chosen to Illustrate Various Aspects of the Social Scene of the Middle Ages*, 1924.

25. "Carlyle was a voice crying in wilderness. Today the new history, whose way he prepared, has come. The present age differs from the centuries before it in its vivid realisation of that much-neglected person, the man in the street, or (as it was more often in the earlier ages) the man with the hoe." *Ibid.*, 12.

26. At the same time, only what is discontinuous is communicated. Stable communities have no history; there is nothing to be told. The past is an impeded past as soon as there is something worth telling. And the same is true for the life of the individual. The person who leads an exciting life does not remember easily. The agitation so typical of the neurotic can barricade the past.

27. Power, *Medieval People*, 167.

28. "Pour donner une idée de l'état où se trouvait alors mon esprit, je ne puis mieux le comparer qu'à un de ces appartements comme on en voit aujourd'hui où se trouvent rassemblés et confondus des meubles de tous les

temps et de tous les pays. Notre siècle n'a point de formes. Nous n'avons imprimé le cachet de notre temps ni à nos maisons, ni à nos jardins, ni à quoi que ce soit. On rencontre dans la rue des gens qui ont la barbe taillée comme au temps de Henri III, d'autres qui sont rasés, d'autres qui ont les cheveux arrangés comme ceux du portrait de Raphaël, d'autres comme du temps de Jésus-Christ. Aussi les appartements des riches sont des cabinets de curiosités: l'antique, le gothique, le goût de la Renaissance, celui de Louis XIII, tout est pêle-mêle. Enfin nous avons tous les siècles, hors du nôtre." Alfred de Musset, *La confession d'un enfant du siècle*, 1835, ed. Garnier, 35.

29. Margaret Mead, *Male and Female*, London, 1950, 187.

30. *Loc. cit.*

31. Charles Darwin, *The Voyage of the Beagle*.

32. The title is, *Principles of Geology, Being an Inquiry how far the Former Changes of the Earth's Surface are Referable to Causes now in Operation*. The first volume appeared in 1830, the others between 1830 and 1833. The letter fragments are from *Life, Letters and Journals of Sir Charles Lyell*, Murray, London 1881, I, 169, 199, and 234.

33. Leibniz, *Nouveaux Essais sur l'Entendement Humain*, 1704; in the Flamarion edition of 1920, this quotation is on 422.

34. "Les enfants n'ont souvent de plus redoutable ennemies que leur parents." Lenba, "La famille nevrotique," Revue française de psychoanalyse, 1937.

35. With these words André Gide quotes Oscar Wilde: "La nature imite ce que l'oeuvre d'art lui impose. Vous avez remarqué combien, depuis quelque temps, la nature s'est mise à ressembler aux paysages de Corot." Gide, *Dostoievsky*, 142. The quotation is a condensation of Wilde's discussion on the changeableness of nature. Also see Oscar Wilde, "The Decay of Lying," *The Works of Oscar Wilde*, Collins, London, 909.

36. René Descartes, *Discours de la Methode*, Deuxieme Partie (1637). Ed. Gilbert, I, 20.

37. Emile Brehier, *Histoire de la philosophie*, II, 1, 54.

38. Descartes, *La Géométrie*, ed. Cousin, 428. ". . . en matière de progressions mathématiques, lorsqu'on a les deux ou trois premiers termes, il n'est pas malaisé de trouver les autres."

39. Descartes, *Principes de la philosophie*, par. 36. "Nous connaissons aussi que c'est une perfection en Dieu, non seulement de ce qu'il est immuable en sa nature, mais encore de ce qu'il agit d'une façon qu'il ne change jamais."

40. Pascal, *Pensées*, fragment 77, ed. Brunschvicq. "Je ne puis pardonner à Descartes; il aurait bien voulu, dans toute sa philosophie, se pouvoir passer de Dieu; mais il n'a pu s'empêcher de lui faire donner une chiquenaude, pour mettre le monde en mouvement; après cela, il n'a plus que faire de Dieu."

41. This excellent distinction is borrowed from the psychologist, G. T. Fechner. Also see his *Die Tagesansicht gegenüber der Nachtansicht*, Leipzig, 1879.

42. See Julien Green. "Cette grosse bête, le canon, me tuera peut-être sans m'avoir convaincu pour cela qu'il existe, alors que quelques notes de Bach semblent soutenir le ciel. Que la lourdeur triomphe en Europe, ce ne sera

jamais qu'une atroce apparence. La vrai demeure hors de toute atteinte." *Journal*, I, 49.

43. ". . . etwas, das der Vergrösserung, Verminderung, der Verschiebung und der Abfuhr fähig ist und sich über die Gedächtnisspuren der Vorstellungen verbreitet, etwa wie eine electrische Ladung über die Oberflächen der Körper." *Die Abwehr-Neuropsychosen*, 1894, *Gesammelte Werke*, I, 74.

44. Freud, *Drei Abhandlungen zur Sexualtheorie*, 1905, *Gesammelte Werke*, V, 117–118. "Wir dürfen nun glauben, dass im interstitiellen Anteil der Keimdrüsen besondere chemische Stoffe erzeugt werden, die vom Blutstrom aufgenommen die Ladung des Zentralnervensystems mit Sexueller Spannung zustand kommen lassen." . . . "Wir bilden uns also die Vorstellung eines Libidoquantums . . . dessen Produktion, Vergrösserung oder Verminderung, Verteilung und Verschiebung uns die Erklärungsmöglichkeiten fur die Beobachteten psychosexuellen Phänomene bieten soll."

45. J. Hughlings Jackson, "Croonian Lectures on the Evolution and Dissolution of the Nervous System," *The Lancet*, 1884. The observations on hallucinations and delusions can be found in *The Lancet*, April 12, 1884, 652.

46. Herbert Spencer, *An Autobiography*, 1904, I, 89.

47. Spencer does not mention God, he only speaks of miracles.

48. Leon Bloy, *Le fils de Louis XVI*, 1900. See also Leon Bloy, "Textes choisis," *Le cri de France*, Fribourg, 1943, 195. "Il est remarquable qu'à une époque où l'information méticuleuse est devenue la sorcière du monde, il ne se rencontre pas un individu pour donner aux hommes des nouvelles de leur Créateur. Celui-ci est absent des villes, des campagnes, des monts et des plaines. Il est absent des lois, des sciences, des arts, de la politique, de l'éducation et des moeurs. Il est absent même de la vie religieuse, en ce sens que ceux qui veulent encore être ses amis les plus intimes n'ont plus besoin de sa *présence*. Dieu est absent comme il ne fut jamais. . . . Cette absence est devenue l'un des Attributs de Dieu."

49. Dietrich Bonhoeffer, *Widerstand und Ergebung, Briefe und Aufzeichnungen aus der Haft*, 1952, 240–241. "Gott als moralische, politische naturwissenschaftliche Arbeitshypothese is abgeschafft, überwunden; ebenso aber als philosophische und religiöse Arbeitshypothese (Feuerbach). Es gehört zur intellektuellen Redlichkeit diese Arbeitshypothese fallen zu lassen bzw. sie so weitgehend wie irgend möglich auszuschalten. Ein erbaulicher Naturwissenschaftler, Mediziner etc. ist ein Zwitter. Wo behält nun Gott noch Raum? fragen ängstliche Gemüter und weil sie darauf keine Antwort wissen, verdammen sie die ganze Entwickelung, die sie in solche Notlage gebracht hat. . . . Und wir können nicht redlich sein, ohne zu erkennen, dass wir in der Welt leben müssen—etsi deus non daretur. Und eben dies erkennen wir—vor Gott! Gott selbst zwingt uns zu dieser Erkenntnis. So führt uns unser Mündigwerden zu einer wahrhaftigen Erkenntnis unserer Lage vor Gott. Gott gibt uns zu wissen, dass wir leben müssen als solche, die mit dem Leben ohne Gott fertig werden. Der Gott, der mit uns ist, ist der Gott der uns verlässt (Markus 15, 34)! Der Gott, der uns in der Welt leben lässt ohne die Arbeitshypothese Gott, ist der Gott, vor dem wir dauernd stehen. Vor und mit Gott leben wir ohne Gott."

50. Jean Paul Richter, *Flegeljahre, eine Biographie*, 1808.

51. H. H. Muchow, *Flegeljahre*, Maire, Ravensburg, 1950. "Von seelischen Pubertätserscheinungen oder von "Flegeljahren" ist in keinem der Lebensläufe die Rede."

52. Ph. Ariès, *Le XIXe siècle et la révolution des moeurs familiales*, in R. Prigent, *Renouveau des idées sur la famille*, 1954, 116.

53. "Christophe Colomb n'a découvert que l'Amérique. J'ai découvert l'enfant, moi!" Quoted by C. Salleron, *La littérature au XIXe siècle et la famille*, Prigent, 67.

54. Charles Péguy, "Le porche du mystère de la deuxième vertu," *Oeuvres poétiques complètes*, Gallimard, 188.

55. Dorothy Kunhardt, *Little Peewee or Now Open the Box.*

56. This too-hasty review is almost entirely concerned with the boy. But the girl, too, rejects a pseudo victory at the beginning of her adolescence. Her pseudo victory, however, is located in the communicative sphere. She begins her adolescence by realizing the emptiness, measured against the scale of adulthood, of her relations with the people around her.

57. If the child does not ask (if he does not ask in any way), it is best to drop every enlightenment. It may be that the child does not trust his parents to answer his questions; in that case he will find someone else. The child has a fine sense of discrimination in his choice of the right person, which the parents should respect. It may be, however, that the child does not want instruction, because he does not feel a need for it. In that case, he should be left ignorant. There are no objections to having a girl made love to while she is still in a state of ignorance, or to having a boy in love although unacquainted with even the preliminaries of sexual enlightenment.

58. J. Green, *Journal*, V, 263.

59. See Ph. Ariès, *op. cit.*, 113.

60. "La sensibilité de l'homme aux petites choses et l'insensibilité pour les grandes choses, marque d'un étrange renversement." Pascal, *Pensées*, 198.

61. Hamann, in a letter to Jacobi in 1786, says, "Vive la bagatelle. Die machen Sie zum Gegenstand, zum wichtigen Gegenstand Ihres Forschens." There is no device more significant for the psychologist. If he wants to find the correct answers to his questions, he will have to search among the small things, the most insignificant things, the trifles. For it is there—and nowhere else—that our existence is occurring.

62. See, for example, Stephan Zweig, *Die Welt von Gestern*, Fisher, Stockholm, 1944, especially Chapter 3. Many more books could be mentioned, which, together, give a poignant picture of the condition of the child in the previous century. It is well-known that these children often worked in a factory from the time they were five or six years old, standing for sixteen or eighteen hours a day—"rhagitiques et déformés, mourant à la peine dans les bagnes industriels en plein essor," Jean Maitron, *Les thèses révolutionnaires sur l'évolution de la famille du milieu du XIXe siècle à nos jours*, in Prigent, *Renouveau des idées sur la famille*, 143. It would carry us too far to go into this in detail. Nor can we discuss the important role machinery played in increasing the distance between child and adult.

63. "At every stage of its discussion the Conference was powerfully influenced by a realization of the ever-increasing need for occupational flexibility—the readiness and ability to engage in new types of work as the old become obsolete." *Education in a Technological Society*, UNESCO, 1952, 43.

64. Thus are described the modern forms of work, which "by their very nature, tend to create new forms of narrow specialization." The words "by their very nature" typify the relation of worker to work.

65. *Ibid.*, 42.

66. *Ibid.*, 50–51.

67. H. Freyer, *Theorie des gegenwärtigen Zeitalters*, Stuttgart, 1955, 140. In these lines I borrowed much from this book: See page 139: "Wir erinnern uns sodann der Verwandlung, die die menschliche Arbeit dadurch erfährt, dass sie unter das System der Maschinen, der Fliessbänder und des bürokratischen Apparates subsumiert wird. Nicht nur die Arbeit des Menschen, sondern er selbst verfällt dieser Subsumption: auch der Rhythmus, in dem seine Glieder schwingen, auch die Antriebe, die ihm wirken, auch die Massstäbe, an denen er sich selbst misst, und die Befriedigungen, die er empfindet. Er wird testbar."

68. Margaret Mead, *Coming of Age in Samoa*, Mentor Books, 149.

69. ". . . the lack of neuroses among the Samoans, the great number of neuroses among ourselves." *Ibid.*, 136.

70. Or three, rather. But the story of the state of being in love cannot be discussed here. It would lead us to too extensive a discussion of part of our cultural history.

71. "C'est un type nouveau: l'adolescent-marié." See P. Ariès, *Familles du demi-siècle*, in *Renouveau des idées sur la famille*, 164.

72. *Idem.*

CHAPTER 3

1. It is really justifiable to say "out of nothing." The views held before 1882 are not important; the knowledge gathered in the care for the mentally ill has an essentially different nature. Pierre Janet's discoveries were made after 1882.

2. Breuer and Freud, *Studien über Hysterie*, 3d ed., 27. The first edition appeared in 1895.

3. Breuer and Freud, "Über den psychischen Mechanismus hysterischer Phänomene," *Neurol. Zentralblatt*, 1893. *Gesammelte Werke*, I., 81.

4. *Gesammelte Werke*, I, 81.

5. Nowadays every peculiarity is a symptom, and what is more, a symptom one should get rid of as soon as possible. In principle one can always get rid of it. One way to get rid of it is psychiatric treatment; and thus treatment is recommended for perfectly healthy and sane people. Apparently our ideal is to make every person alike. That this conception harms every person who has a nature of his own—ultimately, that is, every one of us—needs no explanation.

6. Sandor Ferenczi, "Gulliver-Phantasien," *Bausteine zur Psychoanalyse*, III, 307.

7. G. Bernanos, *Journal d'un curé de campagne*, 255.

8. Only this: "Das sexuelle Moment war erstaunlich unentwickelt." *Vorläufige Mitteilungen*, 15.

9. *Zur Aetiologie der Hysterie* (1896), *Gesammelte Werke*, I, 434.

10. S. Ferenczi, "Relaxationsprinzip und Neokatharsis" (1929), *Bausteine zur Psychoanalyse*, III, 469.

11. "Nobody" is not absolutely correct; it is obvious that the discovery of 1882 was not new for everybody. In another meaning, and certainly in other connections, the distinction between conscious and subconscious can be found even in the pre-Romantism of the eighteenth century.

12. In 1905 Freud spoke of "die Neurosen, welche sich nur auf Störungen des Sexuallebens zurückführen lassen," *Drei Abhandlungen zur Sexualtheorie, Gesammelte Werke*, V, 117.

13. *Meine Ansichten über die Rolle der Sexualität in der Aetiologie der Neurosen* (1905), *Gesammelte Werke*, V, 153. With these words Freud summed up his views of the years 1895 to 1905.

14. *Die endliche und die unendliche Analyse* (1937), *Gesammelte Werke*, XVI, 99.

15. "Zu keiner Zeit der Analytischen Arbeit leidet man mehr unter dem bedrückenden Gefühl erfolglos wiederholter Anstrengung, unter dem Verdacht, das man 'Fischpredigten' abhält, als wenn man die Frauen bewegen will ihren Peniswunsch als undurchsetzbar aufzugeben, und wenn man die Männer überzeugen möchte, dass eine passive Einstellung zum Mann nicht immer die Bedeutung einer Kastration hat und in vielen Lebensbeziehungen unerlässlich ist." *Die endliche und die unendliche Analyse*, 98.

16. See Freud, *Selbstdarstellung*, 1925, *Gesammelte Werke*, XIV, 33.

17. "Als ich dann doch anerkennen musste, diese Verführungsszenen seien niemals vorgefallen, seien nur Phantasien, die meine Patienten erdichtet, die ich ihnen vielleicht selbst aufgedrängt hatte, war ich eine Zeitlang ratlos." *Op. cit.*, 59–60.

18. Maybe not, after all. How easily was the widely-spread belief in the neurosis-provoking effect of maternal deprivation undermined, for example, by Pinneau's study and by the succeeding perplexing exchange of ideas between him and Rene Spitz. See S. R. Pinneau, "The Infantile Disorders of Hospitalism and Anaclitic Depression," *Psychological Bulletin*, 52, 1955, 429.

19. "Der Neurotiker leidet nicht an Reminiszenzen, sondern er macht sie." *Über den Nervösen Character*, 1912, 3d ed. 56.

20. ". . . dann gehorchen wir zunächst dem Drange unserer Patienten, uns von der kritischen Gegenwart möglichst weit wegzulocken. Denn hauptsächlich in der Gegenwart liegt der pathogene Konflikt," *Versuch einer Darstellung der Psychoanalytischen Theorie*, 1913, 76.

21. See, for instance, J. Sadger, Preliminary Study of the Psychic Life of the Fetus and the Primary Germ, *The Psychoanalytic Review*, 1941.

22. A patient of Sadger's, for instance, remembers how, as a spermatozoon, he entered himself as ovum: "I forced myself through and pressed with great

pleasure into the ovum. But when in doing so I lost the caudal filament, a downright sexual satisfaction occurred." *Loc. cit.*, 339.

23. "Ich habe zu entgegnen, dass mir diese angeblichen Fortschritte wohl bekannt sind. Aber ich bin weder von der Richtigkeit der Neuerungen noch von den Irrtümern Robertson Smiths überzeugt worden. . . . Die Arbeiten des genialen Robert Smiths haben mir wertvolle Berührungen mit dem psychologischen Material der Analyse, Anknüpfungen für dessen Verwertung gegeben. Mit seinen Gegnern traf ich nie zusammen," *Der Mann Moses, Gesammelte Werke*, XVI, 240.

24. ". . . this loveliness, mounted on large firm thighs, in its little garden." François Villon, *Les regrets de la belle Heaumière*.

25. It was not at all clear to her contemporaries, though. In an article in the London *Times* of March 25, 1854, John Ruskin wrote: "People gaze at it in a blank wonder, and leave it hopelessly. . . ." John Ruskin, "Lectures on Architecture and Painting," *Works*, XII, 333.

26. "The Victorian lady could dramatize certain emotions in a way that today would be considered silly, if not hysterical. Yet the working girl who was her contemporary was not as likely to faint as was the lady; there would probably not have been anyone to catch the working girl." H. Gerth and C. Wright Mills, *Character and the Social Structure*, London, 1954, 12–13.

27. Freud, *Studien über Hysterie*, 1895, 3d ed., 114.

28. Simone de Beauvoir, *Le Deuxième Sexe*, II, 148.

29. Laura Marholm, *Das Buch der Frauen*, Langen, Leipzig, 1896, 4.

30. This definition is from Amiel, *Journal intime*, II, 40, 26 Décembre 1868. A more perfect definition of the nineteenth-century woman is hard to find. The complete paragraph, which includes a definite distinction between conscious and subconscious, is as follows: "Si l'homme se trompe toujours plus ou moins sur la femme, c'est qu'il oublie qu'elle et lui ne parlent pas tout à fait la même langue et que les mots n'ont pas pour eux le même poids et la même signification, surtout dans les questions de sentiment. Que ce soit sous la forme de la pudeur, de la précaution ou de l'artifice, une femme ne dit jamais toute sa pensée, et ce qu'elle en sait n'est encore qu'une partie de ce qui en est. La complète franchise semble lui être impossible et la complète connaissance d'elle-même paraît lui être interdite. Si elle est sphinx c'est qu'elle est énigme, c'est qu'elle est ambigue aussi pour elle-même. Elle n'a nul besoin d'être perfide, car elle est le mystère. La femme est ce qui échappe, c'est l'irrationnel, l'indéterminable, l'illogique, la contradiction. Il faut avec elle beaucoup de bonté et pas mal de prudence, car elle peut causer des maux infinis sans le savoir. Capable de tous les dévouements et de toutes les trahisons, 'monstre incompréhensible' à la seconde puissance, elle fait les délices de l'homme et son effroi."

31. *Op. cit.*, 110–111.

32. In spite of the *couleur locale*, it cannot be doubted that these words were well understood even outside Germany.

33. See F. G. Stephens, *Dante Gabriel Rossetti*, London, 1894, 38–39.

34. *Op. cit.*

35. Honoré de Balzac, *Memoires de deux jeunes mariées.* What is even worse, Balzac puts these words in the mouth of the future bride's mother. Mothers of those days did not protest; they knew from their own experience that the warning was true indeed.

36. Only in this way can we understand the commotion created by the first woman medical student. To the woman, and especially the unmarried woman, anatomy was esoteric knowledge, man's knowledge exclusively.

37. *Ratschläge für den Arzt bei der psychoanalytischen Behandlung,* 1912, *Gesammelte Werke,* VIII, 381. A few lines before these Freud writes: "Ich kann den Kollegen nicht dringend genug empfehlen, sich während der psychoanalytischen Behandlung den Chirurgen zum Vorbild zu nehmen, der alle seine Affekte und selbst sein menschliches Mitleid beiseite drängt und seinen geistigen Kräften ein einziges Ziel setzt: die Operation so kunstgerecht als möglich zu vollziehen."

38. For this change, see C. P. Oberndorf, *A History of Psychoanalysis in America,* New York, 1953; and Clara Thompson, *Psychoanalysis, Evolution and Development,* 1952, 230.

39. *Nervöse Angstzustande und ihre Behandlung,* 1920, 16–17.

40. Emile Durkheim, *Le suicide,* Paris, 1897.

41. J. F. Scott and R. L. Lynton, *The Community Factor in Modern Technology,* UNESCO, 1952, 15.

42. *Ibid.,* 15.

43. M. Boss, *Körperliches Kranksein als Folge seelischer Gleichgewichtsstorungen,* Bern, 1940, 54.

44. F. Dunbar, *Emotions and Bodily Changes,* New York, 1954, 344.

45. ". . . angina pectoris has evidently increased in frequency, and is encountered more in communities where the strain of life is great and a hurried existence the habit than in leisurely parts of the world." Paul D. White, *Heart Disease,* New York, 1931, 609. Quoted by F. Dunbar, *op. cit.,* 345.

46. J. F. Scott and R. P. Lynton, *Op. cit.,* 15.

47. "Frequent changes of address are typical of industrial society. J. S. Plant, reporting a study of changes of address in a fairly typical and relatively stable county in New Jersey, states that 68 per cent of the families moved at least once in the five-year period 1922–1927." *Ibid.,* 29.

48. T. S. Eliot, *The Cocktail Party.*

49. See R. Prigent, *Renouveau des idées sur la famille,* Paris, 1954.

50. E. Agier, *Désintégration familiale chez les ouvriers,* Neuchâtel, 1950.

51. P. M. Sorokin, *Society, Culture and Personality,* New York, 1947, 345. "Pluralism of 'selves' in the individual as a reflection of the pluralism of groups."

52. Sorokin also uses this example.

53. The manuscript was ready in 1885; the first edition appeared in 1886; see Prideaux' bibliography of the works of Robert Stevenson. For Stevenson's interest in the "double life," see, Alfred Michel, *R. L. Stevenson, sein Verhältnis zum Bösen,* diss. Zurich, 1949, 146. It is interesting to note how the

idea of a dual, or rather a plural existence, which was portrayed by Jean Paul in *Siebenkäs*, 1795, for the first time, spread and became more clear in the course of the nineteenth century. See Wilhelmine Krauss, "Das Doppelgängermotiv in der Romantik," *Germanische Studien*, 99, 1930; and, R. Tymms, *Doubles in Literary Psychology*, Cambridge, 1949.

54. "Nachdem es gelungen ist, das verdrängte Ereignis realer oder psychischer Natur gegen alle Widerstände zur Annahme durchzusetzen, es gewissermassen zu rehabilitieren, sagt der Patient: Jetzt habe ich die Empfindung, ich habe es immer gewusst. Damit ist die analytische Aufgabe gelöst." *Über fausse reconnaissance* ("déja raconté"), 1914, *Gesammelte Werke*, X, 123.

55. Also in the textbooks on psychosomatic medicine. Hence the unprofitable confusion of ideas in this important science.

56. "Cette tendance qu'ont certains à doubler leur vie d'une vie imaginaire, à cesser d'être qui l'on est, pour devenir qui l'on croît être, qui l'on veut être." André Gide, *Dostoïevsky*, 136–137.

57. *Neue Folge der Vorlesungen zur Einführung in die Psychoanalyse*, 1933, *Gesammelte Werke*, XV, 86.

58. "So viel, wie ich mich kenne, scheint mir sicher, dass, wenn man mir meine Teufel austriebe, auch meinen Engeln ein kleiner, ein ganz kleiner (sagen wir) Schrecken geschehe—und, fühlen Sie, gerade darauf darf ich es auf keinen Preis ankommen lassen." Letter 74, *Briefe aus den Jahren 1907 bis 1914*.

59. "Ich fürchte in mir nur diejenigen Widersprüche, die Neigung haben zur Versöhnlichkeit. Das muss eine sehr schmale Stelle meines Lebens sein, wenn sie überhaupt daran denken dürfen, sich die Hände zu reichen, von Rand zu Rand. Meine Widersprüche sollen nur selten und in Gerüchten von einander hören." *Briefe und Tagebücher der Frühzeit*, 1932, 203.

60. "Ein Erzieher muss darauf ausgehen, aus der Schar der ihm anvertrauten Kinder viele und verschiedene Menschen zu machen; es ist besser wenn er in den Fehler verfällt, einen in zwei Menschen, die miteinander streiten, zu zerspalten, als wenn er die landläufige Arbeit fortsetzt, alle seine Schüler zu einer Art Mensch zu erziehen." *Ibid.*, 243.

61. *Over neurotiserende factoren*, Nijkerk, 1955.

62. See G. Friedmann, *Problemes humains du machinisme industriel*, Paris, 1946.

63. No factor touches the individual himself, not one. On the other hand, it cannot be doubted that the individual does or does not have a tendency toward neurotic reactions; how would this tendency show itself, though, if it did not become apparent as a result of a neurosis-provoking appeal from society? It is this appeal that created the tendency; it was not there before. There is no such thing as a potential possibility.

CHAPTER 4

1. See Julien Green, *Journal*, III, 96. "Un homme peut transformer sa chambre en paradis ou en enfer, sans bouger, simplement par les pensées qu'il y loge."

2. That the thinness of the observation does not exclude its richness, or, indeed, induce it, needs no comment. There is no poorer observation than by camera.

3. This example is borrowed from J. von Uexkuell and G. Kriszal, *Streifzüge durch die Umwelten von Tieren und Menschen*, Berlin, 1934, 91.

4. It is obvious that the Bible does not mention an "apple." What is nameless cannot be called *apple*.

5. This anecdote is borrowed from Freud's *Drei Abhandlungen, Gesammelte Werke*, V, 126. His comment is not important here.

6. *Si le grain ne meurt*, 58.

7. *Essays*, II, 10.

8. R. Bultmann, "N.T. und Mythologie," *Offenbarung und Heilsgeschichte*, 1941. "Man kann nicht elektrisches Licht und Radio-Apparat benützen, in Krankheitsfällen moderne medizinische und klinische Mittel in Anspruch nehmen und gleichzeitig die Geister- und Wunderwelt des N.T. glauben."

9. Cardinal Lépicier, *Le miracle*, Paris, 1936, 2.

10. *Idem*.

11. C. S. Lewis, *Miracles*, London, 1947, 158.

12. "On peut entendre de deux façons le fait que Jésus-Christ marche sur les eaux: soit qu'il ait accordé aux eaux la solidarité, soit qu'il ait mis en acte le don d'agilité." Cardinal Lépicier, *op. cit.*

13. Exodus 14:21.

14. Exodus 14:22.

15. Mark 6:5.

16. Mark 6:6.

17. [Le miracle] "n'est que dans la mesure où notre vie spirituelle y est intéressée," G. Marcel, *Journal métaphysique*, Paris, 1927, 79.

18. These words are not entirely justified. I only want to say that eschatology quite often functions like a reversed Cartesianism in theology, and especially in the theory of miracles.

CHAPTER 5

1. "L'expérience n'ayant pas donné grand-chose, je m'avisai qu'à cette époque ma taille était petite et que ma main, traînant actuellement plus haut, ne rencontrait pas les mêmes reliefs. Je recommençai le manège. Grâce à une simple différence de niveau et, par un phénomène analogue à celui du frottement de l'aiguille sur les aspérités d'un disque de gramophone, j'obtins la musique du souvenir. Je retrouvai tout: ma pèlerine, le cuir de mon cartable, le nom du camarade qui m'accompagnait, ceux de nos maîtres, certaines phrases que j'avais dites, le timbres de voix de mon grand-père, l'odeur de sa barbe, des étoffes de ma soeur et de maman." Jean Cocteau, *Journal d'un inconnu*, Paris, 1953, 165.

2. "Wir fühlen um uns einer Sache zu erinnern, wie wir das Gehirn anstrengen zum Mitarbeiten." Jean Paul, *Vorläufige Gedanken, Werke*, LX, 168.

3. "Que la trompette du jugement dernier sonne quand elle voudra, je

viendrai, ce livre à la main, me présenter devant le souverain juge. Je dirai hautement: Voilà ce que j'ai fait, ce que j'ai pensé, ce que je fus. J'ai dit le bien et le mal avec la même franchise. Je n'ai rien tu de mauvais, rien ajouté de bon. . . ." J.-J. Rousseau, *Les Confessions*, I.

4. *Archiv für Geschichte der Philosophie*, V, 1892, 337.

5. "Von der Freiheit eines Christenmenschen," *Martin Luthers reformatorische Schriften*, Deutsche Bibliothek, 94.

6. "Axiomata, wenn es deren in dergleichen Dingen gibt," *Lessing's Werke*, VII, 375.

7. *Dialektik*, 224.

8. *Der christliche Glaube*, 3.

9. It would carry us too far to go into this and to consider the striking similarities between the conclusions reached by psychologists of religion, psychologists, and belletrists.

10. Luther was not the first. It is only logical that the urge to create and fill the inner man at the cost of exterior things was felt by all those who observed with anxiety the wrong use of exterior things. Savonarola was one of these. In his Psalm about the love of God, he spurns objects: they do not contain God, God is to be found in the soul. And also Thomas à Kempis: Blessed are the eyes that are closed to exterior matters but attentive to inward things, *Imitation of Christ*, III, Chapter 1. Only one who is aware of the pulling power of the things, and who, perhaps, feels it personally, writes words like these. The Gospels rather suggest the opposite view. Nor is Luther's reasoning very evangelic.

11. R. M. Rilke, *Von der Landschaft, Ausgewählte Werke*, 1938, II, 218.

12. "Je forme une enterprise qui n'eut jamais d'exemple, et dont l'exécution n'aura point d'imitateur. Je veux montrer à mes semblables un homme dans toute la vérité de la nature; et cet homme, ce sera moi." *Les Confessions*, Book I.

13. James Joyce, *Ulysses*, 1918.

14. *Confessions*, Book II, devoted to the experiences of 1728, the year Rousseau crossed the Alps.

15. "It was Rousseau who, with an extraordinary intensity and power of expression, created the emotion of the mountains. No doubt it existed before him, at least in elementary form; but it was he who molded these elements into a new shape and who forced the new emotion upon us as an exceptional timbre, composed of previously known sounds but determined by a new fundamental tone." E. de Bruyne, *Het aesthetisch beleven*, Antwerpen, 1942, 147.

16. See D. Mornet, *Le sentiment de la Nature en France de J.-J. Rousseau à Bernadin de Saint Pierre*, Paris, 1907, 55. And R. Hennig, *Die Entwicklung des Naturgefühls und das Wesen der Inspiration*, Leipzig, 1912.

17. "Wir stellen uns vor, dass wir ein gewisses Mass von Liebesfähigkeit, genannt Libido, besitzen, welches sich in den Anfängen der Entwicklung dem eigenen Ich zugewendet hatte. Später, aber eigentlich von sehr frühe an, wendet es sich vom Ich ab und den Objecten zu, die wir solcherart gewissermassen in

unser Ich hineinnehmen. Werden die Objekte zerstört oder gehen sie uns verloren, so wird unsere Liebesfähigkeit (Libido) wieder frei. Sie kann sich andere Objekte zum Ersatz nehmen oder zeitweise zum Ich zurückkehren. Warum aber diese Ablösung der Libido von ihren Objekten ein so schmerzhafter Vorgang sein sollte, das verstehen wir nicht und können es derzeit aus keiner Annahme ableiten. Wir sehen nur, dass sich die Libido an ihre Objekte klammert und die verlorenen auch dann nicht aufgeben will wenn der Ersatz bereit liegt. Das also ist die Trauer." *Vergänglichkeit*, 1915, *Gesammelte Werke*, X, 360.

18. The complete paragraph reads, "Von hier aus mag man es selbst wagen, an die Frage heranzutreten, woher denn überhaupt die Nötigung für das Seelenleben rührt, über die Grenzen des Narzissmus hinauszugehen und die Libido auf Objekte zu setzen. Die aus unserem Gedankengang abfolgende Antwort würde wiederum sagen, diese Nötigung trete ein, wenn die Ichbesetzung mit Libido ein gewisses Mass überschritten habe. Ein starker Egoismus schützt vor Erkrankung, aber endlich muss man beginnen zu lieben, um nicht krank zu werden, und muss erkranken, wenn man infolge von Versagung nicht lieben kann." *Zur Einführung des Narzissmus*, 1914, *Gesammelte Werke*, X, 151–152.

19. Charles Morgan, "The Constant Things," *Reflections in a Mirror*, Second Series, London, 1946, 66.

EPILOGUE

1. Chamfort (died 1794).

2. "Universal History, the history of what man has accomplished in this world, is at the bottom the History of the Great Men who have worked here." Thomas Carlyle, *On Heroes, Hero-Worship and the Heroic in History*, 1840, Lecture I. This typically nineteenth-century sentence, matching what David Riesman called an "inner-directed" type of life (*The Lonely Crowd*, 1950) is, in my opinion, still true (although with some reservations) today.

Norton Paperbacks
PSYCHIATRY AND PSYCHOLOGY

Adams, James L. *Conceptual Blockbusting* (2d Ed.).

Adler, Alfred. *Cooperation Between the Sexes.*

Adler, Alfred. *Superiority and Social Interest.*

Adorno, T.W. *et al.* *The Authoritarian Personality* (Abr. Ed.)

Alexander, Franz. *Fundamentals of Psychoanalysis.*

Alexander, Franz. *Psychosomatic Medicine.*

Bernheim, Kayla F. and Richard R.J. Lewine. *Schizophrenia: Symptoms, Causes, and Treatments.*

Bruner, Jerome S. *Beyond the Information Given.*

Bruner, Jerome S. *The Relevance of Education.*

Burgess, Linda Cannon. *The Art of Adoption.*

Cannon, Walter B. *The Wisdom of the Body.*

Donaldson, Margaret. *Children's Minds.*

English, O. Spurgeon, and Gerald H. J. Pearson. *Emotional Problems of Living* (3d Ed.).

Erikson, Erik H. *Adulthood.*

Erikson, Erik H. *Childhood and Society.*

Erikson, Erik H. *Dimensions of a New Identity.*

Erikson, Erik H. *Gandhi's Truth.*

Erikson, Erik H. *Identity: Youth and Crisis.*

Erikson, Erik H. *Identity and the Life Cycle.*

Erikson, Erik H. *Insight and Responsibility.*

Erikson, Erik H. *Life History and the Historical Moment.*

Erikson, Erik H. *Young Man Luther.*

Fancher, Raymond E. *Pioneers of Psychology.*

Fancher, Raymond E. *Psychoanalytic Psychology: The Development of Freud's Thought.*

Finch, Stuart M. *Fundamentals of Child Psychiatry.*

Freud, Anna. *Psychoanalysis for Teachers and Parents.*

Freud, Sigmund. *An Autobiographical Study.*

Freud, Sigmund. *Beyond the Pleasure Principle.*

Freud, Sigmund. *Civilization and its Discontents.*

Freud, Sigmund. *The Ego and the Id.*

Freud, Sigmund. *Five Lectures on Psycho-Analysis.*

Freud, Sigmund. *The Future of an Illusion.*

Freud, Sigmund. *Group Psychology and the Analysis of the Ego.*

Freud, Sigmund. *Inhibitions, Symptoms and Anxiety.*

Freud, Sigmund. *Introductory Lectures on Psychoanalysis.*

Freud, Sigmund. *Jokes and Their Relation to the Unconscious.*

Freud, Sigmund. *Leonardo da Vinci and a Memory of His Childhood.*

Freud, Sigmund. *New Introductory Lectures on Psychoanalysis.*

Freud, Sigmund. *On Dreams.*

Freud, Sigmund. *On the History of the Psycho-Analytic Movement.*

Freud, Sigmund. *An Outline of Psycho-Analysis* (Rev. Ed.).

Freud, Sigmund. *The Psychopathology of Everyday Life.*

Freud, Sigmund. *The Question of Lay Analysis.*

Freud, Sigmund. *Totem and Taboo.*

Frieze, Irene H., Jacquelynne E. Parsons, Paula B. Johnson, Diane N. Ruble and Gail L. Zellmann. *Women and Sex Roles: A Social Psychological Perspective.*

Haley, Jay. *Uncommon Therapy: The Psychiatric Techniques of Milton B. Erickson, M.D.*

Horney, Karen (Ed.). *Are You Considering Psychoanalysis?*

Horney, Karen. *Feminine Psychology.*

Horney, Karen. *Neurosis and Human Growth.*

Horney, Karen. *The Neurotic Personality of Our Time.*

Horney, Karen. *New Ways in Psychoanalysis.*

Horney, Karen. *Our Inner Conflicts.*

Horney, Karen. *Self-Analysis.*

Inhelder, Bärbel, and Jean Piaget. *The Early Growth of Logic in the Child.*

James, William. *Talks to Teachers.*

Jones, Ernest. *Hamlet and Oedipus.*

Kagan, Jerome. *The Growth of the Child: Reflections on Human Development.*

Kagan, Jerome, and Robert Coles (Eds.). *Twelve to Sixteen: Early Adolescence.*

Katchadourian, Herant. *Human Sexuality: Sense and Nonsense.*

Kelly, George A. *A Theory of Personality.*

Klein, Melanie, and Joan Riviere. *Love, Hate and Reparation.*

Komarovsky, Mirra. *Dilemmas of Masculinity: A Study of College Youth.*

Lacan, Jacques. *Ecrits.*

Lacan, Jacques. *The Four Fundamental Concepts of Psycho-Analysis.*

Levy, David M. *Maternal Overprotection.*

Lifton, Robert Jay. *Thought Reform and the Psychology of Totalism.*

Light, Donald. *Becoming Psychiatrists: The Professional Transformation of Self.*

Lunde, Donald T. *Murder and Madness.*

May, Rollo. *Psychology and the Human Dilemma.*

Meehl, Paul E. *Psychodiagnosis: Selected Papers.*

Piaget, Jean. *The Child's Conception of Number.*

Piaget, Jean. *Genetic Epistemology.*

Piaget, Jean. *Play, Dreams and Imitation in Childhood.*

Piaget, Jean, and Bärbel Inhelder. *The Child's Conception of Space.*

Piaget, Jean, and Bärbel Inhelder. *The Origin of the Idea of Chance in Children.*

Piaget, Jean, Bärbel Inhelder, and Alina Szeminska. *The Child's Conception of Geometry.*

Piers, Gerhart, and Milton B. Singer. *Shame and Guilt.*

Piers, Maria W. (Ed.). *Play and Development.*

Rank, Otto. *Truth and Reality.*

Rank, Otto. *Will Therapy.*

Raymond, Margaret, Andrew Slaby, and Julian Lieb. *The Healing Alliance.*

Ruesch, Jurgen. *Therapeutic Communication.*

Ruesch, Jurgen, and Gregory Bateson. *Communication: The Social Matrix of Psychiatry.*

Sullivan, Harry Stack. *Clinical Studies in Psychiatry.*

Sullivan, Harry Stack. *Conceptions of Modern Psychiatry.*

Sullivan, Harry Stack. *The Fusion of Psychiatry and Social Science.*

Sullivan, Harry Stack. *The Interpersonal Theory of Psychiatry.*

Sullivan, Harry Stack. *The Psychiatric Interview.*

Sullivan, Harry Stack. *Schizophrenia as a Human Process.*

Walter, W. Grey. *The Living Brain.*

Watson, John B. *Behaviorism.*

Wheelis, Allen. *The Quest for Identity.*

Williams, Juanita H. *Psychology of Women: Behavior in a Biosocial Context.*

Williams, Juanita H. (Ed.) *Psychology of Women: Selected Readings.*

Zilboorg, Gregory. *A History of Medical Psychology.*

Liveright Paperbacks
PSYCHIATRY AND PSYCHOLOGY

Balint, Michael. *Problems of Human Pleasure and Behavior.*

Bergler, Edmund. *Curable and Incurable Neurotics: Problems of "Neurotic" versus "Malignant" Psychic Masochism.*

Bergler, Edmund. *Parents Not Guilty of Their Children's Neuroses.*

Dunlap, Knight. *Habits: Their Making and Unmaking.*

Featherstone, Joseph. *Schools Where Children Learn.*

Featherstone, Joseph. *What Schools Can Do.*

Gutheil, Emil A. *The Handbook of Dream Analysis.*

Gutheil, Emil A. *Music and Your Emotions.*

Jones, Ernest. *On the Nightmare.*

Köhler, Wolfgang. *Dynamics in Psychology.*

Köhler, Wolfgang. *Gestalt Psychology.*

Köhler, Wolfgang. *The Mentality of Apes.*

Köhler, Wolfgang. *The Place of Value in a World of Facts.*

Köhler, Wolfgang. *The Selected Papers of Wolfgang Köhler.*

Luria, Alexander R. *The Nature of Human Conflicts.*

Russell, Bertrand. *Education and the Good Life.*

Stekel, Wilhelm. *Impotence in the Male.*

Stekel, Wilhelm. *Sexual Aberrations: The Phenomena of Fetishism in Relation to Sex.*